Praise for *The Real McKay*

"In *The Real McKay* the well-respected sportscaster tells all of the astounding stories of his remarkable career."
—*Denver Post*

"The appeal of McKay's book is the memories . . . they were great moments, and it's fun to revisit them."
—*Arizona Republic*

"Relive the most memorable moments in a memorable career."
—*New Orleans Times-Picayune*

"A compelling history of television."
—*Greenwich Time*

"McKay traveled the world in search of the human drama of athletic competition, while serving as the voice of many a television network's sports programs. It's no surprise that he collected plenty of good stories along the way."
—*Buffalo News*

JIM McKAY has been chief anchorman for ABC's *Wide World of Sports* for almost fifty years, and still covers major sports events for ABC, including the Triple Crown of horse racing and the British Open. He is the winner of thirteen Emmy awards and a Peabody Award of Lifetime Achievement, and is a member of the Television Hall of Fame.

✶ THE ✶
REAL McKAY

MY WIDE WORLD OF SPORTS

JIM McKAY

With a Foreword by Peter Jennings

A PLUME BOOK

PLUME
Published by the Penguin Group
Penguin Putnam Inc., 375 Hudson Street, New York,
    New York 10014, U.S.A.
Penguin Books Ltd, 27 Wrights Lane, London W8 5TZ, England
Penguin Books Australia Ltd, Ringwood, Victoria, Australia
Penguin Books Canada Ltd, 10 Alcorn Avenue, Toronto, Ontario,
    Canada M4V 3B2
Penguin Books (N.Z.) Ltd, 182–190 Wairau Road, Auckland 10,
    New Zealand

Penguin Books Ltd, Registered Offices: Harmondsworth,
    Middlesex, England

Published by Plume, a member of Penguin Putnam Inc.
Previously published in a Dutton edition.

First Plume Printing, May, 1999
10 9 8 7 6 5 4 3 2 1

Ⓟ REGISTERED TRADEMARK—MARCA REGISTRADA

The Library of Congress has catalogued the Dutton edition as follows:
McKay, Jim.
    The real McKay : my wide world of sports / by Jim McKay :
with a foreword by Peter Jennings.
        p. cm.
    ISBN 0-525-94418-4
            0-452-28025-7 (pbk.)
    1. McKay, Jim.   2. Sportscasters—United States—Bibliography.
    3. ABC Wide World of Sports (television program).   I. Title.
    GV742.42.M45A3   1998
    070.4'49796'092
    [B]—DC21   98-2646
                                                          CIP

Printed in the United States of America
Original hardcover design by Stanley S. Drate/Folio Graphics Co. Inc.

This book is dedicated to my wife, Margaret, for
making me happy
to our daughter, Mary, and our son, Sean, for
making me proud
and to our grandson, James, for bringing me so much
joy and keeping my eyes on the future, not the past.

Acknowledgments

My sincere thanks go to Peter Jennings, for taking time out from the world news to write the foreword.

For their kindness in checking the facts in the chapters on their respective sports, I thank Steve Nagler (horse racing), Sam Posey (motor racing), and Draggan Mihailovich (Olympics).

For his help in obtaining pictures I am grateful to Frank Mandel of ABC Sports.

For being my agent and friend for twenty-five years, I thank Ralph Mann.

Also, Gerry Gross, for having faith in this book as he did in my previous book twenty-five years ago.

And to Al Silverman, for guiding me through the rocks and shoals of writing a book, as my editor, and in the process becoming my friend.

And to Matt DeVito, simply for being my friend.

Contents

Foreword

by Peter Jennings

To think that Jim McKay and I might have had each other's jobs. You will read in this endearing book that Jim's early ambition, when he was a fledgling journalist in Baltimore, was to be a television reporter and subsequently an anchorman.

I, on the other hand, said for years, not altogether idly, that the man with the really great job was Jim McKay. In four decades *Wide World of Sports* took him several million miles around the globe, to one place after another that I was lusting to see.

We both love sports, and we each believe that sports is about culture and nationalism and politics as well as individual human endeavor. Jim, as you will read here, was often somewhere doing a sports event just as a great news event was about to unfold, and I am reminded at several places in the narrative that his eye for a news story was always very keen.

I have subsequently managed to work in a good piece of the world, but I have only once managed to do it the McKay way. One year Cuba told *Wide World of Sports* that they could send a television team to cover the regional volleyball playoffs between Cuba and the USA. But they wouldn't let ABC send any Americans. "Know anything about volleyball?" asked Roone Arledge, who has given both Jim and me such opportunities. "Not a thing," I said. "But you are Canadian," said

Arledge, "you can at least get into Cuba. Put together a team and get to Havana as quickly as you can."

Those were the days. I played basketball and talked politics with Fidel, managed to see a few dissidents, and came back to New York much enriched by the experience. Eat your heart out, McKay. I also cheered so lustily for the U.S. team that when the time came to insert the commentary track, I could hardly speak. McKay, the unabashed enthusiast, who once lost it and began shouting at an impostor who invaded the Olympic marathon in the final moments, would have understood.

But whereas I had a very short career as a sports commentator, Jim had one of his greatest moments anchoring a news story that absorbed the whole world. His minute-by-minute description in these pages of the Palestinian attack on the Olympic village in Munich at the height of the 1972 Games is so declarative, and so without frills, that I felt as if I were back in the Olympic village. Jim was widely recognized at the time for being wise and dignified under enormous stress, and all these years later, when the tendency to hype everything seems to have taken over, Jim's powerful sense of decorum on a very difficult unfolding story stands out as a model.

Perhaps it's the conceit of age, but as we roll up on the millennium I seem to notice so many talkers on television who can't go very long without repeating themselves. McKay can talk intelligently forever. Twice now I have been assigned to work the opening ceremonies of the Olympic Games with him. The idea was that during the parade of athletes I would give a quick account of the history and politics of the country's delegation and Jim would pick up with the sports connection. I loved it, but McKay didn't need me. He could have done it all with great aplomb, hour after hour.

In the early days of television when there were no video-taped packages to give commentators relief, someone observed that Jim could go an hour and hardly say hello. Try it some time. Readers take note, he is every bit as warm and intelligent in this book, but he writes sparingly and with his usual modesty. In other words, he gets the best out of each story and then moves on.

One of the things that I enjoy most in the book are Jim's lists. His best golfers, best race car drivers, best Olympic athletes. I don't know anyone other than Jim who uses the word hero so unself-consciously. I grew up in Canada, where we Anglos at least were taught that you didn't use the word hero as lightly as, say, Ronald Reagan often appeared to use it. But Jim's heroes are those who he believes have genuinely struggled, not those who have lucked into success. Here again, there is a sweetness of appreciation for athletes that is singularly Jim. When Jim says "Wow" as he sometimes does during a great performance, you somehow know that additional analysis would be redundant.

And don't look here for athletes to be put down or excoriated. This is Gentleman Jim at work. These days so many athletes, not to mention public figures in general, feel, often with good cause, that they are threatened by reporters. Too many reporters seem intent on their own agenda or setting a public figure down a peg. There is such kindness about Jim's nostalgia. Graham Hill's first visit to Indianapolis, just hanging out with Eddie Arcaro anytime, making his way around Muirfield in Scotland with Lee Trevino. Even the frightful Olympic Hotel in Mexico City is forgiven, at least by Jim. The book is chock full of gems that keep me looking for the next one.

Quickly now, who was the ski jumper that careened off the jump into the judges' stand, who has come to represent the "agony of defeat" at the beginning of *Wide World of Sports* all these years? Quickly now. Vinko Bogataj, of course, from Yugoslavia. He didn't do as much damage to himself as Yugoslavia did to itself.

I went to Sarajevo several winters ago. For a while it was as dangerous as any place on earth. The Serb gunners had the city surrounded and were shelling it indiscriminately.

My crew and I arrived on a freezing cold morning, when the mayor had finally and reluctantly given people permission to cut down the city's trees so that they might have some fuel.

People were using primitive axes and handsaws and even files, all the while waiting for the next Serb shell to fall among them. I was quite terrified until a man came up and said, "ABC Sports. I worked with them at the Olympics, don't worry. I'll take care of you. How's Jim McKay?" There I was again, getting by on Jim's connections.

There are so many nuggets here. I love the story of how the great miler Roger Bannister walked off a CBS program on which they thought they had him "exclusively" when he discovered that the program was advertised by a cigarette maker. Thanks to Jim, we're reminded that fifty years ago, Dr. Bannister had it right.

Several years ago at the Kentucky Derby I ran into Jim on the first turn at Churchill Downs. "Now there," I said, "is an institution." It seemed to me that he had been there forever. In fact, it's been a mere twenty-some years. But the love of horses and racing is very powerful here, for Jim and his indispensable wife, Margaret. Jim has only the faintest notion that we have horses in common, but when he writes about his visits with Eddie Arcaro to the Grand National at Aintree, without a doubt the toughest horse race in the world, he reminds me of a story I hope he enjoys.

My teenage daughter is a competitive rider, and several summers ago she went to work on a friend's horse farm in Wales. She came home talking about a horse who was not the Three Day Event horse my friends had hoped he would be, but was pretty darned quick at the track. I was assured that with a small investment and a good trainer he might make it as a steeplechaser. Before I knew it, I had parted with twenty-five hundred dollars, and Elizabeth and I were the proud co-owners of Channel's Gate—Joey was his barn name—who just might, it was hinted, just might make it to the Grand National.

I didn't think much about it, nor could I ever remember what leg we owned—good friends owned the other three—until on a Wednesday night a year later when the phone rang. "Joey's in the National," I heard. That was it. Down tools, out of the office, on to the last two available seats on British Airways, off to Manchester, mad dash to Aintree, to the roughest race in the world without question. And we were owners! It was one of the great days.

Several favorites fell at the first fence. Only six out of forty finished, and Joey had the good sense to pull up and say to hell with it at the twenty-first fence. That was the day I understood Jim's love of horse racing. And I certainly understood Eddie Arcaro's remark to Jim, "No sumbitch is going to get me to ride in that thing."

So now Jim and Margaret, with their gorgeous daughter, Mary, and grandchild not too far away, are settled in at their own Maryland horse farm, wondering was it worth it. Did they do the right thing all those years ago when they, both of them reporters, sat considering whether sports would be an irrelevant way to make a living? Did they do the right thing? They must be kidding.

Preface

Fifty years. That's how long I've been in sports television. More than half a lifetime, the equivalent of twelve and a half presidencies or the same number of Olympiads. People who weren't born when I started have gone to grade school, high school, and college, have gotten married, had children, worked for twenty-five years, and are thinking about their retirement.

And I'm still in sports television.

Our numbers people at ABC tell me that I have traveled some five million miles (that's about two hundred times around the world), by planes, trains, and automobiles, to cover almost a hundred different sports in forty different countries.

I have covered golf in Scotland, tennis at Wimbledon, cliff diving in Acapulco, barrel jumping in the Catskills, lumberjacking in Wisconsin, the Triple Crown of horse racing (Kentucky Derby, Preakness, and Belmont), stock car racing in South Carolina (the Southern 500, "the Daddy of them all"), ski racing in St. Moritz, speed skating in Lake Placid, water-skiing in Australia, baseball in Japan, the Indy 500, gymnastics in China and roller skating in Madrid. All punctuated by eleven Olympics, summer and winter, throughout the world.

And now, I figure, it's time to look back.

As we sit on our farm, at home in Maryland, my wife, Margaret, and I still ask each other, "Did we do the right thing? Was it all worth it?"

And I think back to our conversation thirty-seven years

ago, when an offer came that would make sports my total career. I'd always harbored an ambition to be a network anchorman for the evening news, but here was opportunity coming from another direction.

Our question to each other was:

Would sports be an irrelevant way to spend our lives?

After a few seconds of thought, Margaret, as always, put it in perspective.

"Look, Jim," she said, "all you have to do is be true to yourself as a reporter and you can make something out of TV sports that no one else is doing now. You can make it an inspiration for kids and a thought-provoking matter for adults. You can discover and convey the meaning of what happens in human terms, not just the play-by-play."

It certainly wasn't what she wanted. She could see spending her days and nights alone while I was traveling, stretching out into the future. But she could also see the benefits and she knew that no matter what I might say, underneath I really wanted to give it a try.

So I did.

I have tried to make my job not just the description of what was happening at the moment, but a search for excellence and an exploration of the human character in action. When I've found examples of excellence, as I have so very often, and as you will read about in these pages, I have tried to point them out to the audience and to convince viewers, particularly young people, that excellence is attainable in their own lives.

I never wanted to search for and expose the worst, but to find the best and use it as an inspiration for others to do the same.

In the early days of ABC's *Wide World of Sports*, we presented a number of sports that people had seldom, if ever, seen on television, things like lumberjack championships, surfing, barrel jumping, figure skating, and gymnastics. The thought was that if the competitors could make these sports a major part of their lives with little financial reward, we should be able to interest the viewer in them for twenty minutes on a Saturday afternoon.

Hip people in the industry snickered behind their hands when we gave sports like those the dignity of taking them seriously.

Quite quickly, though, the promoters of some of these events began to read about the large sums being paid for rights to pro football and baseball and decided to try for a piece of the action. Some of them, alas, overestimated their appeal.

Once in the early *Wide World* days, we were going to Acapulco to televise waterskiing. Roone Arledge, who was producing the event, remembered having seen the cliff divers who performed nightly at the El Mirador Hotel. Thinking that it would be a nice throw-in for local color during the waterskiing, Roone called the hotel manager, who told him that he would have to speak to the divers' shop steward, one Jaime Garcia.

Roone was a bit surprised to hear that the divers had a union, but he waited while the call was transferred, and in a minute was speaking with Senor Garcia. Roone explained the proposition. Garcia cleared his throat and said that since the divers were virtually sure that a major motion picture would be made about them and they were also anticipating a big offer from NBC, he would have to receive a rights offer from us of at least $100,000.

Roone told him politely that $100,000 was considerably more than the budget for the entire show, thanked him for his time, and hung up. The next day, he and I flew to Acapulco, where we were met by a local person who was acting as our liaison for the program. He told us that things were in order for the waterskiing. "Oh," he said, "and by the way, I got the cliff divers."

Roone put up his hand. "Hold it," he said. "You had no authority to do that. They want a hundred thousand dollars."

"I know," said the Mexican, "but I got them to compromise."

Roone was annoyed. "There's no room for compromise. I only wanted them for a throw-in. They're thinking crazy figures. As a matter of curiosity, what is the compromise figure? What are they willing to settle for?"

"Ten bucks a dive," the man replied, shrugging his shoulders.

And so it was done, but the divers carefully counted every dive, including practice, and ended up with something like $300 to split among them.

Other "minor" sports have done better.

Thirty-five years later, figure skating seems to be on every channel at least once a month, gymnastics competitions can fill major arenas, and certain minor sports flood the cable channels twenty-four hours a day. And the pay is better than those divers got.

A minor sport like beach volleyball was contested in the 1996 Olympics in Atlanta. Surfing and ballroom dancing will make their first Olympic appearances in Australia in the year 2000.

It's money talking.

No one is more aware of the importance of the bottom line than the noblemen and millionaires of the International Olympic Committee. So, if a lot of people are out there watching surfing on *Wide World* or ballroom dancing on the popular BBC program *Let's Go Dancing*, well, sure, let's put them in the Olympics.

It's an interesting phenomenon to observe that the greater the amounts of money involved, the more greed increases. It is most unlikely that a young figure skater's husband in the old days would have been involved in a plot to maim her principal competitor by hiring someone to shatter her knee. The prospect of instant riches inspired that act.

In the days when Hall of Fame ballplayers like Jimmie Foxx, an all-time Hall of Famer, were making $12,000 a year, they willingly signed autographs for long lines of kids waiting outside the clubhouse door. I know, because I was one of those kids outside old Shibe Park in Philadelphia. Now that the average major league salary is more than a million dollars a year, they charge kids for their autographs. Think about it: Millionaires are *selling* their signatures to children.

A baseball agent recently told me that with many of the players it isn't really the amount of money they're interested in; they just want to see that their signature or their baseball card can be sold for more than the other guy's.

Not long ago, a pro basketball player was asked what his childhood ambition had been. His answer was not that he had hoped to be a college star, or an All-American, or an NBA standout, or the president of the United States. No. His ambition, he said, ever since he was a little kid, was to have a shoe contract.

I don't believe that the sports have changed that much. Their objects and their rules are basically the same. Nor do I feel that human character has changed. It's the money that's changed everything—the money flowing out of television rights—and that has sometimes brought out aspects of the human character that would be better left concealed.

So, do I feel that my way of covering sports is a thing of the past? Not at all. I still search for the positive in sports, and I agree with the late Chief Justice Earl Warren's comment back in the fifties, when he was asked in what order he read the sections of the Sunday newspaper.

"I read the sports section first," he said, "and the front page last."

Why?

"Because on the sports page, I read about mankind's victories. On the front page, I read about his defeats."

I am still seeking out those victories of the human spirit, and finding plenty of them. The negative things I will leave to the evening news.

I have, for instance, never covered boxing because I don't believe it to be a sport. It is the only activity claiming the name "sport" in which a participant's avowed object is to injure another competitor. People are intentionally injured in other sports, but it is against the rules and calls for a penalty. In addition, in boxing, there are the issues of organized crime connections and the exploitation of uneducated and sometimes brain-damaged boxers. In this case, I think that the seamy side overcomes in significance the excellence displayed by the athlete. So I have stayed away from boxing, since I could never give it a dignity I feel it does not deserve.

For instance, in its edition of November 13, 1997, the *New York Times* told the story of Wilfred Benitez.

At 17, he was the youngest champion in boxing history. He became a youthful idol, and a rich man. But his father, Gregorio, who died in 1996, managed and coached Wilfred and his two older brothers. He, and a horde of hangers-on, gambled and drank away all the money.

At the end of his career, two promoters took him from his home in Puerto Rico to Argentina for a final fight, after he had been barred from the ring in his homeland.

They left him, alone, in South America, where he was found two years later, panhandling on the street, mumbling about his glory days.

Today, he lives in a nursing home in Puerto Rico, incoherent, given to rages that could endanger others. His two brothers, less afflicted than he is, live at home, punch-drunk, suffering from memory lapses.

When the *Times* reporter visited him, he stood up, unsteady on his feet, and managed a few punches—left, right—then sat down, closed his eyes, and smiled. "I would like to start boxing again," he whispered.

And they call it a sport.

Has my style changed in fifty years? Somewhat. It has changed as the medium has advanced and the knowledge of the viewer has increased. Today, the American sports viewer is the most sophisticated fan in the world. He or she (the female sports audience has grown tremendously) now knows as well as I do things I had to explain patiently and repetitively thirty-five years ago. So my approach has changed from that of an instructor to that of a fellow fan, reporting events to an equal, not a student.

Two basics of my job have been most important to me through the years. First, to speak to only one person when I look into the lens, because people watch TV as individuals, not as a crowd in a stadium. Second, never to lie to that individual, because his or her belief in me is the most valuable credential I can own.

All of the things of which I speak here didn't strike me as a lightning bolt the first time I sat behind a microphone. They have developed over the course of half a century, the result of all the experiences I have had in all the places I have traveled. This book is an attempt to share those fifty years with you, not the nuts and bolts of the sports, but the personal elements I remember the most—the funny ones, the touching ones, the exciting ones—all of which have combined to make my life the fascinating time that it has been.

I

THE JIM McKAY LIFE

Not All Fun and Games

In all my days in television, some eighteen thousand all told, one day stands out as the most significant of all: September 5, 1972.

It marked the halfway point of my career and the end of an age of innocence for sport.

The place was Munich, West Germany, scene of that summer's Olympic Games. The occasion was the most devastating, most tragic event ever to happen in connection with sport, something that has lingered in the minds of those who were there, or who watched on television, for a quarter of a century.

The Games had moved through their first eight days with Teutonic efficiency, but with a soft, light touch that was totally different from the last German Olympics, in Hitler's Germany of 1936. The organizers had declared in advance that these would be the "serene" Olympics, an attempt to heal some of the sores left by World War II.

The only marching feet heard at the opening ceremony were those of the athletes of 122 nations. German soldiers had been put to peaceable work—building a five-hundred-meter-long rainbow made of balloons. Polite security personnel wearing pale blue blazers looked more like ushers than police.

The afternoon was sunny and pleasant as children circled the track strewing flowers. Even the Soviet team was cheered.

I had one touchy moment as I was doing my on-camera

opening. A very large bumblebee buzzed ominously in front of my nose as I spoke, finally landing on my lapel, where it stayed until I finished. But like everything else that day, it proved in the end to be a serene, unaggressive bee, just minding its own business.

During the early days of competition, the Games were full of symbolism that pleased the organizers. A young American Jew, Mark Spitz, won an unprecedented seven gold medals in swimming—a Jew was cheered in Germany.

A tiny, teenage Byelorussian gymnast, Olga Korbut, a substitute on the Soviet team, suddenly found herself in the spotlight when a teammate suffered a broken arm. With a dazzling performance on the first night of the competition, a disastrous showing on the second night, and a marvelous, redemptive gold medal performance on the third evening, she became an international star and, in the process, drew more attention to the sport of gymnastics than it had ever had before. Perfect. A child from an old enemy nation becoming an Olympic heroine in Germany.

Everyone was looking forward to the beginning of men's track and field and the expected meeting between the great milers, Jim Ryun of the United States, and Kipchoge Keino of Kenya. Valery Borzov, the Soviet running machine, was the favorite in the sprints. Americans also anticipated the performance of Frank Shorter in the marathon and perhaps Dave Wottle in the 800 meters. You may recall Wottle as the frail-looking fellow from Ohio who always ran wearing a golf cap.

The Games were just what the government wanted . . . until that moment in the deep darkness before dawn, just after 5:00 A.M. on September fifth, when eight men dressed in athletic uniforms scaled the seven-foot fence surrounding the Olympic Village. A postman, on his way to work, saw them and, assuming that they were athletes sneaking back into the village after a night on the town, smiled and waved to them.

They waved back.

Minutes later, Tuvia Sokolsky, a coach on the Israeli wrestling team, awoke suddenly from a comfortable sleep. Someone was pounding urgently on the door of the Israeli sleeping quarters at 31 Connollystrasse. No Jew needs to be told what a knock on the door in the middle of the night means. Sokolsky knew instantly that the Arabs had come.

In the darkness, he made out the form of Joseph Gottfreund, pressed against the door, trying to keep out the intruders, and heard him shout to his colleagues, "Get out! Get out! Run away!" Gottfreund, a referee at the Games, had been a successful amateur wrestler in his native Rumania before emigrating to Israel. At the age of forty, he was still a strong man physically, and held out as long as he could, enabling Sokolsky and other fortunate members of the team to escape out the windows. Ten others did not.

The terrorists, their faces concealed by ski masks, armed with submachine guns, pistols, and grenades, burst into the rooms. There was a furious, chaotic struggle during which Moshe Weinberg, coach of the Israeli national team and an Olympics referee, and Joseph Romano, a thirty-two-year-old, Libyan-born weight lifter, were shot and killed. The rest of the unarmed Israelis, nine of them, were forced to stand in a circle, back to back, bound to each other and blindfolded.

Weinberg's body was placed outside. Romano's remained in the room for some time.

When the phone rang in room 1810 of the Sheraton Munchen Hotel about eight o'clock that morning, I thought it must be a wrong number, because this was supposed to be my one day off during the Games, a brief interlude between the end of gymnastics and the beginning of track and field, my two play-by-play assignments. But it was Geoff Mason, right-hand man to Roone Arledge, the president of ABC Sports and producer of our telecast, and I could hardly believe what he was saying, that terrorists had invaded the Israeli quarters, had killed two men, and were threatening to kill others.

Furthermore, he said we would be going on the air, live, to the States, and that Roone wanted me to be the anchorman. "It's still the middle of the night in the States, so I'll call you back in an hour or so when we're almost ready to go."

Margaret and I were quiet as we ate breakfast in our room, hearing sirens from the police cars wheeling around the traffic circle below us on their way to the Olympic grounds. This was too much to fully grasp.

Then, I went down to the hotel swimming pool, a habit I'd developed during the Games, for a wake-up swim. I was still in the water when I was paged. It was Mason again, and his message was simple.

"Get out here," he said. "They're putting us on the air as soon as the network opens for the day back home."

I pulled on my clothes. Only when I returned to our room long hours later and took off my trousers would I realize how completely concentrated I had become on the events of the day. Instead of underwear, I still had on my bathing suit, and it was still slightly damp.

After a thrill ride to the ABC compound with the reckless young German assigned as my driver (later in the day he totaled the little BMW while careening on some errand), I arrived to find a scene of controlled chaos—technicians moving equipment, production assistants rushing around, German border guards, some disguised as athletes, arriving in half-track vehicles outside the studio. Extra armed security ringed the television center. There was a rumor that the center would be the next target of the terrorists.

We couldn't have been much closer to the story. From our studio to the village fence was just twenty-five yards, from the fence to the Israeli quarters another seventy-five.

A camera had been rolled into position atop a knoll outside the studio. It would be the only live camera under our control all day. The pictures from another camera on a tower looking down into the village were available to us, but manned by the Munich police.

In the midst of the bustle Roone sat behind the console, apparently as calm as ever, puffing on his favorite pipe. He would be my link to the world for the next sixteen hours, talking to me through the tiny speaker (called an IFB) hidden in my right ear. As I put on the ugly gold jacket that was our uniform for the Games, I asked him why I would be anchoring the show. After all, Chris Schenkel was our on-camera host. I was assigned to play-by-play, plus the opening and closing ceremonies.

Schenkel would be in for the normal nighttime show, he said. I would anchor the live telecast because of my early background as a police reporter on the *Baltimore Evening Sun*.

This may seem like a rather flimsy credential for the job that lay ahead, but I have always felt that reporting news or sports is basically the same. The reporter gives the facts, after making sure that they *are* facts. Then he places them in context with the location, the time, the weather, and the significance of what is taking place.

The live television reporter is also a storyteller whose function is to point out the twists and turns of the plot that is unfolding, and to alert the viewer to the things that may happen as he watches. In addition, I think he has the responsibility to communicate some of the emotion he feels as an eyewitness.

At the end of the telecast, if the viewer knows as much as I do and feels the emotion that I feel, then I think I've done a good job.

Arledge filled me in on what had happened and what facilities we had in place. They were minimal. We had just the one camera under our control and two reporters inside the village with shaky communication links.

One was Peter Jennings, who had been recruited for the Games by Roone with the promise that it would be a nice vacation for him, a change from Jennings's usual beat of covering the Middle East. Now, Jennings found himself closer to danger than he would have been in Lebanon.

After getting into the village with one of the few carte blanche credentials we had, he holed up on the sixth floor of Building 24, the Italian team headquarters, just fifty or so yards from the unfolding crisis. His only link to us and the world was an ordinary telephone, which technician Bill Blumel had somehow hooked into my earpiece and our outgoing signal.

John Wilcox, a young associate producer, had no carte blanche credential, so he borrowed the uniform and equipment bag of an American boxer, and slipped past the gate guard. In the bag, instead of boxing gloves, was a 16-millimeter film camera and a Telefunken brand walkie-talkie. Since he was assigned to produce film coverage, he had no idea that he would end up as a live, on-air reporter.

Looking for a vantage point for filming, he entered a building he knew was close to 31 Connollystrasse. He entered an elevator and pushed the button for the second floor. Why the second? No idea. Had to push something.

He found the second floor deserted as he walked along the corridor. Hearing water running, he entered a room. It was empty. Someone had just forgotten to turn off the water when they left. He walked out onto a balcony to see where he was and suddenly found himself looking straight into the eyes of a terrorist lookout standing on a facing balcony, no more than fifty feet away. They stared at each other for a moment; then the person, wearing a ski mask, blinked and went back inside.

I went into the studio and settled into the rather uncomfortable chair that would be my position for the next fifteen hours. We went on the air at one o'clock in the afternoon, Munich time (7:00 A.M. in New York), with a number of things to report. The terrorists had set a deadline of noon, after which they would kill all the hostages if their demands were not met. The demands included release of some two hundred Arab terrorists. Now that deadline had passed and they set a new one—five o'clock, after which they would kill one or two hostages every hour.

Chancellor Willy Brandt was on his way to Munich.

Willi Daume, chairman of the organizing committee, had just announced that the Games, unbelievably, would go on. On the monitors in the control room, I could see competition in canoeing and equestrianism. It was bizarre. A hundred yards from where I sat, men's lives hung in the balance.

The sports events seemed like meaningless trivialities from another world as I watched them through the control room glass. Glancing at my studio monitor, I felt I could almost touch the lookouts in front of Building 31—the young one in the hat, chain-smoking as he guarded the door, and the one in the ski mask, popping his head out a window like a character in some obscene Punch and Judy show.

I brought in Peter Jennings, his voice sounding thinner than usual on the telephone line. He felt reasonably sure, he said, that the hostage-taking was the work of an extremist Palestinian splinter group called Black September. That proved to be correct. From Peter's experience, he was surprised that they had killed someone at the outset. Usually, he said, they threatened much more than they carried out.

We saw the upstairs lookout throw a piece of paper out the window. It was another ultimatum, demanding that three planes fly from Munich at staggered times bearing captors and captives, each plane to leave only when the one preceding it had arrived at an unspecified destination.

All we saw on the screen was the front of a building, the lookouts, and an occasional negotiator going in. There were no reports of an agreement. The picture was unchanging, yet the feeling of tension was growing, not only on the scene but, as we learned later, all across America. People stopped their working day to watch—in homes and offices, through appliance-store windows.

From the beginning, I thought of one family certainly watching in Shaker Heights, Ohio. They were the parents and brother of twenty-eight-year-old David Berger, who had emigrated to Israel and become a member of the Israeli weight lifting team. Now he was one of those helpless men, bound together, blindfolded, not knowing if or when they would be executed.

And I would be the person who, in the end, would tell the

Berger family whether their son and brother was alive or dead. I had better be right when I told them.

And so the minutes ticked on.

3:00 P.M.—It's two hours until the deadline; all gates into the village are closed now. We see police snipers dressed in athletes' warm-up suits deploying around Building 31. One of them, tiptoeing along the roof, has an automatic rifle dangling from his hand as casually as if it were a tennis racket.

On the big bank of monitors, we see a volleyball game and a big crowd watching the American heavyweight boxer, Duane Bobick, prepare for his bout. He is a big favorite, who on this day, unfortunately, epitomizes an old saying: "The bigger they come, the harder they fall." If it had been a normal afternoon of competition, his defeat would have been one of the U.S.'s major disappointments. Now, it seems obscenely irrelevant. I wonder how long the IOC will permit the Games to go on.

There's another odd sight, too—athletes still sunning themselves around the pond in the middle of the village.

I interview an Israeli commentator, who has more details. He says that he has seen the body of Moshe Weinberg being put into an ambulance. The body is identified by Weinberg's mother, who is one of the few Jews still living in Munich.

I interview Tuvia Sokolsky, who has escaped thanks to the warning of Joseph Gottfreund. I ask him what he would do if he were in charge of the police right now. Speaking in Hebrew through an interpreter, he says, in a very low voice, looking down at his hands, "I have always said that I would never give in to these people who attack only when they have guns and we do not. But, speaking truly, all I care about now is my friends' safety."

4:00 P.M.—It's an hour until the deadline. At last, the Games have been suspended and a memorial service scheduled for 10:00 A.M. tomorrow in the Olympic Stadium. Mark

Spitz has been flown out for his own safety. The Egyptian team is leaving in sympathy with the Israelis.

4:35 P.M.—The streets around Building 31 are deserted now as the policemen in athletic garb (all volunteers, we are told) silently surround the terrorists. Other police sweep nearby buildings to empty them. Jennings locks himself in the bathroom of the Italian headquarters. Wilcox hides under a bed. Neither is discovered.

Jennings has been our primary source all afternoon, but occasionally we have been able to hear Wilcox. As he talks to Wilcox on his walkie-talkie, Peter holds the device's speaker up to the mouthpiece of his telephone so that we, and all of America, can hear. At one point when he is not on the air, Jennings says to Wilcox, "John, please don't call them Ay-rabs. After all, you're on the air to the States."

"I am? Well, thanks a lot for telling me, Peter!" Somehow, we have neglected to tell John that he is now a commentator as well as a lookout.

4:49 P.M.—It's eleven minutes until the deadline. A few blocks away, the evening rush hour has begun, but on Connollystrasse there is total silence. Jennings reports, sotto voce, that "a colossal number of police and border guards are closing in on Building 31." New York tells Arledge that we must take a station break, of all absurd things. Arledge says no.

4:53 P.M.—I continue to count down to the deadline. We are told that the police chief is coming in a minute to talk to the terrorists. "He'd better hurry," I say. Peter reports that a squad of thirty-five volunteers will storm the building.

4:59 P.M.—Nothing moves. There is no sound except border guard trucks rumbling up outside our studio.

5:00 P.M.—The deadline passes. There is no attack by the police.

5:01 P.M.—Two negotiators go inside. The scene looks like a still picture. Nothing moves for what seems a very long time. I realize that I am talking in a hushed voice, as if praying in church.

5:11 P.M.—Negotiators come out. No word of agreement. They leave behind only one person, a woman, who is carrying on a conversation outside the front door of the building with the young cigarette-smoking guard in the hat.

Later, we find out that the negotiators knew the terrorist-in-the-hat fancied himself as a ladies' man. Thus, the woman negotiator was a person less likely to be captured or assaulted, and just might find out more from the amorous guard.

5:30 P.M.—I report that a crowd estimated at eighty thousand has gathered around the perimeter of the village, but no one in that crowd, no one in the world, can do anything to help the hostages; their fate is controlled by the terrorists. And as the ski-masked lookout sticks his head out again, I wonder aloud to those watching all over America, "What's going on inside that head? If only we knew."

5:46 P.M.—Police are closing in.

5:55 P.M.—I have to report that we are reluctantly leaving the air for an hour. CBS has reserved the satellite for that time and won't relinquish it to us, even though they have no facilities for live coverage of the scene.

During the interval of no television coverage, I continue on radio, a medium rather unfamiliar to me, since I had gone directly from newspaper reporting to TV. I report what I see on my monitor, along with whatever news bulletins come across the wire service machines.

7:23 P.M.—We are back on the air and Jennings reports that flags in the village are at half-staff; he adds solemnly, the mood is one of "immediate expectancy."

8:00 P.M.—The situation has changed dramatically. There will be no attack on the building, and the authorities have agreed to transport the terrorists and their hostages by helicopter to Fürstenfeldbruck, a military airport outside Munich, where a 727 will be waiting to take them to an undisclosed destination. Later we would learn that there was no intention of letting the 727 take off, that six snipers had been dispatched to the airport and would try to pick off the terrorists as they approached the airplane.

By now, darkness has further heightened the tension.

9:15 P.M.—The helicopters take off, their little red identification lights blinking in the darkness. In the studio, we can feel the vibration as they clatter out of the village, only fifty feet or so over the heads of the crowd at the fence. Several thousand people are gathered in that crowd, staring up at the helicopters helplessly. Our daughter, Mary, is there and later says to me, "Dad, they were so close that you felt you could almost touch them. Yet, no one could do anything to help them."

Midnight—It's been three long hours since the last live reports. Nowadays, of course, we would have miniaturized cameras and microphones available to send to the airport, but even they wouldn't have been able to record the scene. The Fürstenfeldbruck airport is closed to everyone but the police. All we get are tantalizing bits from wire services—"Shooting has broken out at the airport" . . . "Unconfirmed report that one Arab has committed suicide, three others killed in shootout, others escaped on foot" . . . "All hostages freed, all terrorists killed" . . . "Previous report too optimistic" . . . "The Jewish Defense League has called for assassination of Arab diplomats all over the world." While delivering these reports, we emphasize that they are totally unconfirmed.

We show tapes from our Volkswagen mobile unit, which has gotten into the village disguised as an ice cream truck. These shots, taken earlier in the day, show demonstrators car-

rying signs saying, STOP THE GAMES; a negotiator banging on
the door of Building 31, apparently fearful for his colleague's
safety; the colleague coming out; the hostages and terrorists
being loaded into buses underneath Building 31 for transport
to the helicopters.

But there is no substantive word of what is happening at
the airport—except for one brief frightening report: "All hell
is breaking loose out here! A helicopter is burning!" This information is handed to me just after I've interviewed Konrad
Ahlers, Chancellor Brandt's press secretary, who has told me
he understands that the rescue effort has been successful.

1:00 A.M.—I am joined in the studio by Chris Schenkel;
Peter Jennings, now attired in a neat double-breasted blue
blazer; and Lou Cioffi, ABC News's recently appointed bureau
chief in Bonn, the West German capital. Cioffi had come
down just the day before with his wife to spend a few vacation
days at the Olympics. Now, he is just back from Fürstenfeldbruck airport, where he went on his own initiative to see what
he could find out.

He tells us that huge traffic jams, caused by rubberneck-
ers, are hindering the efforts of the police. When he finally got
to the airport entrance, he says, he was stopped by guards
but was able to hear an explosion, which he presumed was a
helicopter blowing up, and actually heard bullets whizzing
over his head.

Each report I feed to a disturbed public seems more ominous than the last. But still we have no official word. Have the
terrorists been captured? More important, are the hostages
still alive?

I think of David Berger's family in Ohio, waiting to hear
either the word "alive," or the word "dead."

At the press center, Marvin Bader, our vice president in
charge of Olympic planning, has been camped out for hours,
trying to find out what's happened, if anything, from Hans
"Jonny" Klein, the Olympics press chief. The two men have
gotten to be good friends in the months before the Games, but

now Klein can say nothing. There will be a closed meeting of officials, he tells Bader, then a press conference, at which the Bavarian minister of the interior will report on events at the airport.

So we wait, and wait, and wait.

The meeting seems to go on forever, as we try to make sense in the studio. It is most difficult. Finally, the officials emerge, but a somber-looking Klein shrugs off Bader, saying that the minister himself will have to make the announcement.

4:45 A.M.—It's almost 11:00 P.M. in New York and time for the late evening local news. Things are frantic in the control room, as Arledge argues with New York. We want to stay on the air. New York tells Roone that local news is a sacred cow to ABC's affiliated stations. We will have to leave the air and come back later, he is told.

Mason is on the walkie-talkie with Bader. "We have to know, Marvin!" he shouts. "They're going to cut us off in New York!"

I am filled with mixed emotions as I continue. Jennings fills us in on the background of the Black September group. Roone feeds me every bit of verified information he can come up with. With every passing minute, every pessimistic unconfirmed report, I feel certain that the news will be very bad, but I can't say it until I know for sure.

At the press center, where we have no cameras, the interior minister drones on. Rather than saying immediately what has happened to the hostages, he begins telling the entire story from its beginning early the previous morning. A reporter shouts angrily, "We know all that. Tell us what's happened to the hostages." Still, the man persists.

Bader spots another German official he has gotten to know, Otto Kensch. He draws him aside and looks squarely into his eyes. "Otto," he says, "we have to know. What's happened out there?"

"I can't tell you, Marvin."

"Otto, as a friend, you have to. They're going to take us off the air in New York. We've been covering this story live for fifteen hours, the whole country is watching and waiting, and we have to know."

As the two men stare at each other, Bader sees Kensch's eyes filling up with tears. Then Otto, looking around carefully as the minister drones on, tells Marvin the terrible news.

"They're all dead, Marvin."

"Who is dead, Otto? Who?"

"The Israelis."

The word is flashed from Bader to Mason to Arledge. Roone tells it to me gently in my earpiece as I continue to talk with Schenkel, Jennings, and Cioffi. I interrupt our conversation.

"Gentlemen," I say, "we have the official word from the airport." By my expression, they know the news isn't good, but they don't know just how terribly bad it is.

Even after long years in the business, it is still difficult to realize that the cold piece of glass you are talking to, the camera lens, is actually the eyes of millions of people, each looking at you on their television screen and reacting as if it is a one-on-one conversation.

I look into those eyes, still thinking especially of that family in Shaker Heights, and I know that my own eyes are heavy with sorrow. And I know what I must say.

"When I was a boy, my father told me that in life, our greatest ambitions and our worst fears are seldom realized. Tonight, our worst fears have been realized."

I pause, to suck up air.

"Two of the hostages were killed in their rooms this morning—excuse me, that's yesterday morning. Nine others were killed at the airport tonight."

I pause again, looking for breath. I feel the tears coming and try to hold them back. I hope my voice won't break as I say the next three words. I've never felt this way before.

"They're all gone."

That moment is the closest I have ever come to breaking

up on the air. All the tension and emotion I have been feeling during the long hours of waiting have welled up inside me.

Schenkel, Jennings, and Cioffi look down at the floor as I recount the entire story, from its shocking beginning to its terrible end. In the usually noisy control room, there is total silence.

It is a time without hope.

Other details came in bit by bit. Watching from their hiding places, the police snipers had allowed two of the terrorists to enter the waiting 727, inspect it, and start back to the helicopter. Then they opened fire, killing one of the men. The other escaped to the helicopter and shortly thereafter, there was wild shooting and an explosion from a hand grenade, which destroyed the helicopter and killed the hostages. There was no immediate word on how many terrorists had been killed and if any had escaped.

We left the air shortly after 4:00 A.M. Outside the studio, I looked across the fence to the dark, silent building that had been the focus of the world for the past twenty-three hours. Standing in the dark, in the cool early morning air, I thought of the hostages, all dead now, and recalled a poem by A. E. Housman I had learned in high school called "To an Athlete Dying Young."

Margaret awoke as I walked back into our hotel room.

"You must be exhausted," she said. "But at least all the hostages were saved."

She'd heard the false report German television had aired, then gone to bed. Our telecast was not available in the hotel.

"No, Margaret," I said. "I hate to tell you, but it is the other way around. The hostages were all killed at the airport."

Six hours later, I was in the crowded Olympic Stadium doing commentary on a memorial service. Many of the seventy-five thousand people gathered there had gone to bed after hearing the same false report Margaret had heard—that all the hostages had been saved. They were shocked to find that instead of track and field, which was scheduled to begin that day, they were taking part in what amounted to a funeral service for the eleven slain Israelis. As at the opening ceremony, the weather was beautiful, but the mood was so different—heartbreaking, really. I recited on the air some of the Housman poem:

> The time you won your town the race
> We chaired you through the market-place;
> Man and boy stood cheering by,
> And home we brought you shoulder-high.
>
> Today, the road all runners come,
> Shoulder-high we bring you home,
> And set you at your threshold down,
> Townsman of a stiller town.
>
> Smart lad, to slip betimes away
> From fields where glory does not stay
> And early though the laurel grows
> It withers quicker than the rose.
>
> Eyes the shady night has shut
> Cannot see the record cut,
> And silence sounds no worse than cheers
> After earth has stopped the ears:
>
> Now you will not swell the rout
> Of lads who wore their honours out,
> Runners whom renown outran
> And the name died before the man.

Twenty-four years later, I was awakened again in my hotel room by an early morning call. This time I was at the 1996 Atlanta Olympics and the phone call was from a reporter for the *Atlanta Constitution*. It was an eerie moment as he told me that a bomb had exploded early that morning in Centennial Park, the downtown playground constructed by the city for the enjoyment of the visitors to the Games. A woman had been killed, others injured. Once more, I was hearing news of a disaster at the Olympics. Once again my wife stirred beside me in bed, wondering what this was all about. Once again, just as at the hotel in Munich, the room had pale beige walls and draperies, which were drawn shut against the morning sun.

But there was a difference. The Atlanta bombing, like most acts of international terrorism, was designed to instill fear into the hearts of everyone in Atlanta because of its indiscriminate nature.

Munich was different. It was a targeted event. There was something about it that had the symbolism of a medieval morality play. The terrorists invaded the sanctum sanctorum of sport, the Olympic Village, dressed in the uniforms of Olympians, and proceeded to kill not their enemy's soldiers, but its sportsmen.

In the case of Atlanta, we saw and heard about the result, not the act itself.

In Munich, we were all, reporters and viewers alike, eyewitnesses, and for that reason, almost participants in what happened. We felt not only the possibility of death, but the possibility of salvation.

While the athletes lived, there was hope in our hearts. The cruel outcome erased all that hope.

When we hear of an accident in which only one or two people survive, we tend unconsciously to put ourselves among the survivors. Here, in that last shocking moment, we all knew that if we had been in that room, standing in that circle, bound and blindfolded, we, too, would in the end have died.

In the quarter of a century since then, not a month has passed without at least three or four people approaching me wherever I might be—in an airport, a supermarket, wherever—wanting to talk with me about Munich.

I think that what remains in their minds, and mine, is compassion for the men who died, but also a lingering reminder of our own mortality.

☆

The dictionary defines the word "seminal" as meaning "influencing future events or developments." That was the meaning of the Munich tragedy to my career.

My intention when I started out in television was to become a network newsman, possibly an anchorman, but opportunities kept presenting themselves in sports. I had always loved sports and apparently have a talent for talking about them, but there had been that nagging feeling within me that I had missed a more worthy calling.

I was stunned by the personal response to my coverage of the tragedy.

Walter Cronkite cabled me the morning after, telling me that I had done honor to the medium, my network, and myself. Later, I received a news Emmy and a George Polk Memorial award for my work that day, along with the Officer's Cross of the Legion of Merit from the West German government. I realized that whatever news ambitions still lurked within me had been fulfilled. One day had been sufficient.

Another thing entered my mind looking back on September 5, 1972: I understood more clearly the tremendous power of television. On that day, the people of the United States were indeed united in their reaction to what happened. It stirred their emotions in a way that only live television reporting can.

If they could be moved to anger and sadness, I reflected, they could also be moved to more positive emotions. A young person could be inspired to pursue a talent, no matter how small it might seem. An adult might realize that defeats in life sometimes can lead to victories, that "the human drama of athletic competition" can be translated into the drama of daily living.

So the lesson came to me through the towering tragedy of Munich that I might also find very worthwhile work in my regular job, that of reporting sports. I have found it more satisfying ever since.

This book is about my career, which started in Baltimore a long time ago.

But my life began on Jefferson Street in Philadelphia.

6219-21-23-27 Jefferson Street, Philadelphia, PA

I grew up in the Overbrook section of Philadelphia in the days before they changed our names to Social Security numbers and our hometowns to zip and area codes. More specifically, I grew up in an unusual family compound that found three generations of McManuses, Gallaghers, and Callahans living in the 6200 block of Jefferson Street in the 1920s and '30s.

To understand the way it was you must picture the Royal Poinciana Apartments (where they got the name I'll never know—there wasn't a palm tree within 1,200 miles). The apartments were actually a row of some thirty houses, all connected in the front, but separated in the back by what were called "areaways." Each house consisted of two apartments, one on the first floor, with a nice front porch and a small lawn, the other taking up the second and third floors, with a porch sticking out from the second floor in the rear.

We all lived within four houses of each other. Like this:

6219—The second and third floors were inhabited by my mother's family: her mother, a small German-American woman who ran the show; her father, a retired salesman who kept pretty much to himself; Uncle Kenny, a bachelor, and Aunt Marie, the sister who never married. The rest of my mother's ten siblings were scattered up and down the East Coast, as far north as Boston (my favorite uncle, Jim) and as far west as Cleveland (Joe, known as Uncle Joe Cleveland, to differentiate him from my father, Uncle Joe Philly).

I remember my grandmother for her German potato salad, made with oil and vinegar, bacon bits, onions, and celery seed, and for holiday dinners, where I would sit at the children's table with my sister, Mary Lou, and several cousins. After dinner, my grandmother would retire to the rear parlor, where she would preside from her favorite armchair. Stuffed between the cushion and the chair arm were her cigarettes, which she deceived herself into thinking no one knew she smoked. In the corner was an upright player piano, which we took turns pumping. The piano rolls, tight rolls of white paper with small, rectangular holes punched in them, were all renditions of popular songs of the day.

Grandfather Gallagher, frankly, was rather a rudderless man at this point in his life, unable to hit the road anymore because of illness, but he was good to me and provided my first sports thrill by taking me to meet two friends of his, Ted Lyons and Sad Sam Jones, both pitchers for the Chicago White Sox.

6221—Just across the areaway from the Gallaghers lived my father's sister, Mary, and her husband, Ed Callahan, who resembled Babe Ruth. He had, in fact, been a semipro baseball player with some local repute as a home run hitter. The Callahan house, like my grandmother's, was basically a matriarchal society. Aunt Mary, who worked in her mother's health spa (about which more later), was in charge of all pragmatic matters, like money.

Uncle Ed was a theatrical booking agent, a soft man in a hard business who sometimes loaned his clients more money each week than he took in from them. Among the young performers he started out was comedian Red Skelton, later a major star, who arrived from the Midwest without a dime. Uncle Ed staked him and got him his first booking in the East, as the MC of a marathon dance show.

Once, when an old vaudevillian died, Uncle Ed was notified that he was among the man's heirs. His inheritance turned out to be the old trouper's songs, none of which had been hits.

Uncle Ed never smoked a cigarette or took a drink in his life. His strongest oath was "Goshamighty, Mary!" and his answer to all problems was to run to the store for two quarts of ice cream and a bottle of ginger ale.

There were three Callahan kids: Frank, my favorite cousin; Helene, known as Sister; and little Eddie. In a room on the third floor, in treasured privacy, lived Uncle Ed's bachelor brother, Uncle Frank, a longtime men's clothing salesman at John Wanamaker's department store. At report card time, all the cousins would enter Uncle Frank's room, one at a time, to present their marks and do a short recitation, at the end of which, if your marks were good, you got a silver dollar.

My recitation was, "Jack be nimble, Jack be quick, Jack jump over the candlestick," accompanied by a small leap on the word "jump." Uncle Frank would then tell me the same thing every time.

"Jimmy," he would say, "you are a good boy—quiet and unassuming."

Cousin Frank, who was named after Uncle Frank, did not get good marks, although he tried hard, and we felt sorry for him when he went into the hallowed room. Only years later did we find out that he got *two* silver dollars—for trying so hard.

The Callahan maid, Katie, stormed through the house, scattering dust and kids as she went. She bowed before only two people—Uncle Frank and curly-haired Eddie, who had her wrapped around his little finger, as the saying went in those days.

The Gallaghers and Callahans were not directly related, of course, and in fact, there was a sort of mini-vendetta between them. The Callahans were rather a loud crowd, and this drove my grandfather up the wall, particularly when the sound of the kids' favorite record, Clyde McCoy's "Sugar Blues," drifted across the areaway, as it sometimes did all day long.

6223—This was our address. We lived on the first floor: my father, Joe McManus; my mother, Florence; and my sister and I. Dad had started a successful real estate business in

1928, just in time to be wiped out by the 1929 crash. He was a young man, determined to get his kids raised with a good education, so he found a job with the federal government as a real estate appraiser, a field in which he became an expert over the next thirty years.

My mother did what mothers did in those days: She stayed home, took care of Mary Lou and me, cleaned the house, and cooked the meals. She had a basic mother's feeling toward me. She thought I was perfect, frankly, and that was that. She must have forgotten the day she took me to the circus when I was eight or nine. When she refused to buy me a live chameleon to take home so I could watch it change colors, I closed my eyes and refused to look at the rest of the circus.

Some perfect.

My father was my dad, my friend, my fellow baseball fanatic, and my teacher. He was a strong believer in finding a kid's interest and talent and encouraging him to develop it. He never tried to force me into a career as a doctor, a lawyer, a businessman, or anything else. But when he noticed that, at the age of twelve, I could write a good composition and that my idols were a young sportswriter on the *Philadelphia Record* named Red Smith and the CBS Radio sports announcer, Ted Husing, he encouraged me in that direction.

I still remember the morning he and I were sitting in the family's 1939 Dodge, waiting for the Loyola High School bus. My marks had been sagging recently, and it was time for a lecture, something he seldom gave. When he did, I paid attention.

He didn't scold. He told me how proud he was of me, of how much potential I had. He said I should remember that he would always be on my side, no matter whether the marks were good or bad, whether my behavior was exemplary or disappointing.

But.

Although he would always be on my side and ready to help, he would certainly prefer to be able to be proud of that association, rather than maintaining it simply because I was his son and he loved me.

How could I be a rebellious teenager after that?

Mary Lou was five years younger than I, and more confident in some ways. When I was too shy to collect the money from the customers on my *Collier's* and *Woman's Home Companion* magazine route, she went out and did it for me. And she took my big-brother teasing in good spirit.

Across the areaway from us, at 6225, were a childless couple named Roland and Fanny Bloomer (yes, that was the lady's real name). I am told that I called them Ro-Ro and Fa when I was very small.

Grandmother McManus lived above us, on the second and third floors. Born in Ireland, she had married another immigrant, Patrick McManus, at the age of sixteen. He became a very successful home builder, had in fact built many of the homes in our neighborhood, before dying of pneumonia at the age of thirty-five. Sadly, most of Grandmother's children died before they reached fifty. Uncle Jimmy, after whom I was named, died in his mid-twenties in a flu epidemic, after serving in the navy in World War I.

My grandmother, however, was never to be daunted. With seven children to raise, she somehow started a business catering to the vanity of wealthy Philadelphia women. Today, it would be called a spa, and she might be Elizabeth Arden. She had steam cabinets and masseuses, and all the things that promised instant health and beauty to the ladies of the Main Line. Her clients had names like Warburton, Stotesbury, and Sinickson.

She did very well, well enough to travel to Europe every summer, taking along one or another of her daughters each time. On one occasion, she even flew across the English Channel, when that was still considered an adventure. She was small but had a presence when entering a room, and seemed much taller than she was, with a large frontal area, adorned with ropes of pearls.

6227—Appropriately, there were two apartments (6225

upstairs and 6227 downstairs) occupied by strangers before one reached the next relative. I never really knew who lived in those houses, but they must have felt like besieged villagers, surrounded by McManuses, Gallaghers, and Callahans as they were. I say that the gap was appropriate because when you entered the upstairs apartment at 6227, you entered a different world than the hurly-burly of the other relatives' homes.

The occupants of 6227 were my great-uncle Michael—my paternal grandfather's brother—and his wife, Aunt Til (for Matilda). Uncle Mike had been born in Ireland, but was now a respected Philadelphia lawyer, a religious man who sternly refused to take on divorce cases. He looked a great deal like President Woodrow Wilson, and to enter his house was almost like entering a courtroom. Most of the furniture seemed to be old leather, and the glass-fronted barrister's bookcases were full of imposing-looking law books. The place had a permanent aroma of Uncle Mike's fine cigar smoke as Aunt Til padded about, her hair in neat braids wrapped around her head, always wearing a housedress that seemed to have been pressed within the last ten minutes.

Uncle Mike was the arbiter of all arguments, not only among us cousins, but of all the kids in the neighborhood. His judgment was accepted without question and acted upon faithfully. After all, he was a lawyer and his partner was a judge.

When entering his presence, you took off your cap and lowered your voice. Leaning back in his favorite leather chair, he would allow a wreath of cigar smoke to form over his head before saying to me, "Well, Gim"—he always called me Gim— "what's the problem this time?"

This was the closed society in which I was raised. Summertimes were great. Grandmother McManus rented a place at the shore in Margate, New Jersey, on the same island as Atlantic City, and the McManuses and Callahans used it. We played in the ocean and lay on the beach and flew kites high in the summer seaside breeze.

Once, I stood on the boardwalk, tied three balls of string together, and let out my kite until it was just a dot on the horizon. I was totally engrossed, in my own world, watching the little paper kite shrink almost into invisibility. Then I realized that the sun was setting and that I was going to be late for dinner, with the kite string still to be reeled back in.

I was arm-weary, penitent, and an hour late when I got home. And, as always, I was forgiven.

Cousin Frank and I once walked the length of the boardwalk, all the way to the inlet and back, some fourteen miles, just to prove we could do it. We went to the Steel Pier and the Steeplechase Pier, and one day, the great dirigible *Hindenburg* flew straight over our heads at about two hundred feet in altitude.

There were memorable incidents, small tragedies at the time, like the evening when Grandmother Gallagher sneezed her new false teeth out the window of the car on the way back from the shore, and the time when Uncle Jim's wife, Aunt Mae, fell into the grease pit of a gas station while trying to find her way to the ladies' room. Serious things to the adults, but to us kids they were cause for secret laughter as we sat in the backseat, covering our mouths.

Looking back, there was a negative for me. I think the closeness of the families contributed to my shyness with outsiders, which was so great that when my father was transferred to Baltimore, I asked to stay behind and live with the Callahans. That request was denied, fortunately.

Moving to Baltimore was the key to my later life.

My father suggested that I go out for a lot of activities at Loyola High School until I found ones that suited me, which I did: football, basketball, baseball, dramatics, debating, the school paper—the whole lot. And I made new friends.

By the time I entered Loyola College, I was much more confident and gregarious. College-level varsity sports were beyond my abilities, but I played intramurals, became president and star of the drama club, proved a good debater, and was sports editor of the college paper and P.A. announcer at the basketball games. I was even president of the senior class.

My college career was shortened to three and a half years, accelerated because of the war effort. I went off to midshipman school at Columbia University in February of 1943, served three and a half years in the navy, mostly on escort duty in the South Atlantic aboard minesweepers, then returned to Baltimore and looked for my first real job.

All I knew was that I wanted to be a newspaper reporter or a radio sports announcer.

Television?

There was no such thing in Baltimore, not in the summer of 1946.

The News Business to a New Business

The room was windowless.

In the dark, a clutter of empty boxes and tangled wires could be made out. On top of an empty shipping carton was something that looked like a large 1930s radio, except for the glowing rectangular tube in the upper left-hand corner.

Two men stared at the tube.

One was Neil H. Swanson, executive editor of the Sunpapers of Baltimore, in his mid-fifties, a tall, imperious-looking fellow in shirtsleeves. A cigarette dangled from his lower lip, defying gravity.

The other person was a twenty-six-year-old reporter on the *Evening Sun* named Jim McManus. And McManus was feeling extremely honored to be alone in the room with the Great Man. Swanson was a flamboyant character—quite out of tune with the good, gray Sunpapers—who seemed to see himself as a combination of William Randolph Hearst and Hildy Johnson, the swashbuckling reporter in Charles MacArthur and Ben Hecht's wonderful play *The Front Page*.

Something resembling snow appeared on the tube. The two of us stared at that for a while until suddenly a picture came into focus. It showed people roller-skating in a big, empty arena known as the Baltimore Coliseum.

Swanson smiled, clapped me on the back, and said, "Well, Jim, it looks like we've bought ourselves a television station!"

"We?" At that time, my salary was $65 a week, before taxes.

This was how television came to the city of Baltimore in the first week of November 1947.

My involvement had started unexpectedly several weeks before.

Coming out of the navy after World War II, all I wanted to do was get into the newspaper business. So I started making the rounds. After a few futile interviews in New York, I came back to my hometown and managed to get an appointment with Edwin P. Young Jr., city editor of the *Baltimore Evening Sun*.

The paper wasn't hiring right then, Young said to me, but was I, by any chance, the same Jim McManus who had written a column on high school sports before the war for a small local magazine called *Gardens, Houses and People*?

I couldn't believe that he had even read *Gardens, Houses and People*, let alone that he remembered it. The magazine was basically a women's garden publication that was sent out free to residents of several nice areas in Baltimore. It was my father who had suggested that I talk to the editor of the magazine about a high school sports column. I'll be darned if the editor, Warren Wilmer Brown, hadn't said okay, providing that I would accept a tie each Christmas as payment for my efforts.

Now, seven years later, I'd discovered that the city editor of the *Evening Sun* had read my column. After thinking it over for a minute, he said, "Jim, that was some of the best sports-writing in town in those days—better than those guys over there [gesturing toward the sports department]. But we don't have an opening in sports at the moment, or so the sports editor claims. How would you like to be a police reporter?"

My stomach did a somersault as I pictured myself, press card in my hatband, swaggering into the police station and saying to the captain, "Hi, Chief, I'm the new man from the *Evening Sun*."

"I'd like that a lot," I said.

It was the break of a lifetime, because, in the next year and a half, Ed Young taught me everything I know about reporting. It also led to television—and, oh yes, it introduced me to my wife.

Indirectly, that introduction was made on the first day I reported for work. Mr. Young looked extremely busy when I came in, so I leaned against a pole for about a half hour watching the fast pace of the city room swirling around me. Eventually, Ed Young noticed me.

"Oh, sorry, Jim," he said. "We're a little short on desks, but that reporter is out sick today, so take the desk over there." He was pointing to a chair on the back of which one of the staff artists had written the name "Dempsey" in india ink and drawn a pair of boxing gloves beneath it. I vaguely associated that with sports and thought no more about it until the third morning of my career, when a soft, friendly, feminine voice in back of me said, "Excuse me, but I think you're sitting in my chair."

I turned around and saw, for the first time, star reporter Margaret Dempsey, one of the few women who had been able to make her way on the paper in those benighted days before women's lib. She was rather tall—five feet eight—slender, blond, with a soft, beautiful complexion, green eyes that could never know envy, and a friendly smile that could melt the Rock of Gibraltar. She was wearing a navy blue skirt and a white shirt, open at the neck.

The old *Evening Sun* city room is gone now—the whole building, in fact—but to this day, I stop whatever I am doing to look at her when she wears a white shirt. And when she smiles at me, which is often, my feeling is as new and deep as it was at my first sight of her that day fifty-two years ago.

We quickly became friends, but it took me a solid year before I worked up my nerve to ask her for a date. I was not exactly Cary Grant when it came to such things.

During that year, I moved up to general assignment reporter and was made aviation editor, in lieu of a raise. That meant I inherited a huge stack of press releases from the departing aviation editor and got to attend many boring meetings of the aviation board.

It also got me my first out-of-town assignment, to cover the Cleveland Air Races, which in those days were conducted over a triangular course in the suburbs of Cleveland. One of the World War II fighter planes in the race crashed into a house, killing several people, so I wrote a column headlined "The Romans Would Have Loved It," detailing the crash and condemning the air races as deadly folly. The column was displayed prominently on the editorial page, and within a month, the air races were canceled. I still like to think that my piece may have had something to do with the cancellation.

I was as happy as I could be.

Then, one early fall day, two assistant city editors named Bob Cochrane and Phil Heisler quietly approached three of us—Jake Hay, Dick Tucker, and me—at our desks and asked us to come upstairs at four o'clock.

"Upstairs" was a big, attic-like area, unattractive but private.

"Mr. Swanson has asked us to speak to the three of you," Cochrane said. "As you know, the Sunpapers have never owned a radio station, while the Hearst paper has the most successful station in the area, WBAL. He is determined that this will not be the case in television. We have been very quietly assembling the equipment and technical personnel for a TV station for some time now, planning to go on the air in a month or so.

"Now we have just found out that the *News-Post* [the Hearst paper] has been planning just as secretly and is going on the air in two weeks. Mr. Swanson is determined that we will be on the air before they are."

I wondered what that had to do with me.

He continued. "As I said, we have all the technical gear and personnel, but we have no producers, directors, or announcers. We want you three to serve those functions until we can hire professionals from out of town."

"Why me?" I asked, I suppose with a bit of petulance in my voice.

"Well, didn't you say you were president of the dramatic society at Loyola College?"

"Yes, but . . ."

"That's good enough for now. After all, Phil and I are going to run the station, and we don't know anything about television either. And remember, nobody in Baltimore knows anything about television, except for a few people who have been watching in bars that have those big antennas that can pick up the Washington stations."

Our small group—Cochrane, Heisler, Carl Knopper (the chief engineer), Hay, Tucker, and I—crashed ahead for several weeks, with my mellifluous voice announcing, "This is WMAR-TV, the Sunpapers television station, operating on Channel Two for test purposes."

Swanson appeared often, looking around, pulling his suspenders out a bit with his thumbs, nodding, then going back to his big office, leaving a trail of cigarette ashes in his wake.

Now, we were ready to actually go on the air. We would televise two horse races from nearby Pimlico in the afternoon, then the crew would race in the mobile unit to the Coliseum for a Baltimore Bullets basketball game, where Bob Elmer would be the commentator.

I was the host of the very first Baltimore telecast—the horse races. Joe Kelley, racing writer for the *Sun,* and Dave Woods, the track's PR man, joined me to add racing expertise.

Might they have been TV sports' first "analysts"?

The Pimlico track management, ever wary of the new, untested medium, wouldn't allow us to televise the feature race for fear it would hurt attendance. This seemed an overly cautious attitude, since there were only about a hundred TV sets in the Baltimore area, but we managed anyway with lesser races.

Except for a few camera problems, we thought the show went quite well.

Many years later, I discovered that at least one viewer disagreed with my assumption. He was H. L. Mencken, the revered "Sage of Baltimore," newspaperman, author, and critic.

After watching us at the home of Paul Patterson, publisher of the Sunpapers, Mencken wrote this in his diary, which was not made public until 1989:

"It seemed to me to be a very poor show. . . . I'd not give ten cents for an hour of such entertainment, even if it showed a massacre. . . . The *Sun* announcer, a young man in the sports department, was poor at the job, and there were intervals of complete silence. . . . I can imagine only very stupid people looking at it, at least in its present form. It is not even as well developed as the movie was in the days of *The Great Train Robbery.*"

If there were "intervals of complete silence"—and I believe there were—it was because I became slightly tongue-tied at that historic moment; it was probably the last time that I, or any other TV sports commentator, ever committed that sin. (Then again, some might have considered it a blessing.)

Actually, those of us who participated in that bit of local entertainment history thought the show went reasonably well, except for the moment a workman carrying a ladder walked directly between Joe Kelley and me and the camera. The man's mistake was understandable—in those days, two men with a microphone meant "radio." It never occurred to people that a picture of the scene might be sent through the air.

Except for local news shot with a hand-held 16-millimeter camera, all programs were live, and we had a lot of time to fill. WMAR-TV was the fifth station to join the CBS television network; already on the air were affiliates in Boston, New York, Philadelphia, and Washington. The network itself provided a couple of hours of prime-time programming. This left us with a vast void to fill, which was difficult since, to begin with, we had no studio.

Anticipating that problem, the *Sun* purchased two large, awkward mobile units. These would become familiar objects in the months to come, rumbling through the streets of Baltimore in search of almost anything that moved. Logically enough for a newspaper, the Sunpapers saw television more as a news rather than as an entertainment medium. In most cases, the "news" that could be covered on a prescheduled, regular basis turned out to be sports.

On one notable day, we covered four events with the two ungainly mobile units. One of them was horse racing at a track in Laurel, Maryland, about twenty miles from Baltimore. We then rocketed to the city to televise an amateur hour from a movie theater. The other unit picked up a Navy football game in Annapolis in the afternoon, then followed with a Baltimore Bullets basketball game in the evening. Such a feat would be considered impossible in the high-tech nineties.

Looking back, our equipment was primitive. The cameras were huge, heavy loads—iconoscopes, they were called. The pictures were black and white, of course, and since the iconoscopes were insensitive to the color red, performers were required to wear brown lipstick and a strange shade of heavy tan pancake makeup. Margaret was sent to New York by Swanson to research the makeup situation before we went on the air.

Graphics (supers, they were called then) were made by hand. Individual letters were stuck, one by one, on a piece of cardboard. One camera shot the graphic while another showed, for example, the speaker's face. The graphic bearing the speaker's name was then superimposed on the face. Sometimes the super would be slightly slanty. Occasionally, a thumb would be seen adjusting the card.

I'll say one thing about this job of mine: It was never routine. There seemed to be a surprise a day. During the daytime hours, the station normally fed music and a test pattern, which consisted of a border of dark lines surrounding a drawing of an Indian chief's head. It is an indicator of the novelty of TV in those days that some people used to watch the test pattern, but after a while Cochrane came up with the idea of locking a live camera in place looking out over the busy intersection of Baltimore and Charles streets. It would at least be something to look at.

One particular day, it turned out to be more than that. Before the startled eyes of the few people watching, two robbers ran out of The Hub department store across the street from the Sunpapers, brandishing their pistols as they fled. Seconds later, people ran out of the store after them, shouting and gesturing.

Of course, if you hadn't been watching, you missed it, because there was no videotape at that time. There was something called kinescope, but that was used only to make a very fuzzy reproduction of programs for later telecast or for historical files. But the audience for the locked-in-place camera increased markedly from that day forward.

Somehow, despite all our efforts, television was coming on. On the streets, passersby would stand looking in the windows of television stores, staring at whatever was on. It was like going to the movies free.

Simultaneously, a strange social phenomenon was occurring all over town. The few people who owned TV sets would find neighbors coming to the door, uninvited, asking if they could please watch Milton Berle, Ed Sullivan, pro wrestling, or the Roller Derby, the most popular shows of the early years. The designated hosts would be expected to supply potato chips and maybe even a beer. Why? No one ever had the nerve to ask.

After many weeks of running around town with the mobile units and cramming the occasional show into the O'Sullivan Building Tower, we finally moved into our studio above the *Evening Sun* city room.

The centerpiece of our new local programming became *The National Sports Parade,* sponsored by National Bohemian Beer. It was on five afternoons a week from three to six. I was the host of the first and third hours and directed the middle hour while Bailey Goss, the top local radio sports personality, sat in the host's chair.

The raison d'être of the show, frankly, was to give race results. Baltimore was a big horse racing town (still is), and thousands of players who couldn't get to the track bet with their bookies every day.

Three hours, however, was a long time to fill. And for every half hour there was only one race result to report. So to fill out the time, we did interviews of all sorts and engaged singers and dancers, each of whom was to provide three numbers a day. By the third day, the performers were wearing out. I found myself with twenty minutes of airtime left and no musical numbers ready to go. So I got up and sang a song, fulfilling a lifelong secret ambition. From then on, I sang a song every day, a fact that in time would lead to a major upgrade in my career.

About this time, while spinning around in this brave new world of TV, I finally got up the nerve to ask Margaret for a date. To be sure she would accept, I bought tickets to a Baltimore Colts football game in the new All-America Conference. (The city's NFL glory days were still in the future.)

On the way to the game, I explained that it wouldn't be a close game, that the visiting San Francisco 49ers were a superior team, that all the Colts had was a prematurely bald quarterback named Y. A. Tittle.

"No," Margaret said, "I think it will be a tie."

"Really? And what do you think the score will be?"

She didn't hesitate. "Twenty-eight to twenty-eight," she said.

Well, the Colts fell behind, as predicted by me, and by the fourth quarter were trailing, 28–14—at which point, the remarkable Y. A. launched the first of many impossible comebacks in his long pro career. The final score? 28–28.

Maybe the reason that to this day we seldom quarrel is because, beginning with football, I came to find her so often, and so maddeningly, right.

After that, we went out together for forty-eight consecutive nights, except for one evening. She had promised fellow *Evening Sun* reporter Bill Manchester that she would go to a movie opening with him. I found it rather annoying that the man who would later write *The Death of a President* and so many other best-selling histories was cutting into my act. I didn't tell him then, but you might as well know it now, Manchester.

I persisted, however. I wasn't going to lose this woman.

One afternoon (I was still on the paper at this point) Ed Young called to me across the city room. "Jim," he said, "two guys with submachines just walked into a jewelry store on Howard Street. Get on your horse!" I ran to the door at the back of the city room, and as I opened it, I looked back and saw Margaret sitting at her desk typing. She was wearing that white shirt and navy blue skirt again. And so help me, a ray of sunshine was glinting off her blond hair. Her expression was concentrated and sincere and altogether lovable.

That picture is crystal clear in my mind half a century later.

Whether it was the possibility of sudden death in the jewelry store or what, at that instant I determined I would marry that girl. If I survived the day.

Ed Young interrupted my brief reverie. "Jim," he called, as heads turned toward me from every corner of the room. "Don't get shot!"

In the interest of accuracy, I must tell you that the holdup turned out to be a false alarm. But there was nothing false about my determination to marry Margaret. It was a long and difficult campaign. She was having a marvelous time on the newspaper and had no immediate plans for marriage. But I still persisted, and one day it finally paid off when I went to the B&O railroad station to meet her upon her return from an assignment in New York.

She was wearing a navy blue suit this time, and a navy blue straw hat.

With that beautiful smile that people comment on to this day, she said, "I did a lot of thinking while I was away, and I realized that I missed you very much. I think you're right: We should get married." So. We became engaged on a chilly late March Easter Sunday.

Six months later, we were married at Immaculate Conception Church in Towson, Maryland, at noon on October second, a gorgeous fall day.

Margaret continued writing for the *Evening Sun* and editing the Women's Page (which nowadays would be called Today, Style, Tempo, or some other chic name). I had dragged her into television as my cohost of a panel show called *The Teenage Forum* once a week. I was working on *The National Sports Parade* five afternoons a week, reading the news at 11:00 P.M., and covering various sports events. It was the beginning of a strange and busy joint schedule that continues to the present day.

January 20, 1949, some three and a half months after our wedding, was a day we looked forward to with great anticipation. Margaret was assigned by the paper to cover the inauguration of President Harry S. Truman after his historic comeback victory over Thomas E. Dewey. She would also cover the parade and the inaugural ball that night.

I would be working on it, too. WMAR-TV had agreed to lend me for the day to a new group called the Continental FM Network. FM radio stations were as new as TV, but were considered to be the wave of the future because of their superior sound quality.

For providing their coverage, I would be paid the dizzying fee of $200. Little did they know that I would gladly have done it for nothing, or perhaps a necktie the following Christmas.

The network provided me with a large envelope containing everything I would need—a credential to get to the broadcasting booth, the key to open the booth, a thick stack of notes on the inauguration and the parade to follow. They warned me that I would be on my own. There would be no other commentators ("Can't afford them, Jim"), and no technician on the scene. In the booth I would find a headset and microphone, and a television monitor on which I could follow the events while commenting on them.

Margaret and I got out of bed on the morning of the inauguration at 5:00 A.M.; I'd insisted that we leave plenty of time to make the 6:30 train to Washington. There was some grumbling from Margaret when we arrived at the station a half hour early. All these decades later, I still want to leave too early and she still wants to leave too late. Compromise is the art not only of politics, but of marriage as well.

After the forty-five-minute train ride to Washington, we checked our evening clothes in a locker at the train station (remember, we would need them for the ball), then took a taxi to the Capitol. Both of us had butterflies in our stomachs at the mere sight of the great Capitol dome, the big temporary grandstands, the security people combing the area, and the network TV trucks. This was the first inaugural ever covered on network TV.

Margaret and I separated, agreeing to meet at the railroad station after the parade.

I was surprised to see our commentary booth. It was directly above the inaugural stand, a small cubicle the size of a telephone booth with glass windows on all four sides. On the other side of an aisle was another booth exactly like it. When a guard told me that Douglas Edwards would be working in that one for the CBS network, I was impressed.

I opened the booth with my key and sure enough, there was a mike and headset as promised, and the TV monitor. My orders were to put on the headset at 10:50 A.M. At that time, a technician in a downtown studio would do a mike check and a time check. At eleven o'clock sharp, he would open my mike and I would be on the air for the next five hours.

It was a clear, very cold day in Washington, but in the cramped quarters of the booth, the sun shining in the windows made it very warm. I decided to get a little fresh air and smoke a cigarette in the few minutes remaining before airtime. Fresh air and a cigarette? Sounds ridiculous these days, doesn't it?

At five minutes before the hour, I returned to the booth and turned the door handle. It was locked!

I saw the key lying on the desk, only a foot or two away but useless to me now. I have never again been as close to panic before a show. At eleven o'clock, the technician would open the mike and hear—nothing!

I looked around for help. At the top of the stairs, a fireman stood watch. I ran up and asked him if I could borrow the small ax that hung from his belt.

"Sorry, sir," he said. "I would be fired if I let anybody have that." Then he must have seen the sheer terror in my eyes as I told him the situation. "But if you were to steal it from me for a minute . . ."

While Doug Edwards and the surrounding spectators looked on in confusion, I yanked the ax from his belt, ran down the stairs, and smashed the door window. Then I ran back, returned the ax to the fireman's belt, came back to the booth, reached through the jagged broken window, and opened the door from the inside, cutting my hand and forearm in the process. I had thirty seconds until airtime, just time enough to wrap a handkerchief around my bloody hand and arm before saying, "Good morning. This is Jim McManus reporting from Washington for the Continental FM Network . . ."

As I described the scene preceding the ceremonies, the wind picked up. Frigid air rattled the broken glass and chilled my bare, bloody right hand. It continued for the next five hours, through the inauguration and the parade, which I thought would never end. I also thought I would never be warm again.

But when the voice of a Continental executive came into my headset at the end of the broadcast, saying, "Nice job, Jim. Everything go all right on your end?" I was a happy young commentator. "Oh, sure," I said. "Just fine. Great."

Getting a taxi was impossible. I ended up walking through the cold twilight to the railroad station, where I found Margaret waiting for me. Somehow, she has always found a ride.

I was ready to go home and sleep for a week, but her day had only begun. We changed our clothes in the rest rooms at the station and were off to the inaugural ball. It was a long night as Margaret doggedly pursued one story after another. The one picture that stays in my mind of that night was Governor Jim Folsom of Alabama, known to the nation as Kissin'

Jim, sitting with his feet up on the railing of his box, drinking
Coke out of a bottle, surrounded, as always, by a covey of
twittering, pretty Southern girls.

Eventually, at about midnight, we left to catch the last
train back to Baltimore. End of story? Not quite. Margaret
still had to return to the *Evening Sun* office to write her piece
for the next day's (or by now, today's) paper.

In the empty city room, I sat with my head resting on a
desk while she typed. I was totally out of it by now, and began
to groan as the *tap-tap* of the typewriter seemed to drill into
my brain.

Margaret is a dedicated, careful writer. She will not final-
ize a page until she is totally pleased with it, no matter how
many rewrites it takes. And so it was that night.

Every so often, she would say, "Please, Jim. I won't be
much longer. I can't think with you groaning like that." She
typed and I groaned until about 4:00 A.M. Then, at last, it was
done.

It had been a twenty-four-hour period that neither of us
have ever forgotten, memories we both cherish. It helped
when five or six people told me the next day that they had
heard me on the radio, and when Ed Young, the city editor,
told Margaret that her copy was terrific.

The Sports Parade was Baltimore's first hit TV show. Wives
stayed home in those days, and they watched our program in
large numbers, even though much of it was dedicated to
sports. Just as is true to this day, except much more so then,
it was the personalities they were interested in—big, blond,
hearty Bailey Goss; Joanie Cole, a secretary who started out
handing in scores to Bailey or me and became a regular singing and dancing member of the cast; Bob Dean, a handsome
tenor; Frank O'Brien, the pianist, who developed a bantering
relationship with the hosts, much as Doc Severinsen would a
generation later with Johnny Carson on *The Tonight Show*;
and, presumably, me.

Thanks to the cooperation of theater management, we interviewed many well-known personalities who appeared at the Hippodrome and the Royal on Pennsylvania Avenue. They ranged from comedians (even the already famous Milton Berle) to musicians like Lionel Hampton, who not only came to be interviewed, but gave us an impromptu half-hour concert on the vibes. We interviewed politicians and athletes. A Washington station began to pick up the show, giving us our own mini-network. The cost of such a five-day-a-week, three-hour production would be prohibitive today.

The Sports Parade also gave birth to Baltimore's first animated commercial. The advertising manager of National Bohemian Beer, our principal sponsor, became enamored of a Lucky Strike cigarette commercial that featured marching cigarettes, dutifully performing to martial music, spelling out "Lucky Strike" like a college marching band. Could WMAR-TV produce such a commercial with marching beer bottles?

"Of course," said Cochrane. Considering our lack of big sponsors, whatever National wanted, National got. But how?

Well, Cochrane and Heisler got a couple dozen beer bottles from the brewery, lined them up, and went to work, moving the bottles by hand, punching up single-frame shots with each minuscule move. If anyone on the staff seemed not to be busy, they would put them to work. "Here—you—move these bottles for a while. I need a break."

The commercial took days to make, but it turned out surprisingly well. At least the brewery people were happy, watching the little National beer bottles marching up and down the television screens of the city.

Many years ago, when the so-called road shows dried up for the legitimate theater, someone said that "there is no place to be bad in anymore," meaning there was no place where provincial audiences would patiently watch actors learn and polish their trade. We had the luxury in TV's infant days of being "bad" in almost anything we wanted to try. I was a newsman and sports commentator. I sang and told funny stories. I was host of what must have been television's first courtroom program—*Traffic Court*, starring a real-life traffic court judge, Joseph Kolodny. I dressed up as a gas station attendant for a commercial.

Perhaps my most difficult assignment, and the one that gave me a valuable baptism under fire, was a weekly fifteen-minute interview program called *Know Your Sunpapers Route Owner*. The Sunpapers were delivered then, as they are now, by independent contractors who serviced the various neighborhoods of the city and surrounding counties. Each week, I was required to interview one of them (and his family) for fifteen minutes. How many different ways can you ask someone how early he has to get up in the morning to deliver the papers, or how he keeps them from getting wet as they lie in the customer's driveway?

Remember once again that TV was such a hypnotic new attraction that people actually watched such stuff. It also kept the route owners happy, and taught me how to fill time.

The biggest occasion of our early televising was to be the opening of Baltimore's brand-new airport, Friendship International. It would be the first commercial airport in the East capable of accommodating jet aircraft. The state police estimated that a crowd of 250,000 people would assemble for the great day. With that in mind, aircraft would be utilized for the first time in Maryland history to spot and direct the huge volume of traffic.

There would be a "breakfast flight" of small planes from all over the East, hundreds of them to blacken the sky over Friendship. President Harry S. Truman would fly in to deliver a major address on the runway, where a temporary grandstand to hold some 30,000 people had been erected. The events were scheduled to run a total of six hours, every minute of which we would carry live, totally sponsored by a popular Baltimore eatery, Marty's Restaurant.

Ad Wienert, an announcer later destined for considerable success in New York under the name of Lee Stevens, was sta-

tioned in the terminal building. I was out on the runway, prepared to describe all of the outdoor excitement.

The breakfast flight didn't exactly blacken the sky. Perhaps
a dozen small aircraft showed up; the pilots gobbled their
Danish and left. Instead of the anticipated 250,000 people,
only 2,500 showed up. State police planes circled over empty
highways.

When President Truman arrived in what was the equivalent of today's Air Force One, he took a look at the nearly
empty grandstand, threw away his prepared "major address,"
ad-libbed a few lines about the airport and the "great state of
Maryland," then took off for Kansas City.

We had gone on the air at 8:00 A.M. It was only two hours
later and everything was over—finished! If we could simply
have gone off the air, we could've chalked up the day to experience and that would have been that. However, Marty's Restaurant had bought six hours of programming and was
planning to use every minute of it. Each commercial was
worth money to the station, and we had forty-eight of them
left to do. That meant four hours of ad-libbing for Ad Wienert
and me, and for four hours we threw it back and forth like the
proverbial hot potato.

"Nothing much happening here, Ad. Back to you."

"Jim, let's take another look at the beautiful mural here in
the terminal lobby. See? Now, back to you."

"Thanks, Ad. Those of you who weren't with us earlier may
not realize the vast expanse of this magnificent new facility.
[Camera pans empty runway.] One day jet aircraft will be
landing here regularly. Ad, I'm sure you have something for
us at the terminal, where construction is still under way."

And on and on and on, for four hours.

But we got in all the commercials. There's a sentence that
could sum up the history of television.

Aside from the technical staff, the only television professional we had was a director who shall be called Hal. He had
actually worked as a TV director for two years in Philadelphia,
which in those days qualified him as an old hand. He was also

a nonrecovering alcoholic, which our bosses did not know—until later.

In the early weeks, I seemed to puzzle him. As we sat in Joe Alonso's Bar on Cold Spring Lane after a show (the bar is still there, by the way), he would shake his head and say, "Jim, we must find out what your specialty should be. I can't put my finger on it as yet."

Then, one night we did professional wrestling from the Coliseum. In just a short time, I had fallen a long way from prospective star newspaperman to pro wrestling shill, but an assignment was an assignment and pro wrestling was one of the most popular entertainments on TV in those days. I did try to comment with some objectivity. I didn't call it real blood, because it wasn't. I didn't say a wrestler was groggy when he was obviously playacting.

This approach got me into trouble a few weeks later. A wrestler named Billy Graham took umbrage at my objective approach. In the middle of a match with a 350-pound kindly grandfather known as the Super Swedish Angel, Graham picked up his opponent, walked him to the corner directly over my head, said, "See how fake *this* is, kid!" and threw the Angel at me. The bulky granddad missed me, but landed on my notes with a loud crash. It was the only legitimate move I saw in a year of televising wrestling.

A few nights after the first wrestling show, we covered a sermon by Bishop Fulton J. Sheen (who soon would oust Milton Berle as the King of Television). I did my brief opening and closing comments with what I hoped was appropriate dignity and we were off to Alonso's again.

Several drinks into the evening, Hal looked me straight in the eye with great seriousness. "By God, Jimmy," he said, "we've done it. We've discovered your strengths—wrestling and religion!"

Hal actually was a pretty good director when he wasn't into the sauce too heavily. He certainly looked the part. He was tall and slender and sported a pencil-line mustache just like the movie directors of old. You could picture him in a director's chair with a cloth cap on backward, shouting instructions through a small megaphone.

But he did drink a lot, and in time it was his downfall. The climax came one fine summer day. Hal was assigned to do two shows. In the afternoon, he would direct powerboat racing from the Maryland Yacht Club. In the evening, he would be at the console for our very first studio program.

Now, we still didn't have an actual studio. The attic where we first met with Cochrane and Heisler was in the process of being remodeled into a studio. But for this night's two programs—a symposium featuring the *Sun*'s Washington and foreign correspondents and the aforementioned *Teenage Forum*, on which my wife-to-be and I were the hosts—the same tiny room where I had stood with Swanson to see the first test pictures come in had been made into a makeshift studio. It was so makeshift that the door had to be left partially open to allow room for the camera cables. The director's console was sitting on a table in the hallway. It was a very small space, actually the tower of what was then called the O'Sullivan Building, which Baltimoreans were proud to say was "the tallest building south of New York."

The first show would go on the air at 9:00 P.M., and at 8:55 Hal wasn't there. The correspondents were in place, already beginning to sweat in the un-air-conditioned room. The teenage kids were milling in the hall while Margaret and I tried to quiet them. Everyone was on tiptoe, since the studio door had to be left open.

Cochrane put a hand on the shoulder of Frank Harms, a young former radio disc jockey who was now an announcer for our station. "Frank," Cochrane whispered, "you've been saying that you would like to be a director. Your moment has come. Sit down in that chair and direct. You have four and a half minutes to pull yourself together."

Two minutes later, Hal stumbled in, hair rumpled, eyes a bit out of focus. "It's okay, kid," he said to Harms. "Thanks for standing by for me. I'll take over now."

"No, you won't," said Cochrane, while the teenagers stared

in awe and the honored correspondents craned their necks to see what was going on. "You, Hal, are fired. Frank will direct the show. Now, get out of here."

Hal, head hung low, faded from the scene. One minute later, we were on the air. All went well for the first two minutes or so, until a technician rushed into the crowded hallway. "Mr. Cochrane," he whispered, "it's awful. Somebody has to do something. Hal has climbed to the top of the tower and says he's going to jump!"

Cochrane ran to the ladder leading to the small open parapet that crowned the tower, followed by everyone not otherwise engaged. In a minute, a small knot of scared people stood staring up at Hal, who was poised on the edge like a platform diver. "Don't try to stop me, Bob," he said. "It's all over for me. I've ruined the show and ruined my life. It's best for everyone if I jump."

Cochrane sighed in annoyance. "God damn it, Hal," he said. "If you're going to jump, shut up and jump. We're trying to do a show downstairs."

Somehow, Cochrane's commonplace tone and words took all the drama out of the situation. Hal climbed down without a word.

The question was not quality of programming, but quantity. We found a bonanza of quantity in an event sponsored by the *Evening Sun*—the municipal swimming championships. I was the sole commentator, aided only by a thick handful of heat sheets and lane assignments. The event started in the morning and ended when, quite literally, the evening sun went down. There were about a hundred races in all, and I can see the swimmers still, paddling back and forth endlessly while I prattled on.

When the station began to carry the Baltimore Orioles' minor league baseball games in the spring of 1949, I was assigned to develop a pregame show. Since the city's glory days in baseball had taken place before the turn of the century, I conceived a show that would come out of the 1890s. A girl singer, Marian Carle, and I appeared in period costume, pursuing a flimsy plot (which I wrote). As the plot moved (slowly), we would weave in songs of the nineties and stories of the great Orioles of those times.

Not all of our time-fillers were without merit.

One of them, *The Johns Hopkins Science Review*, later became a network staple for a time. It was the precursor in many ways of today's PBS science and nature programs. I was the producer and host, working in conjunction with Johns Hopkins PR man Lynn Poole and whatever scientists were involved each week.

Working with the scientists was fascinating, but I found that it could be dangerous to assume anything without talking to them first. One week, the theme of the show was "The Creation of the Universe." I opened our meeting.

"In the beginning, there was nothing. Right?" I said.

The scientists nodded assent.

"So, I think we will open on a blank, black screen, and I will say, 'In the beginning, there was nothing. . . .' "

"Hold it," said one scientist.

"Hold it? I haven't started yet."

"Yes, you have. And you have it wrong. 'Nothing' wasn't black. It was white."

I haven't argued with a scientist since then.

In the midst of all this oddly assorted activity came a phone call from WOR-TV in New York, offering me the opportunity to do a show. Sure, the subject matter was again pro wrestling, but the price was right—$500—and it was, after all, New York!

I took the train there in the afternoon and met the producer, director, and production assistant at a restaurant on the ground floor of the RKO General Building, where WOR-TV was located. The assistant was a student from Fordham University, freelancing in the new medium, hoping for a break. His name was Vin Scully, later to become the voice of Dodgers baseball.

We all got so engrossed talking baseball (Scully really knew his subject even then) that we were almost late for the wrestling, which was to take place in a tawdry little bullpen called the Sunnyside Arena in the borough of Queens.

The sponsor was a discount house called Friendly Frost, and the ad agency had come up with a bizarre idea. They had a young woman dressed in a snowman's suit (abbreviated, of course) stashed in a storeroom with a black velour curtain behind her. During the matches, they would superimpose her over the wrestlers and she would appear to torment them, making faces and poking them with her icicle. Unfortunately, she couldn't watch the monitor and do her act at the same time, so she appeared to be making faces in the wrong direction and poking the icicle into thin air. Frosty, as she was called, would not be invited back.

The whole show was pretty much of a disaster, but for better or worse, I had made my New York TV debut.

I took the last train back, which I found was, literally, the milk train, stopping at every station on the long road from New York to Baltimore. The trip took six hours, but Margaret and I had saved a hotel bill and were five hundred bucks richer.

Looking back, I guess we were tired most of the time, between her schedule and mine, but we were having such a good time that we just didn't notice.

And, my career kept careening in all different directions.

When I was pressed into service to help WMAR-TV get on the air, I figured my place in it would be as a newsman. I was a reporter—first in the police districts, then on general assignment—and I assumed that would be my role on television. As I watched the nightly network news programs grow in popularity and their hosts, people like Douglas Edwards and John Cameron Swayze, become familiar national personalities, I had a new dream: that one day I would be a top network anchorman.

It was a distant dream, because Margaret and I were happy where we were, and being summoned to the network seemed an unlikely prospect.

Then, out of the blue, everything changed.

One afternoon I came out of the studio after *The Sports Parade* to find the station manager, Ewell K. Jett, standing with a short, stocky man. His graying hair was combed straight back. A cigar stuck out of his mouth aggressively.

"Jim," said Mr. Jett, "I want you to meet Dick Swift, of CBS."

With no preliminaries, as if it were a scene from a 1930s Hollywood musical, the man took my hand and said (I remember the words precisely), "Hiya, kid. How would you like to do something like this in New York?"

What could I say? The man was actually asking me in one brief sudden question, "How would you like to have your life and your wife's life changed forevermore? How would you like to leave the town you love for the most competitive, unfeeling place in the world? How would you like to have eleven years of frustration, followed by thirty-three years of very slowly rising success? How would you like to have a job that would keep you traveling the world much of the time while Margaret stays home raising two children, handling all the family financial affairs, and still trying somehow to keep her career alive?"

Had I known all those question were being asked, I'm not sure what my answer would have been. As it was, all I could come up with was "Well, thanks. I'll have to check with my wife."

Which I did.

You must realize that Margaret was one of the paper's stars. She loved her work, the paper, and her colleagues with a true passion. Now, I was asking her to give it all up for a totally uncertain future in New York. (And indeed, it would be a lonely life for her at the beginning, since we had no children yet.)

Her answer was simple: If that was what I wanted, that

was what we would do. Her career? She would figure out something when we got there, she said.

I called Dick Swift and told him I was ready to give it a try, assuming that he meant to use me on a sports and/or sports interview show. We heard nothing from New York for two months.

Margaret suggested I call them back. I said they would call me when they were ready. Maybe, I reasoned, they had just changed their minds. Finally, she said, if I wouldn't call Swift, she would.

So I did.

He seemed surprised when I asked him if he was still interested. "Hasn't Dick Doan called you?"

"Who's Dick Doan?"

"My program director. Hasn't he called and told you that your show goes on the air in three weeks?"

The answer, of course, was no. Swift went on to explain that it would be a variety show, an hour and a half long, five days a week, in the afternoon.

"You and your wife better get up here!" he said.

With a confidence born of naïveté, we made a quick house-hunting trip to Connecticut. Later, Dick Swift would say, "You were house-hunting? I can only promise you the show will be on the air for thirteen weeks." Well, if we hadn't thought we would make it a permanent arrangement, we wouldn't have come at all.

We decided on an apartment in Greenwich, Connecticut, thirty-five miles from New York City in a new garden-style development called the Putnam Park. Although it was still under construction, Margaret selected a nice corner apartment that they assured us would be ready in a week.

Just to be sure, Margaret called the manager the day before we were to make our historic move. Everything was ready, he said.

So we gave the moving people the go-ahead, and the next morning Margaret carefully placed her freshly ironed cottage curtains in the backseat of our Pontiac convertible. She could hardly wait to hang them. Shortly, she felt like hanging the manager instead.

When we pulled up in front of our new home, we noticed large gaping holes where the windows should have been. Going inside, we saw nothing but dusty pink paper where the floors would one day be, but weren't now.

Thank heaven for Margaret. I don't know what I would have done, but she simply sought out the manager and let him listen as she used his phone to call the Berkshire Hotel, across the street from CBS in Manhattan. She reserved a room starting that night, until an open-ended departure date.

"Oh," she said. "And send the weekly bills to the manager of the Putnam Park Apartments in Greenwich, Connecticut." She hung up and looked at the manager.

"Well," he said. "Okay . . ."

Margaret said, "Just let us know when the apartment is totally ready. And will you find someplace for me to store my freshly ironed cottage curtains?"

With that, we were off to the Berkshire Hotel. That night, we were able to look out our hotel room window and see the CBS Building, catty-corner across the intersection of 52nd Street and Madison Avenue.

For better or worse, we were in New York City—the big time.

"If We Can Make It There . . ."

An early morning in 1950, Margaret and I went out to Greenwich to make sure the apartment builders were at work. They were. The next morning, we took the train back to New York for my first day of work at CBS.

The taxi we took from Grand Central Station was one of those big old De Sotos that used to roam the streets of the big town. They featured a sunroof long before regular cars had such luxuries, the better to view and be overwhelmed by the skyscrapers rising to the heavens like a suffocating concrete forest. This wasn't Baltimore, for sure.

I thought of the 1930s Hollywood musicals about show business, where some innocent young couple from the boondocks would be seeing New York for the first time, determined to make their way on Broadway. That was our situation, and I said to my wife, "Margaret, corny and immature though it may be, I have to do it."

"What are you talking about?" she said. "Do what?"

I stood up, poked my head through the sunroof of that old taxi, and said, "Hello, New York. I'm not afraid of you!" Sure.

I dropped Margaret at Saks Fifth Avenue—now, that was something I was *really* afraid of—and faced my clouded future alone.

Walking into the CBS Building that morning was a daunting experience in itself. Compared with today's mammoth "Black Rock" building on Avenue of the Americas, it was a modest structure, but it certainly impressed me. Even the ornately dressed doorman scared me, until I asked him where I might find Dick Swift. "Well, laddie," he said in a pleasant Irish brogue, "that should be easy enough," and he gave me directions. I came to know him as Mike Donovan, the nicest doorman on Madison Avenue, and the most relaxed. He even called CBS's chairman, William S. Paley, "laddie."

My meeting with Swift, the general manager of WCBS-TV, and Dick Doan, his program director, featured a couple of depressing surprises. First of all, they wanted to change my name. In those days, when radio still reigned, the networks had a custom of "owning" names. For example, CBS owned the name "Galen Drake," who offered a homespun philosophy every day. In five or six large cities, there were actually different Galen Drakes, all with similar voices, tailoring their philosophies to their individual audiences.

Also, if the network got into a contract dispute with the "talent," as we were euphemistically called, it conceivably could let the person go, find another guy with a similar voice, and give him the "house name."

You couldn't change Galen Drakes on television, but that didn't seem to bother Swift. As a radio man, he was used to the old way, so he stuck with it.

He gave me a serious, Galen Drake look.

"You," Swift said, "will be Jim McKay."

"Why McKay?" I asked him. I liked my own name just as it was. The thought of James K. McManus disappearing into thin air didn't please me at all, and I knew would be even less pleasing to my parents, and to Margaret, who had easily taken to the liquid sound of my real surname.

"Well," Swift said, "Dick Doan thinks that now we can call your show *The Real McKay*." He was all smiles as he said, "Sort of a play on words, you know. Like 'The Real McCoy.' "

I asked myself why they didn't just call me Jim McCoy. But at that moment I wasn't about to argue with them about anything. This was to be my first break into the big time, so I figured I'd better bend on the name. But then I got crunched when they explained about the show's format. "See, Jim," Swift said, "we hired a consultant to create the show and invent a personality for you. And they came up with a great idea."

"What would that be?" I asked cautiously.

Swift said, "Jim McKay's Peanut Stand."

I looked at my two would-be bosses, my blue eyes about to pop out of my face. My voice rising in wounded indignation, I said, "Jim McKay's WHAT?!"

"Peanut stand," Dick Doan said. "See, you'll have a peanut stand on wheels, and you'll wear a little pointed hat. Your 'customers' will turn out to be the people you interview. People walking along the street will be the entertainers on the show. And, of course, you'll take off your little hat now and then to sing a song." With a big, smug smile on his face, Doan pumped me on the shoulder. "Don't you love it?"

Somehow overcoming every timorous bone in my body, I said, "No. I don't think I can do that."

Bracing myself for an angry retort, I was surprised to hear Dick Swift say, "Okay. I'm not crazy about it myself. You think up something that you can be comfortable with, and let us know tomorrow. Meanwhile, I have an office for you. Unfortunately, this building is full, so you'll be just across the street. The guy we've hired as producer is working up on the borscht circuit right now, so he won't be here until next week, but we do have a production assistant for you. Name's Frank Moriarty. He's over in your office right now. Why don't you go and get acquainted?"

"Jim McKay" headed over to his office, all awonder about the world of television, and there was Frank Moriarty, a pink-faced, red-haired kid from New Jersey, about five years younger than me, just out of Fordham University. Moriarty was sitting in a straight-backed oak chair at an old oak rolltop desk. Along with two other straight chairs, they were the only pieces of furniture in a very large office. No rug, no draperies, no name on the frosted glass door. It was just this kid and I, trying to figure out what we were supposed to do with ourselves.

We talked for an hour or so, mostly getting acquainted

with each other, then decided we would call it a day. We discovered we had locked ourselves in the office, and neither of us had a key, or a clue on how to get out. Mercifully, there was a phone that worked, or we would have been stuck there until the cleaning women arrived after dark. Still, it was more than a little embarrassing having to call the boss on Jim McKay's first day at work in the big town to ask him to release us from house arrest.

That night, across the street from CBS in our room at the Berkshire Hotel, Margaret and I talked about my projected life as a purveyor of peanuts. As usual, she got to the heart of the matter. "Well, of course, that's out. It's absurd. You're a reporter, not a clown. They have to let you be the guy Swift saw on the show in Baltimore and liked."

I agreed, so we talked about alternatives to a peanut stand. "How about a living room?" Margaret said.

"What do you mean?" I asked.

"You know, a living room," she said. "You don't need any trick, phony locations. Just Jim McKay, if that's what they insist on calling you, interviewing guests on a sofa in his living room. Television is an intimate medium. You're going into people's living rooms, so why not welcome them to yours?"

Margaret, an interior decorator at heart, went on to furnish the living room. Nothing modern, just a nice sofa covered in a warm fabric, some comfortable chairs, a big hooked rug, and a Morris chair for me. A Morris chair? That was an old-fashioned chair, made of wood, that could lean back like a modern outdoor chaise longue. From the Morris chair, Margaret assured me, I could talk with my guests and the members of my cast and occasionally get up and sing a song.

The next day, I immediately popped the idea to Swift and Doan. Now, people's wives don't create sets, not on TV. But mine did. And after much thought and discussion, they could see nothing wrong with Margaret's set. They agreed to it and I formally agreed to be Jim McKay.

The set was in place by the time our producer arrived from his summertime borscht-belt stint in the Catskill Mountains.

Like Frank Moriarty, this guy was tall and red-haired, his face flushed from a summer under the sun. He had a smile that never stopped, displaying two rows of large, gleaming teeth. His name was Jack Lescoulie, who later would be second banana to Dave Garroway on the *Today* program.

I was surprised that they gave me a writer, since I normally ad-libbed all my comments. It was explained that he would come up with ideas for little skits. The writer's name was George Roossen, a large, easygoing young man who at one time had written the *Little Orphan Annie* program for radio in Chicago. George was a graduate of Swarthmore College, which is known as the Harvard of Pennsylvania. I never found out exactly how he had wandered from Swarthmore to *Little Orphan Annie*, writing such gems as the opening song: ". . . always worth a sunny smile, now wouldn't it be worth your while, if you could be like Little Orphan Annie. 'Arf,' says Sandy."

Bit by bit, person by person, the show began to come together. Our little group—Lescoulie, Roossen, Moriarty, a director named Ned Cramer, and I—would sit in a big empty room and audition singers and dancers. That was fun. I felt a bit like those great old Hollywood character actors, Eugene Pallette or Charles Coburn, playing the big movie producer. One or the other of them would invariably say to Phil Silvers, who was playing the stage manager, "All right, Sid. Tell the third girl from the left to come back. The kid has talent."

I actually learned a lot during these auditions. For instance, I discovered that almost every singer performed a song called "I've Got a Crush on You, Sweety-Pie," while making goo-goo eyes at Jack Lescoulie. Singers do not live by talent alone.

A few days before we went on the air Dick Swift did me a huge favor: He set up an appointment for me to see Arthur Godfrey. At that time, Godfrey was the biggest name in radio and television. Swift had heard him on the radio in Washington, D.C., some years before and brought him to New York.

Now, Swift said to me, "I think you can be the next Arthur Godfrey. So I want you to meet him."

A little background may be in order if you are not old enough to remember Arthur Godfrey. He had been a sailor in the U.S. Navy, the guy on his ship who played the ukulele and led the singing on long trips at sea. One night in the late 1920s in Baltimore, Godfrey and his pals, on liberty, were in a bar, drinking and listening to an amateur hour on WFBR, a local station, when one of his shipmates pointed a finger at Godfrey and said, "I dare you to go up and try to get on the show." Godfrey just smiled, went on, and was so good that the station offered him a job. As soon as he could get his navy discharge, he took the job.

In time, he moved to a Washington station and became the "morning man," spinning records and talking and doing commercials—his way. Godfrey was the first to make fun of his sponsors and get away with it. It started with a furrier—his name was Zlotnick—whose store featured three stuffed polar bears standing outside the door. Arthur started telling his audience that they could always spot Zlotnick's place by "the mangy old polar bears outside." Zlotnick was furious at Godfrey, until he found that business was getting much better.

I've never forgotten that story. In fact, forty-six years after my interview with Godfrey, I walked into a shoe store in Towson, Maryland, and standing in the corner was an immense, mangy, stuffed polar bear. While waiting for the shoes I had left to be repaired, I told the owner, Dick Rudolph, the Zlotnick story.

Rudolph patiently smiled as he listened to me, then said, "That isn't a similar bear. That's *it*. That's one of Zlotnick's bears. Old Harry Weiss, a friend of mine, bought the three bears at a going-out-of-business auction when Zlotnick closed down, and gave me one. Harry did things like that. He was quite a character."

At the time of my appointment with Godfrey, he was the hottest thing in the entertainment world. He was doing a radio show five mornings a week, an informal nighttime TV variety show called *Arthur Godfrey and His Friends*, and another nighttime TV program, an amateur hour. He had a full deck, and more. So I was understandably nervous as I was ushered into his office in a building just across the street from CBS on 52nd Street. He was sitting behind a big desk, wearing a Hawaiian sport shirt. His hair was as red as I had been told (you couldn't see its color on the black-and-white TV of those days), and he had a friendly smile on his face. But I was nervous because he had this reputation for being arrogant in person, demanding of his performers, rude to outsiders.

He put me at ease immediately.

"Sit down, kid. I hear you started in Baltimore, too." Then he recounted the story of how he began his career in the late 1920s by going on the amateur show, strumming the ukulele and singing.

"Well," I said, "Dick Swift has this idea that I can have a career as spectacular as yours, and he thinks you might give me some advice."

"Sure," he said. "Swift brought me to New York, too. He's a good guy. You want advice? Okay."

Then he hunkered down, his eyes boring right into mine.

"First, always be yourself on television. That camera has an X-ray quality to it, son; it spots a phony every time, and there's no escape. To be yourself is your only chance, for better or worse, in TV. And, another thing, never talk to more than one person when you look into the camera lens. To the viewer at home, it appears that you are talking to them, one-on-one, not to a great crowd. That individual may be multiplied by millions, but to each one watching, it is just them you are talking to."

If that advice sounds a bit basic, let me assure you that I think of it before every show I do, and it has served me extremely well. The TV camera does have that "X-ray quality." Haven't you sometimes seen an actor or actress, for example, whom you have admired in the movies or on the stage, come off as totally insincere when being interviewed on television?

You would think that his or her acting ability would enable that person to fool you, but it doesn't, not on TV. That's why what some critics call "talking heads" actually provide some of the most interesting programming on the air. The human face in close-up reacting in an ad-lib situation is fascinating, from an athlete just after competing in a major event to a witness on the stand, live, as in the O. J. Simpson trial.

I have this vivid memory in my mind going back to 1980 and the Lake Placid Winter Olympics. I see this tight shot of a young Soviet hockey player's face, immediately after his team has been defeated by a hugely underdog United States team. It was on the screen no more than one second—just one, but his expression of total disbelief, his mouth literally hanging open, will probably remain in my mind forever. That's the awesome power of television.

So, on *The Real McKay* what they would see was what they would get. I hope that has been true of me ever since.

☆

In those early days, Margaret and I tried to figure out how rich we were going to be. First of all, my base salary would be $500 a week, which was more than twice what we had been making together on the *Evening Sun*. Of course, we were not yet aware of how much more it would cost us to live in the New York area.

But there was another more exciting consideration. I would receive $25 for each commercial sold on the show. Since there were twelve availabilities every day, if the show sold out, I would be making more than $100,000 per year, including my base pay. In 1950, $100,000 was equivalent to about half a million today. It was probably just as well that we did not have the foreknowledge that only two or three commercials a day would actually be sold.

But to us, the future now seemed to have no limits. The show would go on the air with a guarantee of only thirteen weeks, but that was in small print, which we chose to ignore. We were in New York with an hour-and-a-half show, one to two-thirty, five days a week on CBS's flagship local station. What more could we ask?

Television was already growing so fast in 1950 that the networks were using any studios they could find. The problem was that radio studios just weren't suitable for the visible medium of TV. Our show was assigned to an ornate old place on East 58th Street called Liederkranz Hall, which originally had been the property of a German singing society but was now occupied by CBS Records. The hall had the finest acoustics of anyplace in Manhattan and CBS recorded its revolutionary new 33$\frac{1}{3}$ RPM, long-playing records there.

But along came the invading horde of TV, ousting the record makers, dividing the hall into four studios, and thereby ruining the famed acoustical quality of the hall. The need for studio space bedevils TV to this day and here and there, you can still find programs being shot in old movie theaters or abandoned hotel ballrooms in Manhattan.

Our show's debut was set for August 14, 1950, on CBS's flagship station, WCBS-TV, Channel 2 in New York. The time slot seemed set, but in the year to follow, the show would end up in twelve different time periods at lengths varying from a half hour to an hour and a half. It was a time of experimentation. WCBS-TV had been existing until this point by riding the coattails of the network, picking up the network shows while providing no local programs of its own. We would be the first.

We had one day of rehearsal before our big debut and I discovered I didn't have a clue about what was going on. See, television was beginning to develop its own inside language in New York, and I neither spoke nor understood it. I felt like a greenhorn who had just stepped off the boat. Here I was sitting with producer Lescoulie, who had a clipboard in his lap and was saying, "First, our schedule for tomorrow. At nine we have facts time." Facts time? All I could think of was that it was a time when we would all sit down and talk over the "facts" of the show. So I simply nodded assent.

Then, however, I heard him say, "And at ten o'clock, we have no facts time."

Now, he had me.

I had to swallow my pride, admit to my Baltimore provincialism, and ask him, "What do you mean, *no* facts?"

Lescoulie gave me his famous grin, teeth gleaming in the rehearsal hall lights. "It's *F-A-X,* Jim; it means the facilities we will use—cameras, microphones, lights, our set, the furniture, everything necessary for the program. The nine o'clock rehearsal will be with fax, then at ten, while the crew makes whatever technical adjustments are necessary, we'll have no fax, just a run-through on our own to make sure we have all the moves right."

For our first show, Lescoulie booked two young singers who were just coming down from the Catskills to try their luck on Broadway. The idea was for me to talk to them, find out their background, and listen to them sing. Some months later, we would bring them back to our show and find out how their careers in the big town were going. As it turned out, Jack had selected two good candidates from the hundreds of youngsters who had performed in the mountains that summer.

One was Barbara Cook, a pretty slip of a lass, later to be costar of *The Music Man* with Robert Preston, singing "Goodnight, My Someone" in a beautiful, youthful soprano. Today, forty-seven years later, Barbara is still pleasing audiences from coast to coast, belting out her songs in a style that has always been emotionally engaging.

The young man was Jack Cassidy, later a father of two talented sons, Sean and David, and a star on Broadway and TV until his early death.

From day one, a jolly, roly-poly regular singer-pianist named Mac Perrin proved to be a big asset. He even wrote our opening theme, words and music, which the entire cast sang as we came on the air for that first show and every show thereafter:

Brighten your day with The Real McKay, *here's a show just meant for you. We're gonna chase all your blues away, gonna make you feel just like* The Real McKay. *We've got old songs, and O new songs—a little conversation, too. Now is the time to introduce to you* [glissando on the piano]—*the Real* [another glissando]—*McKay.*

That was my cue to walk onstage and open the show. The first song I sang, to get things going, was an old favorite of Margaret's and mine, "It Had to Be You." Then İ brought on the people who would be our regulars. A little dancer named Sandy, whose last name I have unfortunately forgotten forty-seven years later, did a ballet number; Mac Perrin and I did a rousing duet of "On Behalf of the Visiting Firemen"; a black-haired young singer, Ellen Parker, sang a ballad; we did a skit, the contents of which escape me, perhaps mercifully; and I interviewed Barbara Cook and Jack Cassidy.

I felt the show went all right, but I wasn't sure until Dick Swift called immediately after it was over to say he thought it was great. Feeling almost secure, I took Margaret out to an expensive restaurant for dinner that night.

We found out very soon, though, that fame does not come quickly in New York—although Margaret thought that perhaps it had when she got into a taxicab just a few weeks after the show went on the air. She dropped me off at CBS, then continued on in the taxi. The driver asked Margaret, "Who was that guy? He looked familiar."

"Well," Margaret said, anticipating our first compliment in the big city, "who do you think it was?"

"I don't know," he said. "Let me think. . . . Wait a minute, I've got it."

Smiling, Margaret asked him, "Okay, who was it?"

"You know, that guy in the crime movies. Always plays the psychotic killer. Peter Lorre, right?"

The show did slowly build a loyal audience, and people seemed to like the format: me interviewing people, from actors and authors to politicians and police chiefs; Mac Perrin and me singing duets together; me singing ballads like "One for My Baby." But the show wasn't achieving the skyrocket success that Dick Swift had envisioned.

Then I got lucky again.

A couple of months after *The Real McKay* went on, Swift, who was general manager of the station, decided to insert a five-minute sports segment into the 11:00 P.M. local news. Because of my *Sports Parade* experience in Baltimore, Swift let me do the new sports segment, the first of its kind in New York. So I found myself doing not only the daytime show but also the short evening effort.

I had three and a half minutes to give all the baseball scores from both leagues, along with the other sports news of the day. Thank God there were only eight teams in each league in those days, but it was still a challenge. I also did a live commercial during the sports segment for Piel's beer. In those less restrictive days, I was actually required to take a sip of the beer on camera from a frosty glass, then smile a satisfied smile.

In the end, it was those quickie sports shows that kept my CBS career alive. After about a year and a half, *The Real McKay*, which had been shortened to a half hour (from 6 to 6:30 P.M.), was canceled in favor of local news. I was kept on, now doing two sports shows, at six and eleven.

I also made friends at CBS Sports. John Derr, the director of sports, and his successor, Bill MacPhail, gave me assignments on horse racing, pro football, track and field, the Orange Bowl parade, and other special events.

So I was kept busy on an erratic basis during my eleven years at CBS. At one point, I was doing the six and eleven o'clock shows, got about five hours' sleep, then returned to the studio for *The Morning Show*, CBS's first effort to compete against NBC's *Today* program. Walter Cronkite was the host, and I was the sports man and second banana, doing sidewalk interviews and other remote telecasts.

Before the *Today* show made it, the conventional wisdom was that morning TV would never work. Radio was still king in the morning, and the thought of climbing out of bed to sit still and watch television defied reason.

Until Dave Garroway came along.

Garroway was a tall, professorial-looking fellow in horn-rimmed glasses and a bow tie who seemed to have the perfect pitch for the early morning mood of America. He was low-key all the way, a manner perfected as a midnight disc jockey in Chicago, where he would murmur soft, romantic philosophy between tasteful jazz recordings.

Today was pure Garroway, with his own special effects. For example, there was his sign-off: With his right hand casually raised, he'd intone, "This is Garroway saying so long, with some love—and peace." But he had help. He was attended by an attractive assistant called the Today Girl; the announcer was our old friend Jack Lescoulie; and at the show's height, a chimpanzee named J. Fred Muggs, added—uh—zest to the mix.

After a succession of about a dozen Today Girls, a young woman working in the anonymous role of a writer on the show was finally given her chance. Barbara Walters featured brains instead of the glamour of her predecessors, and went on to starry heights on television.

By and large, our new CBS show fought a losing rearguard action against *Today*. We were far behind them in the ratings, but once in a while, we had a success. One such success caused my career to take a turn.

Roger Bannister was a young British doctor who, in the spring of 1954, became the first person to run the long-sought sub-four-minute mile. It was world news. The handsome Bannister's picture appeared on the front page of newspapers around the world, gasping for breath as he broke the tape.

A few nights after the Englishman's great achievement, the doorbell rang at our apartment. It was after midnight and we were already asleep (I had to get up at 4:30 in the morning to do the show) but Margaret went to the door.

The caller was Hugh Beach, a onetime English professor turned New York character and one of the segment producers

for *The Morning Show*. Hugh, for reasons that were never explained, liked to be called "Meathead" (to him I was "Burrhead" because of my crew cut), and he spoke in a manner that
was half Down Maine and half Damon Runyon.

"Mahgret," he whispered. "A thousand apologies, but I
must borrow the use of your sofa for a few hours."

"All right. But why?"

"Because your husband and I are going out to Idlewild
Airport [now JFK] to score a major journalistic coup."

He explained that he had stayed late at the office working
on a segment and that, as he'd left, he'd passed by the Associated Press teletype machine and noticed a "Note to Editors."
It said that a man resembling Roger Bannister had boarded a
BOAC flight bound for New York under a presumably assumed name. No confirmation. On this tiny tip, Hugh had
taken it on himself to order up a CBS mobile unit to be ready
to go at the International Arrivals Terminal at dawn.

And so he and I left the apartment in the depressing darkness of early morning. Half asleep, I noticed that another ten-
ant was leaving our building at the same time. I recognized
him as the producer of a successful prime-time program
called *I've Got a Secret*, and wondered vaguely where he was
going at this ungodly hour.

The mobile unit was waiting for us, fired up and ready to
go, but the overnight flight from London was reported to be
about two hours late. That meant Bannister, if in fact it was
he, would arrive between 8:30 and 9:00 A.M., and we signed off
at nine. Remember, there was no videotape in those days; we
would get him live or not at all.

As we waited, the producer I had seen leaving our building
bustled into the waiting room and immediately approached
Hugh Beach. "I saw your mobile unit out front," he said.
"What are you guys doing here?"

In his best Runyonesque manner, Hugh said, "We are
awaiting the arrival of Roger Bannister, who, you may have
heard, recently ran the world's first sub-four-minute mile. My
colleague here, Mr. McKay, is going to have the first American

television interview with him, live on the CBS *Morning Show*, as soon as he steps off the plane. It will be a major journalistic coup."

Meathead smiled proudly. The producer blanched.

"You can't do that! I'll call the network! [His program was also on CBS.] He's ours! We're paying his fare!"

"First class or tourist?" Hugh asked.

"Tourist."

"Tourist?" said Meathead. "Tourist? Now, that is tacky, but it doesn't concern us. We are here simply to do our duty as newsmen, to interview the world's most famous man of the moment before anybody else does."

"Livid" was the word for the producer. He hollered, at the top of his voice, that Bannister was to be the mystery guest that night on *I've Got a Secret*. The show had negotiated quietly for several days, had arranged for the airline to put an assumed name on the manifest, and was prepared to give a large donation to Bannister's favorite charity, since Roger was the purest of amateurs and would accept no cash.

Meathead shook his head sadly, mumbling something about being embarrassed for CBS that one of its programs would insult Bannister by flying him over in tourist.

We waited and waited, while the producer fumed.

At long last, at about 8:45, a cool-looking young man strolled out of Customs into the view of our live camera. It was Roger Bannister all right. He was as unruffled as a proper Englishman is expected to be, his hair carefully combed, his eyes alert despite the long overnight flight in tourist class. He was carrying a small athlete's duffel bag as I approached him, microphone in hand, praying silently that he wouldn't walk past me to the waiting, outstretched hand of the nearly hysterical producer.

"Excuse me," I said. "I'm Jim McKay and we are live on the CBS *Morning Show*. May I ask you a few questions?"

"Of course. Delighted."

Whereupon he gave me about five minutes of an extremely

articulate description of the world's first sub-four-minute mile.

The coup was accomplished.

The producer, muttering something about calling the chairman of the network to protest this, grabbed Bannister and hustled him off.

I threw it back to Walter Cronkite in the studio. He complimented us on our enterprise. Meathead smiled.

There is a postscript to the incident. Bannister was whisked to a secret rehearsal of *I've Got a Secret*, a skeleton run-through of the guests and the secrets to be revealed on that night's show. All went well until they started screening the commercials.

Suddenly, the mannerly Dr. Bannister interrupted.

"Excuse me," he said. "Is that a cigarette advertisement you're showing?" (If you are too young to remember, cigarette advertising was the most lucrative source of network revenue before it was banned.) Told that it was indeed, the good doctor explained apologetically but firmly that he couldn't possibly appear on a program sponsored by a cigarette company. He was, after all, not only an athlete but a cardiologist, and a firm believer that cigarettes were a primary cause of heart trouble.

Dr. Bannister promptly returned to England. We had not only the first, but the only interview with him on American soil. And all free of charge.

Working with Cronkite and Bil and Cora Baird, the puppeteers, on *The Morning Show* was a rewarding job, but combined with the evening sports shows, it was wearing out both Margaret and me, particularly since we now had a little baby girl named Mary, born on Memorial Day, 1953. Mary was beautiful and extremely determined. She would not go to sleep, despite the best efforts of Margaret and the pediatrician, who assured us that, if allowed to "cry it out," Mary would eventually sleep. This was not true. Margaret ended up holding her through much of the hours between midnight and five, so that I could get some sleep.

Margaret's life had changed more dramatically than mine. After being a star reporter and editor on the *Baltimore Evening Sun* (one of the first women to achieve that status on the paper), she was now a mother and pretty much confined to our apartment. But she found a way to put her creative talents to work. She had by this time started a syndicated newspaper column, which gave her some spending money and some professional satisfaction.

Her idea was simple enough—a weekly profile about television personalities. It is hard to believe today that it was an original idea at the time, but indeed, no one was writing such a column. In point of fact, several syndicates turned down Margaret's proposal, including one executive who said, "Nobody wants to read about television."

She finally sold the idea to the Bell Syndicate. After a year or so, in which she realized that she was paying the syndicate 50 percent of the profits for very little work on its end, she decided to syndicate it herself, which she did quite successfully to some one hundred papers around the country, from the *New York World-Telegram and Sun* to the *San Francisco Chronicle*. Between writing the column, taking care of Mary, and handling all our finances, she was far busier than I.

The combination of the 11:00 P.M. sports program, *The Morning Show*, and Mary's sleeping habits finally forced us to press the panic button. Something had to give, and we decided it logically should be the local sports, from both a monetary and prestige standpoint. First, however, I had to be sure that *The Morning Show* would stay on the air, since its ratings vis-à-vis *The Today Show* were shaky.

So I went to see Sig Mickelson, president of the CBS News division. I asked him if I was safe in giving up the local programs and continuing with just *The Morning Show*. He said that I was, that the show had been promised a run of at least a year, and that he was very pleased with my performance.

So we gave up the 11:00 P.M. sports show—but two months

later *The Morning Show* went off the air. In its place came a promising young comedian named Jack Paar. Paar didn't improve the ratings, but the show certainly improved his career. NBC saw his work, liked it, and made him the host of *The Tonight Show,* succeeding Steve Allen.

CBS Sports had decided to put a strange program on that fall, looking for a way to compete with NBC's college football package. It decided to do a television version of CBS Radio's successful college football roundup, which flashed from one stadium to another. The inimitable Red Barber was the anchorman of the radio show. He gave scores of other games and then threw it to reporters on the scene, where they did play-by-play of short segments.

For television, however, CBS did not have the rights to originate anything in the stadiums. So it put me behind a translucent panel—in silhouette—doing play-by-play segments of various games. I was given a bare-bones report from the wire services, on which I was expected to expand as if watching the game in person, giving it full dramatic description. As I talked, CBS would put up a still picture of the player making the run or throwing the pass. I felt ridiculous doing it, but it was, as they say, a living.

It also led to something else.

The director of the football show was Byron Paul, an intense, enthusiastic man who had begun his career some years earlier as a soundman for CBS Radio. Among other things, he was the one at the controls when Mayor Fiorello La Guardia read the funny papers—comic strips, if you prefer—to the children during a newspaper strike, thereby cementing La Guardia's place in history. Byron was also the person who discovered Dick Van Dyke doing a local show in New Orleans. He became Van Dyke's mentor and adviser in New York, and later in Hollywood.

Shortly after the football show ended its predictably unsuccessful run, Byron was hired to direct an afternoon program on the network called *The Verdict Is Yours*. It would simulate courtroom cases, using real-life lawyers questioning actors. There would also be a role for a host-reporter, who would ad-lib his part from the "pressroom." Based on his experience working with me in silhouette, Byron told the producers that I was not only the best man for the job, but the only one.

Almost simultaneously, I was hired by WCBS Radio to be the host of *This Is New York*, a successful program originated by Bill Leonard, who by now was moving up the executive ladder and in time would become president of CBS News.

So I was back to a very busy schedule, rehearsing the courtroom show in the morning, doing it live in the afternoon (again, there was still no videotape at this time), then racing across town to tape three or four interviews for that night's *This Is New York* (there *was* audiotape). The interviewees ranged from Maurice Chevalier to Adlai Stevenson to ephemeral personalities from the daily news.

I recall Stevenson, who was twice the Democratic candidate for president, as the most gracious of my interviewees. I talked with him in his permanent suite at the Sherry-Netherland Hotel, where he had hung beautiful paintings everywhere, including the kitchen. It was a bit of a scoop to get the interview, but I was crushed when I returned to the studio and found that there was nothing, I mean *nothing*, on the tape. Ruth Alban, my assistant, who had set up the interview in the first place, had more nerve than I did. She called Stevenson back, explained the situation, and asked him if he would do the whole interview over again. And he did!

Are you sort of getting the impression that my career had been slightly unfocused at this point? You would be correct.

Sports sort of looked like my future, but at that time was not lucrative enough to be my only source of income. On the other hand, *Verdict* paid extremely well, but had no long-range future for me. It was a velvet-lined rut, and now was cutting me out of sports entirely.

In 1960, Mary was seven years old, and our son, Sean, was five. We had bought a house in Westport, Connecticut, an expensive community, so I just couldn't afford to give up my courtroom career.

That year was the most miserable of my life. I felt that I was being well paid for walking on a treadmill, that my news ambitions would never be fulfilled and that I was blocked from progressing in sports. It really got to me. And suddenly, I began to feel extremely nervous for no good reason. I was full of frustration and anger at the situation. I had a recurrent dream, perhaps as often as once a week, in which I was trying to reach a stadium to do commentary on a game. But my feet began to drag in the dream, as if my shoes were stuck in some clinging substance. I could see the stadium, but no matter how hard I tried to run, I stayed in the same place.

The studio and New York itself began to feel like my enemies. I started to feel irrationally insecure walking the streets of the city, to the point where I asked Margaret to come with me and stay while we taped the shows.

It was the worst possible timing, because right at this point, CBS asked me to work on the 1960 Winter Olympics in Squaw Valley, California, the first ever to be televised in this country. It would be a great event, with Walter Cronkite as host. I would do commentary on ski racing, one of the biggest events in the Games.

Two days later, on a Sunday morning at home, I showed Margaret my hands. They were shaking and I didn't know why. Margaret called a neighborhood doctor, who assured me that I was just burned out, that a couple of weeks in Florida and some new tranquilizing pills he would give me would get me straightened out in no time.

That advice almost ended my career. Margaret booked us a room in the famous Breakers Hotel in Palm Beach (where she scrounged the money from I still don't know), and we left by train. (My problem had also made me terrified of flying.)

The very thought of riding a ski lift or walking down a mountainside made me feel dizzy. So we told CBS that I had pneumonia and couldn't go to the Olympics.

I thought I had missed my biggest opportunity.

I had depression, all right, which was made worse by my having to watch Chris Schenkel do the ski racing, which would have been my assignment. (I couldn't have known that Chris and I would go on to do several Olympics together at ABC, which, in 1960, hardly had a sports department worthy of the name.)

As for the Florida trip, it was a total failure. Most of the time, all I could do was cry, for no apparent reason. I pictured myself in some mental hospital, and begged Margaret to somehow make sure I didn't wind up in one.

I was plain scared, but, as always, Margaret looked for an answer. When we got back to Connecticut, she found a smiling, soft-spoken psychiatrist in Fairfield named William O. Sires, and made an appointment for me. On the morning of the appointment, we woke up to a heavy snowfall, which looked to me like a perfect excuse to stay home. But not to Margaret.

"We're going to Fairfield," she said, "if we have to walk."

Well, we didn't have to walk, but it was a rather dicey seven-mile drive to Fairfield through the storm. I'm glad she made me take it, because it became one of the most important trips of my life.

Dr. Sires looked not at all like Sigmund Freud. He was a chubby, round-faced country boy from Hagerstown, Maryland, who just happened to be the perfect person for me to talk with—no scientific phrases, no fancy office, just two men talking in a decently appointed room over a supermarket in a small Connecticut town.

On my first visit, I said, "Am I supposed to lie down on the couch?"

"That's entirely up to you" was his answer. So I sat in a chair.

He asked to see the pills I had been taking. When I gave

them to him, he murmured "Wow," then threw them in the wastebasket. "They're a depressant," he said. "Enough to make you cry." So *that* was it.

Of course, there was much more. He encouraged me to do most of the talking, but when he spoke, it was pure common sense backed up by the several psychiatric degrees framed on the wall. Occasionally, as I talked on, he would say, "Gee, that's enough to make you angry, isn't it?"

My problem was unresolved anger and misplaced guilt, some of it dating back to my childhood. From Dr. Sires, I learned how to stop burying problems in my unconscious, how to mentally put them up on the wall, look at them directly, figure out where they came from, then deal with them.

Today, I would be said to have "emotional problems." In 1960, it was just called a good old-fashioned nervous breakdown.

Slowly, through April and May, between the sessions with Sires and the constant strong presence of Margaret, I began to feel a lot better. I am convinced that without those two, the rest of my career probably wouldn't have happened.

But I couldn't help thinking about losing that Olympics job and probably blowing my career in sports.

And then, one early June afternoon in 1960, I had a most unexpected phone call from Bill MacPhail, head of CBS Sports. "How would you like to be the studio host for the Rome Olympics?" he asked. It was a bolt from the blue, just the providential boost that I needed at that moment. Naturally, I jumped at the offer. When I told Margaret, it was her turn to cry.

The logistics for televising an Olympics were different in those days. A team of on-scene commentators was in Rome. They described the events, which were recorded on videotape, then flown to New York, where they were edited and put on the air.

I sat in an eerily lit studio located in a loft atop Grand Central Station in New York, in front of a spooky-looking urn with a flame leaping from it. The studio looked more like a funeral parlor than an Olympics anchor position.

I was excited about the job, but from the beginning things were badly organized. The tapes arrived from Rome erratically, sometimes with commentary, sometimes without even a guide script for me to use as I ad-libbed my way through the events. Sometimes the tapes were frozen from their long trip in a cold cargo hold, and the producer and I would have to hold them against our bodies to warm them enough to be edited. We had no format. The whole first night's show was a journey through chaos. I began to wonder if my "big break" might have been the worst thing that could have happened to me.

The show aired at eight in the evening, but in the daytime I went out to the airport to interview returning medal winners. I remember standing at the door of a plane as a young boxer, who had just won the gold medal in the light heavyweight class, emerged. He was friendly, with a sweet smile on his face, but seemed somewhat shy. His name was Cassius Marcellus Clay, later known as Muhammad Ali.

The entire first week of the Olympic telecasts was a disaster, visually and production-wise. At that point, a high-level meeting was held, at which the sports executive responsible for the New York end of the telecast was put on the griddle. He blamed the problems on me. Fortunately, a friend of mine was also at the meeting. He defended me and had Bob Allison, a news department producer, assigned to the show to pull things together. If my friend hadn't been there, I probably would have been fired.

Allison and I got along just fine. At our first meeting, he asked me what he could do to help me. "Give me a format," I said. He immediately doused the dismal studio flame, handed me a tight format for each evening's program, and made a few other changes; the show improved and all turned out well.

But life in those days was one surprise after another. For example, the network suddenly decided to move *Verdict* to Hollywood. Margaret and I are simply not the Hollywood-type couple. We think the town is ugly, the lifestyle pretentious, and the whole scene immensely unconducive to raising children. So we said no, whereupon the network asked us if we would just go out there for a month to break in a new host for the show. We agreed, on the condition that Margaret could go with me, first class, on the new luxury jet Boeing 707 and that we could stay in a bungalow at the Beverly Hills Hotel for the month, all expenses paid by CBS.

I guess we had a good time on the trip, but frankly, only two things come to mind when I think back to it. One is that American Airlines served hot fudge sundaes for dessert on the plane, something it does to this day. The other is that the entire airport terminal in L.A. consisted of a small, green adobe-style building with a waiting room about the size of the average Hollywood star's bedroom. Every time I go to the coast in the nineties, as the plane rolls down the runway, I check to make sure that the building is still there. It is, squeezed in among the huge terminal buildings and hangars of today.

Back in New York that autumn, I was now, at last, free of the professional constraints that *Verdict* had put on me. I was feeling relaxed. All the fear and anger was gone, but there was, as always, a problem. CBS had no sports assignments for me until the Masters golf tournament the following spring. I was, to put it bluntly, out of work.

Enter, as always, Margaret. Suddenly, her column was our only source of income. She used it to pay our bills, with no complaints.

The long winter stretched ahead, with only the Masters to look forward to in the spring. After that, CBS had promised nothing. We thought about going back to Baltimore, which Margaret would have loved, but she knew that I would feel like a loser if we did, so we stuck it out.

The World Opens Wide

It was Masters time in Augusta, the first week in April of 1961, and I was having a lovely time walking the course, following different groups, making notes for the telecast that was to come, when Bob Drum came by. He lived up to his name—huge, fierce-looking, gravel-voiced, but sentimental. It was Drum, a golf writer from Pittsburgh, who had first alerted the world to the presence of a golfer named Arnold Palmer. Drum had also been the first member of the writing press to give me the time of day when we television types first came to the Masters in the mid-fifties. We had not been welcomed as brothers by most of Bob's colleagues.

Now, as he passed by on his way to follow his man Palmer, he growled, "They're lookin' for you in the pressroom, pally."

"Why?"

"I don't know. That's your problem. Some guy named Ron Aldrich from New York has been calling you."

Aldrich. I didn't know any Aldrich, but as I walked back to the pressroom, I recalled a new producer at ABC who had called me in California last fall when I was out there breaking in the new man on *Verdict*. His name was Roone Arledge—how could you forget such a singularly original moniker? This person, Roone, had called to see if I would be interested in doing a little bowling show after *The Friday Night Fights* called *Make That Spare*. It would have an "accordion" time period. In other words, if the fight ended in an early knockout, *Make That Spare* would run fairly long; if the fight went the distance it would be short, with hardly enough time for a strike, let alone a spare.

It wasn't much of a show, but one that was welcome to a guy facing the bleak desert of unemployment when he got back East. I'd have taken it, but it was not to be. They hired a popular singer of the time, Johnny Johnson, who was also a bowling aficionado.

Now, here, sure enough, was Arledge on the line again from New York, along with another fellow named Chet Simmons, Arledge's co-equal at the ABC sports department at that time. Putting a finger in my free ear to keep out the clatter of typewriters and the din of reporters yelling across the pressroom, I heard Arledge, who did most of the talking, ask if I might be interested in a new show and tell me that they were checking the availability of a number of people for a summer replacement show they were planning.

"What kind of a show?" I asked, instantly interested.

"It's a summer replacement show," Roone said.

"What?" I said. It was terribly difficult to hear him over the noise in the pressroom.

"A summer replacement show," he shouted. "Twenty weeks. We'll be covering a number of sports not normally seen on TV."

A guy standing behind me, waiting for the phone, was now shifting impatiently from one foot to the other. But I wasn't going to let this one go.

"Sounds interesting," I gulped, trying to sound interested, but not desperate.

Then, in a major piece of understatement, he said, "I think I should tell you it will require a certain amount of traveling."

"I think I can make myself available, Roone," I said. "It really sounds like a job I would like. Of course, I'm committed to CBS to finish the Masters, and I would have to consult with my wife."

"That's great," he said, but then backed off a bit. "Remember, we're talking to a number of others, too. We'll get back to you."

That was it.

I did not tell him that after the Masters I would actually be unemployed. And I had to wonder if his last comment was another version of the famous show business brush-off line, "Don't call us, we'll call you."

For the next several days I got caught up in our telecast, and I had almost forgotten the rather casual call when I was paged again. This time I was sitting in the pressroom making some notes for the day's telecast. It was eleven o'clock in the morning.

"Jim, Roone Arledge. Well, you're our man for the *World of Sports* show. How much money do you want?"

Just like that.

I gulped, and hoped it sounded like a pregnant pause.

"Well, uh, can't we talk about that part when I get back to New York?"

I was stalling. I had no agent at the time, and Margaret was doing any negotiating that was required. I certainly wasn't going to prostrate myself at Roone's feet without first talking with her.

"No, it can't wait," Arledge said. "We're having a press conference in half an hour and we want to announce that you will be the host."

A press conference? To announce *me*?

It didn't seem like a time to procrastinate, so I straightened my shoulders, took a deep breath, and said, "How about a thousand dollars a show?" To me, that was a lot of money—twenty thousand bucks, guaranteed for the summer.

"Okay," Arledge said. Immediately, I knew I'd made a mistake, had given a lower figure than I could have gotten. I'd known I should have left it to Margaret, but it was done. And besides, Roone Arledge had thrown me a life preserver just as I was quite possibly about to sink under the waters.

It would be nice to say that at that moment I envisioned this show (he told me it would be called *World of Sports*, but the name was later changed to *Wide World of Sports* because somebody else held title to *World of Sports*) running forever.

Uh-uh. I was looking only as far as the summer run and the much-needed paycheck. It would have taken a true clairvoyant to imagine that my association with Arledge would last more than a quarter of a century, and that today I would still be working for ABC Sports.

The road to my being hired to do *Wide World* was littered with the kind of coincidences of which life and careers are made. Arledge, Simmons, and a couple of other people were sitting around one day brainstorming about possible hosts for the show. One of the others at that session was Hugh Beach, the onetime English instructor who called himself "Meathead" and who had been with me through the Roger Bannister incident when we were both working on the Cronkite morning program at CBS. Hugh had left CBS and now was a producer with ABC.

The meeting bogged down when it seemed that most of the commentators whose names came up were occupied with local baseball jobs for the summer. Then Meathead interrupted. "Excuse me, chaps," he said, "but Burrhead would not do you wrong."

"Burrhead?"

"You know, Jim McKay, the guy with the really short crew cut."

Roone remembered having talked to me about the little bowling show, and I guessed he liked the idea of a burrhead running *Wide World*.

Then I got another break. A few years before, a man named Edgar J. Scherick, whom I had met when he was a salesman at CBS Sports, started a little independent company called Sports Programs, Inc. The company's first show was an hour and a half fully devoted to the opening of a new harness racing track called Roosevelt Raceway. Since he had known us at CBS, Scherick hired Chris Schenkel and me to be the commentators on the show, which aired on ABC's flagship New York station, WABC-TV, at eight o'clock on Friday night. That should give you some idea of the quality of programming ABC was sending out in prime time in the fifties.

On the program, I'd show the viewers how beautiful the paddock was, then throw it to Chris, who would explain how efficient the concession stands were. We'd go back and forth like that, ad nauseam. We did manage to show two races, using the track announcer's call. The hour and a half seemed like an eternity, but it represented the first income for Sports Programs, Inc., and Scherick was pleased.

In time, ABC contracted with Scherick to have his company do all its sports programs, and so he was the one Arledge had to convince that I was the man for the new summer replacement show. Scherick remembered the harness track opening and a couple of other things I had done for his company and gave his okay to my hiring.

A week later, I was in a meeting at Sports Programs, Inc., with Arledge, a director named Bill Bennington, and a production assistant named Chuck Howard. Our initial show, Arledge explained, would be a television first. We would televise, live, two of the country's most important track-and-field meets, the Penn and the Drake Relays, on the same day, cutting back and forth between them as the events unfolded. I would be the overall host in Philadelphia for the Penn Relays. My expert commentators would be Jesse Abramson, the track-and-field writer for the *New York Herald Tribune,* and the Reverend Bob Richards, a well-known pole vaulter of the time. Bill Flemming and Jim Simpson would comment from the Drake events in Des Moines, Iowa.

So three weeks after I got that first phone call in Augusta, I was in Philadelphia, the City of Brotherly Love and my birth, at Franklin Field, where I had seen my first sports event at the age of twelve (Penn vs. Navy in football; I remember that the game was won on a field goal kicked by Midshipman Slade Cutter, who later became an admiral).

It was a dank, dreary morning when I arrived at Franklin Field on April 29, 1961, to be greeted by the news that in the torrential rain of the night before, two of our four cameras had been incapacitated by waterlogged cables. The gravel track was firm in some places, soggy in others. (Today's weatherproof Tartan track was still a few years off.) The pole vault and high jump pits were full of wet sand, a far cry from the air-filled plastic landing surfaces of the future. (The vaulting poles themselves were still made of bamboo.)

The events of the two track meets were not particularly exciting that day—what was exciting was the mere fact of the telecast, the novelty of showing two sports events live and simultaneously from different parts of the country. After all, it had been only a few years earlier that Edward R. Murrow had opened the first *See It Now* program by showing a shot of the Atlantic Ocean side by side with a shot of the Pacific. See how it could be done by this marvelous technical leap forward called television?

Still, nobody paid much attention to our first *Wide World of Sports*. The ratings were miserable. Television watchers were much more engaged with two pivotal events of the sixties—the Soviets putting the first man in space and the ill-fated Bay of Pigs invasion of Cuba. But we kept going.

A couple of days after the relays, I boarded a plane of the British Overseas Airways Corporation (now simply British Airways) for my first trip across the Atlantic Ocean. During World War II, I had spent a couple of years in the South Atlantic and had sailed back and forth between Norfolk, Virginia, and Brazil, but I had never been to Europe. Nor had I ever seen a professional soccer match. Now, I would do both, going to London for Britain's F.A. (for Football Association) Cup Final, the climax of a season-long soccer elimination tournament and one of England's top sporting occasions.

Despite a language barrier, my navy time in Brazil had been, in many ways, similar to the United States; at least they drove on the same side of the street as we do. England, I thought, would be even more familiar. I was in for a series of shocks.

The first shock was to my stomach. I made the mistake of accepting a glass of canned orange juice that was offered to me about an hour before our red-eye overnight flight was scheduled to land at Heathrow Airport. The ersatz orange juice, coupled with a particularly strong cup of instant coffee, brought on an attack of heartburn that I can remember and almost taste three and a half decades later.

Then I was buffeted by the cockney accent of the passport control man. It would have been difficult for Eliza Doolittle herself to understand what he was saying. And even the signs in the airport validated George Bernard Shaw's statement that the English and the Americans are divided by a common tongue. Instead of EXIT, the sign read, WAY OUT. Where the attendants were mopping the nearly empty terminal in the early morning, a small placard said simply MIND THE FLOOR. Another one I haven't figured out to this day read, PLEASE DISREGARD THIS NOTICE.

At the Grosvenor House hotel in London, pretty fancy for me, the desk clerk presented me with a room key that, judging from its size, might have been used to lock the little princes into the Tower of London. A young gentleman in formal clothes escorted me to my room. Within minutes of his departure, I had disrobed and fallen into a deep sleep between linen sheets. Although the ailment had not yet been identified in 1961, I was in the first stages of diurnal dysrhythmia, later called jet lag. It was 8:00 A.M. in London, but inside my body it was still three o'clock in the morning, F. Scott Fitzgerald's "dark night of the soul."

Two hours later, I was awakened by the telephone, which sounded more like a fire bell. It was our director, Bill Bennington, who had preceded me to London by a day. "All set for lunch?" he asked. At the word "lunch" my stomach sounded a fire bell of its own.

"What lunch?" I asked.

"Lunch with the BBC guys," he said. "They want to welcome us and go over the format for the show. We're meeting them at an Italian restaurant near the hotel in half an hour."

Lunch turned out to be a preordered meal of spaghetti and meatballs accompanied by not wine, but "bitter," a dark, flat sort of beer. There were six or seven BBC "chaps," one of whom, Kenneth Wolstenholme, was one of their top soccer ("football" to them) announcers. He would be doing the play-by-play on the F.A. Cup Final for us, while I asked the questions that our American audience would like to hear answered. He started to explain the rudiments of the game to me, then interrupted himself. "I hope you won't bring up Belo Horizonte on the program," he said.

My first reaction was to wonder if that was some battle of the American Revolution I had forgotten about. Then I remembered from my navy days that Belo Horizonte was an inland city in Brazil.

"I'm sorry, Kenneth," I said, "but I don't know what you're talking about."

"Oh, come now, Jim. You're taking the mickey out of me. Surely you remember Belo Horizonte. You Yanks will never let us forget it. Every British schoolboy knows of that tragic day."

I was really baffled. "Kenneth," I said, "I don't know what 'taking the mickey out of me' means, and I don't know what happened in Belo Horizonte, either."

Kenneth sighed. "Oh, very well, Jim. I suppose you're going to make me say it, even though the words stick in my throat. At the World Cup in 1950, in Belo Horizonte, Brazil, the United States defeated England, one to nil, in the biggest shocker in football history!"

No matter how hard I tried, I couldn't convince him that not one American in a thousand, including me, had ever heard of such an event, and wouldn't have realized its significance even if word had reached their ears.

Eventually, lunch was finished, amid profuse shaking of hands and promises of total cooperation. Walking back to the hotel through Grosvenor Square Park, in front of the new American Embassy I spied one more British sign to add to my collection. Instead of CURB YOUR DOG! it said, much more gently, PLEASE DO NOT ALLOW YOUR DOG TO FOUL THIS GRASS.

Then we stumbled back to my room for another two hours' sleep—my heartburn and I.

The phone rang the next morning at 8:00 A.M. I had lain

awake half the night, exhausted but unable to sleep, but at that moment, I had just reached the deepest part of my erratic slumber. It was Roone Arledge, just off the overnight flight from New York, asking me to join him for breakfast.

I stumbled into the lobby. There was Roone. For a guy who had just gotten off the red-eye, he looked fresh and fit and ready to go for the day. Roone then, as now, was a chunky, strong-looking man with a full head of red hair. His smile was boyish but his eyes were canny, measuring each person he met. I have long had the feeling that Roone committed to a life plan when he was about twelve years old and has followed it perfectly ever since. I feel this even though he often gives the appearance of being very disorganized and indecisive. Through his career, he has left a long trail of confused and defeated people who thought they could outsmart this smiling, friendly redhead.

Puffing on his favorite pipe that morning in London, he was full of enthusiasm and ideas. We spent the whole day preparing for the next day's match, and that night he dragged me to dinner at one of the Wheeler's Fish Houses, where he ordered—for both of us—Scotch salmon with horseradish sauce, Dover sole adorned with tiny shrimp, a couple of bottles of excellent white wine (he is something of a connoisseur), and an English trifle (an ironic name for a heavy dessert). All of which led to another restless night for me but the sleep of a baby for him.

I was dragging as we left the hotel for Wembley Stadium, and so was my enthusiasm for my new job. But it returned when we reached a pub called the Green Man, perched atop a hill, looking down on the great crowd gathering and the stadium itself, originally built for the 1948 Olympic Games. We stood on a terrace outside the pub, where the BBC had gathered some "old boys," aging veterans of previous F.A. Cup Finals. I interviewed each of them, soliciting from the old warriors the flavor of the Cup's history and meaning. Then we drove down to Wembley Way, where the spectators were streaming in, most of them dressed in the colors of their favorite team—blue and white for the favored Tottenham Hot-spurs, red and white for the underdog team from Leicester City. Some wore crazy hats in their colors; many displayed their loyalty in scarves and sweaters. The more dignified set-tled for a simple rosette pinned to their lapel or a tiny ribbon hanging from their bowler hats.

Youngsters waved pennants and shouted their loyalty to any who would listen.

This was before British soccer crowds had become tyran-nized by hooligans, who broke windows and tore out seats in trains coming to the games, then drank and fought their way through the afternoon, sometimes with deadly results. As in all such cases, the hooligans were a small minority, but vocal and physical enough to throw a cloud over the sport in Brit-ain. Because of such abusive behavior, British fans were banned for a time from games on the European continent.

It has always baffled me how soccer, a low-scoring, often cerebral sport, could inspire such base emotion. Some experts on human behavior think it has nothing to do with the con-test, that it is simply a convenient venue for displaying aggres-sion. Hence the necessity for barbed-wire fences surrounding the playing fields, and tunnels for the escape of referees in some South American countries.

If Wembley Stadium is the holy of holies, the lush grass of the playing field is the altar cloth. On the day before the match in those days, the players were allowed only to *walk* on the field, and in civilian clothes, not uniforms.

We were there to talk with some of them. Our most inter-esting player interview was with Danny Blanchflower, captain of the Tottenham Hotspurs, who was trying to lead his team to "the double," meaning to win both the league champion-ship and the Cup, the climax of a season-long knockout com-petition staged concurrently with the regular season.

I found Danny to be a bright, attractive, charismatic Irish-man who was both a bon vivant and a spokesman for the sport. He also had a mind of his own, which was dramatically displayed on one occasion when he had been selected as the week's surprise guest on the English version of *This Is Your Life*. Younger readers may need a word of explanation. *This Is Your Life* was originally an American program, hosted by a man named Ralph Edwards, onto which a guest was lured each week on some pretense, only to find that the show was to be the story of his or her life. It was a huge hit on American television over the years, and the British version became just as popular. But when Blanchflower walked onto the set and was suddenly greeted by the host with "Danny Blanchflower, *this is your life!*" he shook up the host and the whole nation watching the live telecast. He said, "The *hell* it is!" then turned on his heels and left.

But I will always remember him as he was that day at Wembley, full of life as he directed his men to their triumph over Leicester City, then took a victory lap of the stadium, holding up the Cup to his followers while wearing its lid on his head like a great silver cap.

How sad it was to read thirty-some years later that this vibrant, quick-witted man had died of Alzheimer's disease while still in his early sixties.

Blanchflower was not the only hero that day at Wembley. The Hotspurs' opponent, Leicester City, had an unexpected one of its own. His name was Len Chalmers, a journeyman player with nowhere near the reputation of Blanchflower. Late in the first half, he was cut down on the heavy turf, obviously in great pain. But he limped his way through the remainder of the period. In those days, no substitutes were allowed in professional soccer and if you left the game, you could not return. Leicester would have had to play one man short if Chalmers couldn't come back for the second half. To the surprise of the crowd, he did return, and played through the entire second half—with a broken leg!

My BBC colleague, Ken Wolstenholme, kept referring to him as "poor old Chalmers" for the rest of the game. But he managed to limp up to the Queen's box to receive his runner-up medal with his teammates.

If there is anything we can learn from the British, it is how to put on an impressive ceremony, and we learned it that day at Wembley. Unlike some of our postchampionship celebrations, conducted in the locker room with players pouring champagne on one another's heads, the Cup winners form a neat line and march up red-carpeted steps to the Queen's box. There, Her Majesty, or in some years the Duchess of Kent, gives each player a medal and the Duke of Edinburgh shakes each one's hand. The monarch then gives the Cup to the winning captain, and the crowd roars. The team descends the steps and takes that dramatic victory lap, carrying the captain on their shoulders as he displays the Cup to the huge audience, pausing dramatically at the end of the stadium filled with their followers.

All this was going on while I was getting to know Roone Arledge somewhat better and finding that his thoughts about covering sports were very similar to my own. I have always believed that sports, like politics, business, or anything else in life, is about the human beings involved and their reactions to critical situations. At the F.A. Cup Final, I had tried to do that by concentrating much of my commentary on Danny Blanchflower, directing his team on the playing field like Patton deploying his tanks at El Alamein, and Len Chalmers, gamely playing on against all odds.

Few Americans remember the game that was played that day, but all these years later, I am still approached occasionally by some viewer who asks, "Whatever happened to 'poor old Chalmers'?"

Roone and I flew back to the States together, he squeezed against the window in the back end of tourist class, I sitting bolt upright in the middle seat between him and a snoring Englishman whose head kept lolling onto my shoulder. That was years before ABC finally relented and let us go first class.

On that flight, Roone's head was abuzz with creative ideas about the show. He talked about cameras at the bottom of a swimming pool, of sitting on a "cowcatcher" attached to the front of a moving mobile unit, of hanging from a two-hundred-foot crane. But mostly he talked about something on which we totally agreed—that the most important thing in sports was not the technical achievement or the world-record time, but the human beings involved: who they were, where they were from, how they got to this moment, how they might handle it, why it was so important to them—all the personal dreams and insecurities with which the viewer could identify.

I had never met anyone whose approach to sports was so similar to my own. We would seldom disagree while he was in the control room and I was on the air during the next quarter-century. This human approach expanded from *Wide World* to our coverage of ten Olympics and, in time, to all networks' coverage of sports.

The emphasis on the person involved in the sport would be particularly important in some of the lesser-known sports we would be introducing on *Wide World*. The viewer might not know or care about a particular sport, but if we could get him interested in the person playing it, then interest in the sport itself might follow.

That summer, we introduced our viewers to bowling in Paramus, New Jersey; pro tennis in Mexico City; sports car racing through the French countryside at Le Mans; fast-pitch softball in Clearwater, Florida; waterskiing in Pine Mountain, Georgia; stock car racing in Daytona Beach, Florida; gymnastics in Dallas; track and field in Moscow; baseball in Japan; rodeo in Cheyenne, Wyoming; hydroplane racing in Seattle; swimming and diving in Philadelphia; golf on the Old Course at St. Andrews, Scotland; and a pro football exhibition game in San Diego, during which we pioneered the idea of putting a microphone on the quarterback. The name of the quarterback was Jack Kemp—uh-huh, that Jack Kemp.

We weren't received as conquering heroes by the network. In fact, we nearly were canceled in the middle of that first summer and were only saved by the favorable publicity given to our coverage of the U.S.A.-U.S.S.R. track-and-field meet. That, and the support of ABC president Tom Moore, who had gone to Moscow with us.

Just about the time I was beginning to wonder what I

would do when the summer replacement series was over, Tom told us that he was going to put the show back on the air as a regular series the following January, after a fall hiatus.

And, mirabile dictu, he would pay me my salary during the fall, for doing nothing, if I would remain available to be the show's host!

Would I be available? Indeed. And the next year I began the show that was to be called ABC's *Wide World of Sports*. Where I would stay ever after.

II

THE McKAY RANKINGS

The Olympics: A Story about Heroes

h ero, *n. one who is regarded as having heroic qualities and is considered a model or idol . . . (in the Homeric period) a warrior-chieftain of superior strength, courage, or ability.*

Strength, courage, ability; model, idol. These are the qualities embodied for me in the word "excellence" as I pursue my career in sports TV.

And that is why I have titled the first chapter in this part of the book, "A Story About Heroes." It concerns the Olympic Games, the ancient—and modern—symbol of athletic achievement and international friendship. The traditional birthplace of sports heroes.

But the word applies also to the other sports, my favorites, that I've covered through the years, and that you will read about.

At the end of each chapter, I rank my personal sports heroes—men and women who embody *all* of the heroic qualities, not just one.

It was an unlikely group of Americans who staggered into the Olympic Stadium in Athens in 1896. Some of them were young Ivy League runners and jumpers from prominent Eastern families. Others were Irish-Americans from Boston. They were all led by Robert Garrett, a wealthy Princeton University student from Baltimore, who had conceived the idea of challenging Europe's best.

Their entrance was the end of a long and tiring odyssey, one they had undertaken together because, despite the disparity of their backgrounds and appearances, they shared a common goal. They had traveled on a tramp steamer for weeks to Italy, where they picked up a ride on a battered old hulk that limped across the Adriatic Sea, finally dumping them in a small Grecian seaport, exhausted and still short of their goal. Then they boarded an overnight train and rode it for ten hours to Athens.

They were the first American Olympic team, arriving just in time for the opening ceremony of the first modern Games. Olympics officials were surprised to see them, having assumed that the Americans weren't coming or had gotten lost somewhere in transit. But they had made it, dirty, disheveled, and weary as they were.

There was no television, no radio, no jet airplanes swooping over the stadium to salute the athletes. And there was no great excitement back in the U.S. about this revival of an ancient Greek custom. Most of the country's citizens, including newspaper editors, thought of this business in Athens as strictly a European affair.

But the young Yanks shocked them when James Connolly, a triple jumper, still staggering a bit on his sea legs, won the first gold medal to be awarded in modern Olympics history.

It was a story worthy of the inspirational boys' books of the time. It might have been called, "The Rover Boys at the Olympics."

And when the Yanks continued on, winning nine of the ten events in which they were entered, their country finally awoke to the stature of their achievements. In those long-ago games, they started an American tradition of Olympics track-and-field excellence that endures a century later.

It continued with little Johnny Hayes winning the marathon in 1908 when Dorando Pietri of Italy was disqualified; Jim Thorpe, the Native American marvel, taking the decathlon in 1912, only to have the medals stripped from him when it was discovered he had played a summer of semipro baseball; Charley Paddock being dubbed "the World's Fastest Human" when he won the 100 meters at Antwerp, Belgium, in 1920; with Jesse Owens, a young African-American, embarrassing Hitler with his victories and his dignified demeanor in 1936; Bob Mathias winning the decathlon as a teenager and later becoming a U.S. congressman; Rafer Johnson, who had spent years of his childhood living in a railroad boxcar, winning the decathlon a decade later. The achievements have gone on without interruption—Bob Beamon's superhuman long jump in Mexico City; Carl Lewis's two gold medals in the 100 meters (one because of the disqualification of Ben Johnson) and his four consecutive long jump golds. All of these great athletes followed in the footsteps of that first team in 1896.

In the decades since I first sat in a New York studio as television host for the 1960 Rome Games for CBS, sixty-four years after those first modern Games, I have covered Summer Games from Mexico City, Munich, Montreal, and Los Angeles, and Winter Games from Innsbruck (twice), Grenoble, Lake Placid, Sarajevo, and Calgary.

And as always in my career, I remember personalities much more vividly than medal counts and world records. And each Olympics provides at least one, often unexpected, hero or heroine.

So, forgive me, but this is a chapter about heroes.

INNSBRUCK—1964

If we are to judge by the price paid for television rights, no event has grown over the past three decades as fast as the Olympic Games. For the Winter Games of 1960, CBS paid $50,000. Four years later, for the Winter Games of Innsbruck, ABC paid $500,000, a tenfold increase. It was thought by many to be a ridiculously high figure.

Today, the Olympics go for more than $300 million, and for all the Olympics from 2000 through 2008, NBC paid several billion dollars.

The bidding process for the 1964 Winter Games was a remarkably informal one compared with the complicated, formalized procedures of today.

Roone Arledge and Chet Simmons, then the two top executives of ABC Sports, flew into Munich, where they rented a limousine to take them to Innsbruck and across the Austrian border in the Tyrol, just a few miles from the Brenner Pass leading to northern Italy. The driver happened to be a young man named Kurt Fuchs. He spoke his own brand of English, learned entirely by listening to U.S. Armed Forces Radio and by chauffeuring American tourists.

Upon arrival in Innsbruck, Arledge and Simmons had their first informal meeting with Herr Professor Wolfgang, chairman of the Innsbruck Olympic Organizing Committee. Professor Wolfgang said that no interpreter would be needed, since he spoke perfect English. It sounded a bit less than perfect to the Americans, but they went ahead, discussing some rather complicated aspects of the proposed coverage. Wolfgang kept nodding assent.

In time, he looked at his watch and halted the proceedings.

"Well, gentlemen," he said. "It is interesting what you say, but my clock tells me that I must go now. So I bid you hello."

Hello?

Obviously, an interpreter would be needed for the next meeting. But who? The only person available was at the wheel of the limousine. And so Kurt Fuchs became the interpreter for the rights acquisition of the 1964 Winter Games.

It was as if some Austrian group came to the United States to bid on the European rights to the World Series and brought as their interpreter the taxi driver who'd brought them in from the airport.

But Fuchs got the job done. It was the beginning of a long

professional and personal relationship between him and the people of ABC Sports.

Our coverage of the Games themselves was a far different and more primitive process than is allowed by today's space-age technology. The telecasts would be almost entirely on tape, although two short segments would be sent live through the new marvel, a communications satellite. The satellite of those days whirled around planet Earth at a mind-boggling speed, rather than being anchored at one spot in space. This meant that it was available for use at any given spot on Earth for about a three-minute window as it passed overhead. So we sent only a very short portion of the opening ceremony and another brief segment on the last day live to the U.S.

The heart of our operation, though, was a battery of video-tape machines. The Austrians assigned the machines space in the basement of the brand-new ice arena, a cold, damp, and depressing area. More important than the ambience was the fact that fresh cement dust kept drifting down and settling into the tape machines. As the operators recorded the events, they had to keep blowing their breath into the whirling cylinders to keep the cement dust from clogging them up.

Our method of getting the tapes back to the U.S. was also rather primitive and uncertain.

Each night, at something like 3:00 A.M., a recently retired U.S. air force colonel, Jim McNu, loaded the show into the trunk of his rental car and began a lonely drive over the mountains and through the snowstorms to the Munich airport. He had to make it in time to put the tapes on Pan Am flight 101 to New York. One flat tire or one impassable snowstorm and we would have been out of business for that day.

Innsbruck was our baptism in Olympics coverage. The black-and-white coverage of that time now looks as ancient as silent movies. When we returned to Europe four years later for another Winter Games, we would be televising in what was unfailingly referred to as "living color."

If Innsbruck was our team's baptism, my personal baptism came by way of an unexpected event one unseasonably warm morning.

I was standing in a crowd by the outdoor speed skating rink when a technician from ABC Radio approached. "Jim," he said, "I can't find my announcer and I notice on the start list that an American is skating next. Will you do the commentary for me?"

I was actually on a busman's holiday watching the 500-meter sprint. This was my one scheduled day off during the Games, but I took the microphone and consulted the start list. The skater was Terry McDermott, U.S.A. I knew his name, and I also knew that it appeared he had no chance of coming close to a medal.

Yevgeny Grishin, the favorite from the Soviet Union, had put up a good time early on, when the ice was hard and fast. It was equaled by another Soviet skater and a Norwegian. Now, with the sun beating down, the surface was soft, almost slushy.

I described the run on audiotape, and was glad that I did, because Terry McDermott, skating through the soft, water-covered ice, won the gold medal in an amazing upset. Afterward, I sought him out and asked him what he did for a living.

"I'm a barber," Terry said, "in Bay City, Michigan."

Terry McDermott was the only gold medal winner for the United States in those Games.

However, two young American ski racers did provide a bit of Olympics history. Billy Kidd and Jimmy Heuga became the first male Americans ever to win a medal in Olympics ski racing, Kidd taking the silver and Heuga the bronze in the slalom event on the penultimate day of competition.

GRENOBLE—1968

Long before the NFL experimented with instant replay to review decisions on the field, the facilities of ABC Sports were used to decide an Olympic gold medal. It was at the Winter Games of Grenoble, France, in 1968.

Jean-Claude Killy, the young, handsome hero of France, was trying to win all three gold medals in Alpine skiing. It was a feat accomplished only once before, by the legendary Austrian Toni Sailer. The pre-games build-up to Killy's attempt had been unceasing, relentless. Huge crowds climbed the courses as he won first the downhill event, then the giant slalom. Only the slalom remained, on the final day of competition, with just one serious competitor for Killy to worry about.

Karl Schranz, of Austria, had always been cast as the heavy in the rivalry. He had a dark, serious, almost threatening look about him, as contrasted to Killy's ruddy, smiling face and friendly manner. Schranz even dressed in dark colors, like the bad guy in a Western. Now, he faced Killy on Killy's turf, with thousands of Frenchmen waving the tricolor and singing the "Marseillaise" as the competition began.

In their minds, it was World Wars I and II all over again, the Frenchman against the German-speaking Schranz.

Killy took the lead on the first run, and the cheering echoed through the mountains. One run remained; soon the three gold medals would be his. But fog had rolled in between the runs, a heavy, wet blanket that made it all but impossible to see the course. The spectators at the bottom could only listen to the cheers farther up and wait for the racer to appear. Killy made it to the bottom, holding a ski pole in the air and smiling as he crossed the finish line. Now, only the hated Schranz could spoil France's long-awaited day of victory.

The crowd at the bottom was silent, listening for a report from the public-address system as Schranz started down. For a while there was nothing. Where was he? How was he doing? Then the metallic voice from the loudspeakers told the startling news: Schranz had missed a gate, skied off the course, and would be disqualified!

There was pandemonium. Media people swarmed around the smiling Killy; French flags waved everywhere. A scattering of polite, sympathetic applause greeted Schranz when he finally coasted across the line. But if you looked closely, you could see that his head was not hung down in crushing defeat. Rather, he had the look of a man on an urgent errand. He skied quickly over to the officials, and as he talked to them, he pointed up the hill with a ski pole. The officials huddled, then an announcement hushed the crowd. The result was not official. Schranz was requesting a rerun.

The basis for his urgent claim was that a policeman, Schranz said, had skied out in front of him as he was making his way through the fog and forced him off the course. It was a tough call.

The officials' decision was to give Schranz a provisional rerun, then to view our videotape, the only visual record of the contested incident, before making a final ruling. The crowd was confused, angry, and unruly as Schranz made his way back up the course.

The Austrian pushed off into the fog again as our cameramen strained their eyes to follow him. It was a smooth run this time, too smooth for the crowd below. When he reached the finish line, there was stunned silence, mixed with some whistles of derision. His time was better than Killy's. If his claim of interference on his first run held up under the video review, he, not Killy, would be the winner, and the quest for the third gold medal would have failed.

The officials marched to our TV truck, concerned looks on their faces, and asked if they might review the tape. I stood with Roone Arledge in our crowded tape room as they watched it, over and over. The camera lens sees more clearly than the human eye in fog, since it requires less light, so the belief was that it would reveal what had really happened.

For more than an hour, the officials asked to have the tape rolled, again and again, conferring after each viewing. On the tape, there was another figure visible as Schranz skied off the course. But had he actually caused the racer to miss the gate?

The spectators grew restless, stamping their boots in the snow to stay warm, running the concession stands clear out of sausage and Ovomaltine. They were not a happy group.

Finally, the officials broke up their meeting. The reason for the long delay was that there was considerable disagreement among them about what they were seeing on the tape. In the end, the vote was only 3-2 in Killy's favor. Two French judges and a Swiss had voted to disqualify Schranz; an Englishman and a Norwegian had voted to uphold the Austrian's rerun. They left the truck to the jeers and whistles of the crowd and went to the P.A. announcer, who, in crisp French tones, gave the news to the spectators.

"After a thorough review of the videotape," the announcer said, "the officials have decided that—the protest is denied, the rerun is canceled, Monsieur Killy of France is the winner!"

To the French, it was national vindication. For the officials, it was an escape from a possible lynching. For us, it was a television milestone, the first time our medium had been used to determine the outcome of an event—and an Olympic event, at that.

☆

It was at Grenoble, also, that a new American Ice Queen emerged. Tenley Albright and Carol Heiss had assumed that role in the 1950s, when television coverage was minimal.

Tragedy struck the next generation of American skaters when their plane crashed in Belgium on their way to the 1961 World Championships in Prague. The championships were canceled for that year and the United States had lost a promising and heartbreakingly young group of figure skaters.

Now, in Grenoble, a new queen appeared, skating beautifully in a diaphanous green dress before a worldwide TV audience, in "living" color. She was Peggy Fleming, daughter of a newspaper pressman for the *Los Angeles Times*. She was young, just nineteen, very pretty, and seemingly shy (though not in actuality; you don't skate the way she did in Grenoble by being shy).

She was the perfect story for the revival of American skating. Her mother even made her skating dresses.

As far as skating style was concerned, she wasn't an innovator; she was more of a classical stylist, one of the last of a breed. Soon, she would be succeeded by waves of tiny youngsters, 100-pound marvels who could do six or seven triple jumps in their program. Peggy didn't have a single triple in her Grenoble program. Her skating was about beauty, not acrobatics.

She and Jean-Claude were the shining stars of Grenoble.

MEXICO CITY—1968

If ever an Olympics seemed doomed before it began, it was the Games of Mexico City in 1968. When the International Olympic Committee announced that the Games would be held there, there was shock, dismay, and disbelief in the world athletic community.

The complaints were varied. First of all, the Mexicans had very little experience in international sports. The marathoners would die trying to run twenty-six miles in polluted air at an altitude of 7,300 feet. It was a poor country, so it would never be able to finance the Games. There weren't enough athletic facilities or the skilled workers to build them. There weren't enough hotel rooms.

But Mexico had the Olympics, and as the time approached for them to begin, the outlook for these Games got worse. The Soviets invaded Czechoslovakia, so that the Cold War was now raging on. Days before the start of the Games, student riots broke out in Mexico City. Some were machine-gunned in the streets.

More was to come when the Games began—the Black Power demonstration on the victory stand by American medal winners Tommie Smith and John Carlos; money reputedly placed in the running shoes of other Yanks.

My personal situation wasn't much more pleasant. On my way to Mexico, I had to give a speech in New Orleans, so Margaret was going to fly down separately and meet me in Mexico

City. At some airport (I think it was Houston), I called her to make sure everything was all right.

It wasn't. Our daughter, Mary, had been rushed to the hospital with what they thought was appendicitis but turned out to be an ovarian cyst. So instead of meeting me, Margaret would sit at Mary's bedside for thirty-six hours straight, then spend the rest of the Olympics nursing her back to health at home.

Then there was the matter of our hotel. Ah, that hotel, the Hotel del Angel by name, with the accent on the last syllable as pronounced in Spanish. Our Olympics logistics man had entered into the deal innocently enough. It was a brand-new hotel, still under construction when our man agreed to book us there. Don't worry, he was told, everything will be ready for the Olympics. It will be a state-of-the-art establishment. Everyone on staff will be fluent in English. Fully air-conditioned, excellent restaurant, fully stocked bar, the works.

In fact, the hotel was far from finished when we arrived. Cement dust was everywhere. The elevator worked—occasionally. Air conditioning kept the temperature at a consistent 85 degrees. This made it necessary to open the windows in order to sleep. But just outside our hotel was the bus terminal, where great gasping diesel behemoths moaned and groaned all through the night. If the noise didn't keep you awake, the smell would.

But despite all of these negatives, a remarkable thing happened once the Games began. A picture emerged of a small country trying to say to the world, "Look, we know all the things that have been said about us. But we want to show you that a poor country can put on an Olympics, not as big perhaps as other nations might manage, but a good Olympics nonetheless."

And that Mexico did.

The spirit of the Games was set when a seventeen-year-old Mexican named Felipe Muñoz won a gold medal in swimming. When Felipe came out of the pool, someone put a huge sombrero on his head, then the crowd picked him up and carried him around and around the pool in a victory lap that looked like it might never end.

Then high drama erupted at the finish of an event that normally elicits yawns from the crowd—the 20-kilometer walk. The Soviets were heavily favored, and when the leader entered the stadium after walking twelve and a half miles through the smog of Mexico City, sure enough it was a Soviet, Vladimir Golubnichiy. And the crowd yawned. Entering second, another Soviet, Nikolai Smaga. Yawn.

But then arrived the unexpected moment. Into the stadium came José Pedraza Zuniga, a thirty-year-old woodcutter from the mountains of Mexico, who had never seen this many people gathered in one place for any reason. And now, the crowd was on its feet, all cheering for him. He was so inspired that he went into a sprint walking mode, passed the second-place Soviet, Smaga, and threatened to pass Golubnichiy.

As they came down the stretch, excitement went into high gear. José didn't quite catch the lead Soviet, but he had won a silver medal, Mexico's first medal ever in track and field. José stretched his arms wide in thanks to God and the crowd, then buried his face in his hands to cover the tears streaming down his face.

There were many thrilling moments in Mexico—Lee Evans's world record in the 400 meters; George Foreman carrying his little American flag around the ring (the same George Foreman who was still a heavyweight contender almost thirty years later). But none could match what happened one damp, overcast morning in the Olympic Stadium, an event that we of ABC Sports almost missed.

We had two crews working in the stadium, one covering the track events, the other handling the field. Chuck Howard was producing the track segments. On this particular morning, Chuck was preparing for our events, which wouldn't start until a bit later, when he noticed that the long jumpers were getting ready to start their competition. He also noticed that our field event crew was nowhere to be seen, so he had our technicians start things up on a crash basis.

It wasn't a very exciting scene. The misty overcast made for a dull backdrop. The stands were only about a third full. We were just covering for our colleagues in case something unexpected happened.

Then Bob Beamon came down the runway and flew into history.

It was evident that he had done something special as he landed in the pit, because he bounced up with a big smile. Then he looked at the measuring device. He fell to his knees and burst into tears.

He had jumped two feet farther than anyone in the world ever had, in an event where progress is usually made in inches, or fractions of inches. It was the shock of the Games. Later, the naysayers would claim that the high altitude was the reason for the unbelievable distance. If so, why didn't other jumpers do the same thing? The best in the world were there. The record stood for more than twenty years, and for quite a while, it looked like it might stand forever.

The Games got better as they went along, but the same could not be said for our hotel. Consider the fact that director Andy Sidaris was considered lucky because he broke his leg. Why? Because the broken leg got him out of our hotel and into a Class A establishment elsewhere in town.

There was the case of Tony Triolo. Tony is a big, fierce-looking guy who actually has a kindly, forgiving temperament that makes him a pleasure to be with. He is one of the best sports photographers in the business, usually for *Sports Illustrated*. In Mexico, he was moonlighting, working for ABC.

For the first week or so, he chuckled over the hotel accommodations while others fumed, but slowly he began to smolder. He sent a suit out to be cleaned—and they washed it! When it came back, the trouser legs came up to his knees. The jacket wouldn't have fitted a ten-year-old.

Tony lost it.

He called the desk, got someone on the phone who ur

stood just a bit of English, and explained that if someone didn't get him a new suit, there would be trouble. When the man at the desk said that would be impossible, that he would have to take it up with the dry cleaner, Tony spoke with a quiet menace.

"Then," he said, "I am going to start throwing furniture out the window until you change your mind. I will start with the television set, since it doesn't work anyway!"

He threw the television set out the window. Then a chair.

When the second object hit the pavement with a loud crash, several men came running to Tony's room, begging forgiveness and promising a new suit—two, if he wanted.

The elevator was a cause of constant annoyance. When it ran, which was sometimes, it often stopped between floors. This happened one afternoon to the wife of Parry O'Brien, the former Olympic gold medalist in the shot put who was working with us as a commentator on the field events. Mrs. O'Brien was trapped for several hours with two Mexican workmen, who spoke not a word of English.

Finally, Parry returned from his day at the stadium and was told of his wife's predicament. Looking at the massive steel elevator doors, he drew himself to his fullest height and said, "Give me a broom." The broom was gotten. Parry then wedged the broom handle into the crack between the doors, put his hands in the narrow opening, and pulled, uttering a shot-putter's scream as he did.

The doors flew open and Parry, with great dignity, leaned into the elevator shaft and said, "And now, my dear, let me assist you."

He pulled his disheveled, terrified wife from the shaft, patted her soothingly, and escorted her to their room.

It is difficult to describe the state to which the hotel had reduced us all. There seemed to be some strange formula whereby the hot water stopped when the elevator worked, and vice versa. I finally cracked one night when I tried to take a shower before going to bed. The water was ice cold, which I should have known since the elevator was working.

Inspired by Tony Triolo's success, I called the desk and got the one guy who spoke that bit of English—the same man Tony had spoken to.

"Listen to me carefully," I said, "and repeat what I say."

"Sí, senor."

"I have no hot water. Repeat that," I said.

"You have no hot water."

"If I do not have hot water within ten minutes. . . . What did I say?"

"If you do not have the hot water within ten minutes . . ."

"I am coming downstairs . . ."

"You are coming downstairs . . ."

"And I am going to *kill you*!"

"Senor," he said. "I will come with the hot water."

A few minutes later he appeared, followed by several attendants carrying buckets of steaming water. It wasn't a shower, but it was better than nothing.

It was, in the end, a successful Olympics. Not one I would care to repeat, however, filled as it was with challenges, the last of which came in the final hours of the final day.

Once again, Chuck Howard and I were preparing for a telecast, in this case the closing ceremony, which was to be held in the Olympic Stadium. Roone Arledge was in the main television center downtown, coordinating everything.

About two hours before the ceremony was to begin, Chuck got a telephone call from Roone telling him that there had been a power failure in the TV center, that the only communication working was the telephone, and that the only TV line working to the States was ours at the stadium.

"Tell McKay to start talking," Roone said. "He's going to have to fill until we get the power back. They say it should only be a few minutes."

I talked . . . and talked. I reviewed all the happenings of the Games after explaining the power failure. I told what was coming in the closing ceremony. Nothing from Roone.

I had been talking for more than a half hour when Chuck's

phone rang again. It was Roone, telling him to apologize to me for putting me on the spot, but there was still no power.

"Jim must be running out of things to say, isn't he?" Roone said.

"Roone," said Chuck, "you should know Jim better than that. He's hardly said hello." Which, I hope, was supposed to be a compliment.

I continued to talk over the only picture we had, the empty stadium, until, in time, the power came back on.

Two hours later, the stadium was full. The crowd was a happy one as it filed in, each spectator having been given a tiny straw sombrero to wave at the athletes. The athletes themselves, however, were not very happy.

The tradition had been for all the athletes to march in the closing ceremony, to wave at the crowd one last time, and to mingle with their fellow competitors in an informal celebration. But in Tokyo four years earlier, some athletes had thrown little remembrances up into the emperor's box, meaning it as a friendly gesture. Some people on the IOC had interpreted the action as disrespect and a new rule had been put into effect for the Games of Mexico City. Only six athletes from each country would be allowed in the closing parade. This meant that the rest would have to sit in the stands as mere spectators. And there they sat, unhappily, as the ceremony began.

There came a point where the marimbas began to play an old Mexican folk song. Two athletes leaped over the low railing separating them from the field. Then four more. Then twenty. Then all the athletes took their cue and streamed onto the field and began to dance with each other. I particularly remember a Nigerian boy in a long white robe dancing with a blond Finnish girl.

The marimbas played in the background. There was a soft, rustling sound. I wondered what it was, then realized that it was coming from the crowd, who were waving the little straw sombreros in farewell to the athletes.

I looked down at my notes and saw the words to the folk

song being played by the marimbas. It was a story similar to the legend of the swallows coming back to Capistrano. In obvious reference to the athletes, it said that they would soon fly away, that they would be sorely missed, but that we hoped they would one day return. It wondered if the athletes were lonely for their homes. And then I read the last line over the air.

It said, "I, too, am lonely. But oh, my God, I can't fly."

It was a moment for both tears and laughter as the athletes kept dancing to the music and waving back to the sombrero-brandishing crowd. No planned ceremony could have equaled the feeling of the athletes' impromptu defiance of the new rule.

I thought of all the touching moments of the Games. Of Bob Beamon weeping in disbelief at his great achievement. Of young Felipe Muñoz smiling his broad smile under that huge sombrero. Of "old" Bill Toomey winning the decathlon. As he came down the stretch, I had said, "After two long days of competition, thirty-year-old Bill Toomey still has a kick left. Here he comes, running in the footsteps of Bob Mathias and Rafer Johnson, running in the cold and the dark, in the breathless air of Mexico City, *winning the decathlon!*"

With all the problems and inconveniences, it had been a worthwhile Olympic Games.

There was a footnote. About a year later, an ABC Sports crew went to Mexico City for some other event, and shortly thereafter I received a postcard. It was signed, "The Concierge, Hotel del Angel," and the card read, "Senor McKay. Your laundry is ready."

MUNICH—1972

The Israeli tragedy, as I have written, will always loom large and dark over the Summer Games of Munich, but those Games were also the scene of some remarkable athletic achievements.

The seven swimming gold medals won by the young American Mark Spitz may stand forever as an all-time record. His achievements provided a joyful period for the American contingent in the days before the terrorists scaled the fence of the Olympic Village and put an ugly and permanent stain on the Games.

In the end, in a sad irony, Spitz had to be spirited away from Munich on the day of the tragedy. Because he is Jewish, the authorities feared for his life.

The other big story, in the early days, when the Games looked like they would fulfill the organizers' hopes of a "serene" Olympics, was provided by a pint-sized girl with a crooked little smile from the Soviet Union (today, her country is known as Belarus).

We hardly knew the name of Olga Korbut on the first night of competition in women's gymnastics. We knew only that she was a substitute on the Soviet team who had been put into the starting lineup when another girl suffered a broken arm. But as the athletes were warming up, I was startled by a yelp from our gymnastics analyst, Gordon Maddox.

"Wow!" he cried.

I said, "That's an interesting analysis, Gordon, but what's it about?"

Gordon, always an enthusiastic type, shouted, "That little kid! The one warming up on the uneven bars. She just did something I've never seen before!"

"Not by any gymnast, ever?"

"Not by any human!"

The gymnastics that night were to be recorded on videotape but, because of time constraints, the plan did not include showing little Olga. However, our producer, Doug Wilson, picked up his phone line to Roone Arledge in the control studio and pleaded for more time, which was granted.

And a good thing it was, because little Olga Korbut, four feet ten inches tall, weighing in at eighty-five pounds, became a world celebrity in the course of a performance that lasted exactly thirty seconds.

The enthusiasm of Gordon Maddox didn't wane during the performance.

"Oh my—*wow!*" he shouted, in another brilliant analysis, as Olga flew around the bars.

The next morning, I later learned, commuters around the world—on Long Island Rail Road trains in New York, on cable cars in San Francisco, and certainly on the Moscow subway—were talking about "little Olga," no last name being needed. The combination of her performance, Gordon's enthusiasm, and the charisma she exuded as she smiled her crooked smile and waved to the crowd when the marks were shown had combined to make her the sudden star of Munich.

But the story had only begun.

Two nights later, in the individual all-around competition, working on the same uneven parallel bars, Olga made a mistake, became confused, and finally dropped from the bar without completing her performance. The smile of the first evening changed to tears as she fled, sobbing, to the arms of her coach.

The delight of the worldwide audience now also changed, to sympathy. Could she face the final night of competition on the individual pieces of apparatus?

Yes.

In a performance worthy of the most hardened veteran, she won a gold medal on the balance beam, then climaxed her Olympics trilogy by winning the final event, the floor exercise. As she danced around the floor, whirling and jumping, the crowd cheering her on, I said, "She looks like a little child, playing in the sun."

She had earned her playtime.

At the halfway mark of the Games, the terrorists provided their bloody exclamation point. Many thought the Olympics should have been halted at that juncture in respect to the slain athletes, but others felt that a cancellation would, in a sense, constitute a surrender to the terrorists.

The Games did go on and, surprisingly to me, regained at

least a measure of their competitive spirit, particularly in the marathon, at the Olympics' end.

Frank Shorter, an erect, slender young American, was thought to have a chance of becoming the first of his nationality to win the long race since little Johnny Hayes had been given the gold medal on a disqualification in 1908. This time, our cameras followed the runners all the way, documenting their every step, a far cry from the coverage in the early Olympics years, like 1904 in St. Louis, when the American Fred Lorz was able to hitch a ride in an automobile and briefly be declared the winner until the news of his cheating leaked out.

Sitting with me in the stadium commentary booth, following the runners on a monitor, was Erich Segal, a young Ivy League professor whose novel *Love Story* had been a runaway best-seller, and whose avocation was long-distance running.

He looked the part of a professor—small, with bushy hair and an intense, serious manner. But when talking about his avocation, he became another person—smiling, enthusiastic, and eager to communicate the gospel of running to anyone who would listen. To the derision of some experts, he had flatly predicted that Frank Shorter, who had been his student at Yale University, would win the marathon for the U.S.

Wishful thinking? Perhaps.

But sure enough, as the race entered its final stage, the leader was none other than Frank Shorter, his hair still in place, his neatly trimmed mustache unwilted, as befitted a Yale man.

Erich could hardly contain himself. As we did the live commentary, he told us of Frank's dedication and devotion to the mystical world of long-distance running. I was just giving a bit of Frank's background, that he had actually been born here in Munich as the son of a U.S. Army doctor, when a runner entered the stadium to the cheers of the capacity crowd. My stomach did a double reverse somersault as I realized that the runner wasn't Frank. Frank was still a quarter-mile or so from the stadium.

Was it possible? Had our cameramen made an unforgivable mistake and missed the lead runner? And who was this guy?

He was blond-haired, pink-faced, wearing a blue and yellow shirt and shorts, and smiling broadly as he waved to the crowd, wearing number 72 on his chest. I quickly looked down at the start list in front of me and gratefully found that there was no number 72 in the race.

By the time I opened my mouth to explain, Erich was in full flight, live by satellite, standing up and shouting, "That's not Frank! That's not our man! That guy's a fake, an impostor! This is awful! I've seen this kind of thing before in bush league marathons, but this is the Olympics! Get rid of him!"

He seemed to be shouting more to the crowd and the officials than to our TV audience, but he certainly communicated the message. I thought that I performed very professionally, of course, speaking quietly and explaining what had happened in logical terms, while calming Erich—until the next morning.

On my way to the stadium then, I passed through our tape room, where someone was editing the marathon finish for a highlights show. Suddenly, the sound of my own voice attracted me, and I could scarcely believe what I heard.

It was I, not Erich, screaming, "Yes, they should throw that bum out of here!"

The impostor, we learned, was a German student playing a prank. He had simply lurked in hiding outside and, at the propitious moment, run through the gate into the stadium. He had torn the number 72 from a Coca-Cola billboard that read, OLYMPIADE MUNCHEN, '72, TRINK COCA-COLA.

He was lucky, in fact, that he had not been shot. In the aftermath of the terrorist murders, there were fears of another attack, and armed security people were everywhere. Had one of them known that the man was an impostor, they might well have opened fire.

It says something about the value of honest, heartfelt expression that the analytical commentary I remember best and most fondly from Munich are Gordon Maddox's "Oh my—

WOW!" and Erich's angry—and legitimate—reaction to the impostor.

But even today, my pleasant thoughts of Munich are submerged under a deep-seated sadness. The pictures of the terrorists, one in a hat, the other in a ski mask, standing watch outside the Israeli quarters, and of the helicopter lifting the hostages and their captors off into the night, still appear in my dreams.

INNSBRUCK REVISITED—1976

In 1976, Roone Arledge and I went on a press trip to Innsbruck not long before the Games had been moved there on an emergency basis when the voters of Denver turned down the right to hold them. We were sitting in a car driven by Kurt Fuchs, who had served as interpreter when Arledge was getting the rights to the first Innsbruck Games. Just as we were about to get out of the car, Roone suddenly turned to me and said, "McManus [he usually called me by my real surname], I want you to be the studio host of these Games."

Believe it or not, I resisted at first.

I said, "Roone, I already have my assignment to do ski racing. I enjoy doing that, and I'd rather be outdoors on location than cooped up in the studio."

Arledge gave me a disbelieving look, then his well-known ironic chuckle.

"Jim," he said, "you must be out of your mind. Host of the Olympics is the best job in television sports. Believe me, you'll be glad I'm making you do it."

We shook hands, and I had the job that would define my career.

Innsbruck in '76 had its golden moments. In the winter of the American bicentennial year, it seemed that people were more interested in Dorothy Hamill's haircut and Franz Klammer's gold ski suit than other important matters. They were the hero and heroine of the Winter Games.

Peggy Fleming's performance in Grenoble had accelerated the growth of figure skating as a sport, but Dorothy Hamill in Innsbruck took it a step further. Her "girl next door" image, her shy smile, and the way she tossed her hair all made her a major entertainment figure, more like a movie star than an athlete.

After the Games, she had her own prime-time TV special, which incidentally gave me an opportunity to sing and dance (well, actually, skate—sort of), just as I had on *The Real McKay* and elsewhere years before. I acted in a skit with Gene Kelly, and sang and skated to "Pick Yourself Up, Dust Yourself Off, and Start All Over Again."

Hollywood did not beckon.

If Dorothy fixed herself in the firmament of American stars, Franz Klammer made himself the central figure of his home country in one exciting, explosive run down a mountainside in the Olympic downhill ski race.

As he stood in the starting gate, Klammer was as much on the spot as Jean-Claude Killy had been at Grenoble in 1968. He wasn't just the favorite—his countrymen had decreed that he would win the race, that this two-minute run would be the centerpiece of the Games of Innsbruck. Nothing else would do.

The point was emphasized by Franz's tight-fitting golden ski suit as he pushed off. The suit was a silent promise from the skier to his people.

This time, it was gold or nothing.

With Bob Beattie and Frank Gifford providing memorable commentary, Klammer's run was a sight to remember. His style was not graceful, but a brutal attack on the mountain. Time after time, it appeared that he had lost it, that he would fly off into the trees or skid to the bottom, helplessly out of control.

Somehow, he held it all together, and when he flew across the finish line, holding his ski poles high above his head, winner of the gold medal, he was for the moment king of the Tyrol and emperor of the skiing world.

Early in the Games, Margaret and I had developed a ritual in Innsbruck. We had made friends with the owner of a small restaurant downtown, explaining that I had only a short time for dinner between the afternoon events and my nighttime stint as Olympics host for ABC. He understood, and escorted us to a table in a large upstairs room. We were the only people there each night, so we had solitude and service.

On the evening of the Klammer victory, we were having a predinner drink at our secret table—Scotch for me, grapefruit juice for the abstemious Margaret—when a group of seven or eight people was brought upstairs, talking and laughing as they arrived. I wondered why our peaceful hour was being interrupted, until I saw that one member of the group was Franz Klammer himself! Instead of the golden suit he had worn in the afternoon, he now had on a pair of jeans and the red and white parka of the Austrian team.

The rest of the group were members of his family, including his parents and his brothers. At the only other table in the room, some twenty feet from ours, they drank beer, smiled, ate roast pork and sauerkraut, and toasted Franz over and over in German, none of which we understood. We didn't have to. This was a private family celebration for the man who was being sought all over Innsbruck by his fans and the international press.

It must have been a strange sight: the big room, and just the two tables.

After a time, Klammer recognized me. Margaret and I raised our glasses and made our own toast to him in English. He came over and, as he did, two of his brothers got up and left the room after talking briefly with the father.

"Where are they going?" I asked Franz.

Matter-of-factly, he shrugged and said, "Well, it is quite a distance to our farm, and, gold medal or no gold medal, somebody has to be home to milk the cows."

I liked the priorities. First the family, then the cows. And only then, the rest of the world, waiting outside.

MONTREAL—1976

International politics provided a chaotic opening to the Summer Games of Montreal.

The delegation from Taiwan wanted to carry a placard announcing themselves as the Republic of China in the opening ceremony, but the Olympics officials said no. Taiwan said it was "Republic of China" or they were going home.

And they did go home.

At the same time, twenty-eight small nations said that they were going to boycott the Games in protest against a New Zealand rugby team's tour of South Africa, which at that time was banned from international sport because of its apartheid policies.

And the small countries went home, too.

Sports clairvoyants then prophesied that the Games would degenerate into a contest between the two superpowers, the U.S. and the U.S.S.R. Their crystal balls, it developed, were terribly clouded.

In the running events of men's track and field, the 100 meters was won by Trinidad and Tobago; the 200 by Jamaica; the 400 and 800 by Cuba; the 1500 by New Zealand; the 5000 and 10,000 by Finland; and the marathon by East Germany. All small countries.

And although the United States certainly provided its share of heroes—Sugar Ray Leonard in boxing and Bruce Jenner in the decathlon, for example—the superstar of Montreal was a fourteen-year-old, ninety-pound female gymnast, Nadia Comaneci of Rumania, another small country.

Picking up where Olga Korbut left off four years before in Munich, the shy Nadia outscored the scoreboard with a perfect mark of 10 (the electric board only went as high as 9.9, so it showed 1.00 for her 10, but the public-address announcer

explained it and the crowd had a new international heroine).
Before the spotlight left her, she had scored seven 10s and
won three gold medals.

Even the pronunciation of her name became a matter of
controversy. Was it pronounced "Coh-ma-neech-ee" or "Coh-
ma-neech"? We finally asked her, on camera. She lowered her
eyes, smiled softly, and said, "Coh-ma-neech, Nadia."

Her life after the Games paralleled the chaos of her country as the dictatorship of the brutal Nicolai Ceausescu frac-
tured and fell. But in time she came to America, and later
returned to Rumania for her fairy-tale wedding to the American gymnast Bart Conner.

LAKE PLACID—1980

The winter of 1980 did not seem like a time for celebration
in the United States. The Cold War continued in all its fury.
American hostages were still being held in Iran. President
Carter's popularity was plunging as he seemed helpless
against the will of a Middle Eastern Islamic fundamentalist
called the Ayatollah Khomeini. American pride was at a low
ebb.

But the tiny village of Lake Placid, New York (pop. 2,700),
was committed to play host to all the nations of the winter
sports world in the Olympic Winter Games. Lake Placid had
held the Games successfully in 1932, but these were different
times. Many more countries were involved and the all-around
logistics in the day of television and expanded press coverage
were much more complex. Security was now a major consideration. There was great doubt that the town could handle it
all.

There were no high-powered sports organizers running
the show. The president of the Lake Placid Olympic Organizing Committee was a onetime fireman, and now the pastor of
the local Methodist church, named Bernie Fell. Art Devlin,
onetime ski jumper and a local motel owner, was vice presi-

dent. The treasurer was a farmer named Favor Smith, who said the secret of raising cows was to speak to them softly, as to a lady.

If you were to read the accounts of some American sports columnists covering the opening days of those Games, you might think that the occasion was more a failed experiment in mass transportation than an athletic event. Accustomed to the luxury of baseball and football press boxes, with their comfortable chairs, the constant flow of information that is placed in front of them by public relations people, and the free food before and after games, they were unprepared for an Olympics, where the press buses are seldom on time, where you freeze in your big-city clothes while waiting for them, and where you find upon your arrival to cover the ski races that to reach the best vantage points you must simply climb up the mountain.

Some of them wrote for days about the inadequacy of their accommodations.

To be sure, I speak as a man who spent the Games in the comparative comfort of my host's chair in our ABC studio, but the press bus controversy still seems a bit outsized almost two decades later.

As always, the pre-Olympics forecasts proved inaccurate.

Our most difficult job on television would be the coverage of hockey. By the nature of the Olympics schedule, we would inevitably be covering a lot of the sport, but the American team, it was thought, probably wouldn't even qualify for the medal round. It would be difficult for Al Michaels and Ken Dryden to make it interesting for the American audience. In the pre-Olympics seedings, the U.S.S.R. was placed first, the Americans seventh.

This was the same U.S.S.R. team that had beaten the NHL All-Stars, 6–0.

And just before the Games began, the two Olympic teams had met in Madison Square Garden and the Soviets had prevailed by 10–3. United States coach Herb Brooks blamed the embarrassing loss on his poor game plan. But the Soviet coach, Viktor Tikhonov, made a more prescient statement: "We've got the feeling," he said, "they have a lot in reserve." It was taken as a polite statement to save face for the Americans, but later events proved otherwise.

Before the Games, the team seemed not to have an outstanding player, so our producers selected goalie Jim Craig as the subject for an "Up Close and Personal" profile, mostly on the premise that we would see a lot of him as the Soviets fired the puck into the net.

At their Massachusetts home some months before the Games, Jim's father spoke of his late wife, of how she had come home from the hospital and called her children into her room separately and told each, in a special way, that she was dying of cancer and had no more than six months to live. He told of how she had spent her final months knitting a very individualized sweater for each of the children.

Those were hard times for the family. The mother's death had been followed by the father's loss of his job running the food concession at a local school, after many years of service.

Jim came to his dad after finishing his collegiate career at Boston University, the father told us, and said that he had great news—the NHL's Boston Bruins wanted to offer him a contract.

"I knew," the father said, "that Jimmy was pretending that he would accept the pro offer just to help out with our financial situation at home, so I said to him, 'Jim, you're not fooling me. Pro hockey can come later. Right now, you're going to fulfill your ambition and your mother's: You're going to play in the Olympics for your country.' "

Then Jim told us, "I model my life after my father. He's the greatest man I know."

Some months later, in the chaotic moment of the greatest upset in sports history, the U.S. victory over the Soviet Union at Lake Placid, someone draped an American flag over Jim Craig's shoulders. As Al Michaels shouted, "Do you believe in miracles?! *Yes!!*" and Jim's teammates climbed all over each other in joy, the young man turned toward the stands, jammed with ten thousand screaming spectators. We were fortunate enough to have a close-up camera on Jim at that moment and, although we couldn't hear him, all America read his lips as he said, "Where's my father?"

It was a classic moment of priorities, of first things first.

A few years later, when Jim was hired as an executive by the Marketing Corporation of America, he hung a picture on the wall of his new office, directly behind his chair. It was of his father.

No one could have predicted that America's Eric Heiden would win all five gold medals in men's speed skating—one of history's greatest Olympic feats—much less that his achievement would be overshadowed by the performance of the U.S. Hockey Team, of all unlikely people! No upset in sports history—anywhere, anytime—compares with the win over the U.S.S.R.

But it was more than that.

It regenerated patriotism, a fading quality at the time. Our daughter, Mary, was at the game, having arrived in Lake Placid just in time to make it to the arena. Afterward, Mary, a child of the disillusioned 1960s, said, "Dad, it was unbelievable. The last time I saw that many American flags in one place, they were burning them!"

People remember where they were and what they were doing when they either saw or heard about the amazing accomplishment. As the game was being played, I sat cheering in my chair in the studio. Time after time, members of our technical crew in the control room leaped up and high-fived each other as Roone Arledge, producing the telecast, shouted, "Guys! Guys! We're trying to do a telecast here! Sit down!" But he was smiling as he said it.

A vivid memory of that night, alongside Mike Eruzione's winning goal in the 4–3 win, was a scene that took place around midnight.

"Look at this picture, Jim," Roone whispered through the little hearing device in my ear. On my monitor, I saw a shot of several hundred young people, walking down Main Street past Pete's Pizza and the movie theater, where the marquee advertised the current attraction, *Saturday Night Fever*. As they walked toward our camera, they were carrying a big American flag and singing "God Bless America," loud and clear.

"We haven't heard that song in a long time," I said.

A bit later, I talked to captain Mike Eruzione, a warm, pleasant, twenty-five-year-old Italian-American with a New England accent that would do credit to a Cabot or a Lowell. Mike was one of the few members of the team who was out of college. Before he was selected for the Olympic squad, he had been playing for the Toledo Gold Diggers of the International Hockey League, a professional team, but not exactly the big time.

"Mike," I said, "I've heard you say that you and your teammates really didn't have the physical ability or the talent to beat the Russians. Then how did you do it?"

Mike hesitated for a moment, then said, "Look, Jim, we had played sixty games together before the Olympics, and in the process we had become like brothers. I know it isn't considered cool to say things like this nowadays, but we were able to do it because we loved each other."

SARAJEVO—1984

I should have known that my memories of Sarajevo would, in the long run, be sad ones. The area has been a sad place since the Romans first rolled over the native Illyrians three hundred years before Christ.

Five hundred years ago, Sarajevo fell to the flashing scimitars of the Ottoman Empire and was dominated by them for almost four centuries. Later, it was under the thumb of another empire, the Austro-Hungarian, until the fateful day when the Serbian student Gavrilo Princip stood on a street corner and fired his gun, killing Archduke Franz Ferdinand and his wife and igniting the bonfire of World War I.

During World War II, the Nazis came and hanged citizens in the streets as a warning to the rest of the people to behave themselves.

Still, it seemed that a rather tranquil, if dull, time awaited me when I was assigned to cover the World Table Tennis Championships there in the spring of 1973. I had experienced quite enough tension and sadness at the Munich Olympics the summer before.

I wondered why producer Doug Wilson, a perpetually happy sort of guy, had a somber look about him when he met me at the airport in Sarajevo early one morning.

"Jim," he said, "there has been a report overnight that terrorists are headed here from Belgrade. Their main target is the Israeli team again, so the organizers of the championships have already sent the Israelis home, saying that they couldn't guarantee their safety. Secondary targets are believed to be any Americans on the scene, particularly the team members and the TV people. That's us."

In the hotel lobby, I saw soldiers on duty, holding automatic weapons at the ready. To get into the elevator, I had to show my passport and room key to an armed guard. And when I reached my room, I found my personal guard sitting in a chair outside the door, gun in lap. I lay awake all that night, finishing an entire book, the name of which I don't even remember.

The security measures worked—the terrorists never appeared and the championships went on without a hitch, except for the absence of the Israeli team. I developed a fondness for the historic old town, especially for the marketplace, where the old shoeshine man would let you take his picture for the equivalent of thirty-five cents, and where hookahs and fezzes were sold side by side with Hershey bars and Coca-Cola. It could have been the scene for a movie where Peter Lorre and Sydney Greenstreet were secretly peddling some stolen diamond, pursued, of course, by Humphrey Bogart.

East met West here more intimately than anywhere I had

been. Several times a day, the sound of bells from a hundred churches would blend with the sound of the muezzins, summoning the faithful to prayer from the minarets of a hundred mosques. Over the course of five hundred years, Christians, Muslims, Orthodox, and Jews had learned to get along—or so it seemed.

Eleven years later, I was back for the Olympic Winter Games of 1984. They were exciting—little Scott Hamilton, who had almost died of a growth-stunting disease called Schwachman's Syndrome as a child, winning the gold medal in men's figure skating; the beautiful East German, Katarina Witt, in ladies' skating; the English ice dance couple, Torvill and Dean, with their unforgettable performance to Ravel's *Bolero*; Bill Johnson, the onetime juvenile delinquent, becoming the first American man to win the downhill ski race; Debbie Armstrong, of Seattle, winning the giant slalom in a big upset; the twin Mahre brothers, winning gold and silver in the slalom on the final day.

It was a friendly Sarajevo during those weeks. I remember the lady who came out of her house during a sudden rainstorm and gave an umbrella to some passing, and wet, American athletes. When they said they would bring it back, she waved them off and said, "Keep, keep." The children of the town were everywhere, politely begging for an ABC pin.

Still, the historic hard luck of Sarajevo did rear its head, this time in the form of a blizzard that canceled the ski events for the better part of a week, causing us to televise more luge and figure skating school figures than we had ever hoped to see.

I think back on Sarajevo these days, of room 210 in the old Bosna Hotel, my home for the month of the Olympics. There is no room 210 anymore. I think of the dining room, where John Denver gave us an informal concert during dinner one night. There is no dining room now. There is no hotel.

And John Denver is gone, killed in an airplane crash in Monterey Bay in 1997.

I think of the mountain where the ski racing took place,

remembered now not for that wondrous event, but as the place from which the Serbs bombarded the city day after day, night after night.

I wonder if the umbrella lady is alive today, or if she might have perished when the marketplace became a holocaust one fine shopping day. And the children. Some of them must have become teenage soldiers in the fighting. Were they killed?

And I think of the Zetra Arena, scene of the figure skating and the closing ceremony. It, too, was destroyed, and some of its wooden seats were used to make coffins for the bombing victims buried in the cemetery across the street.

During the Games, it was a parking lot.

LOS ANGELES—1984

If Sarajevo was heavy with history, Los Angeles, later that year, was the Olympics of *right now*, all glitz and glamour, state of the art, Hollywood on parade.

The opening ceremony featured a man flying around the stadium propelled by a rocket belt, a fanfare by a hundred trumpets, singing by a chorus of a thousand banner-towing airplanes, fireworks, and dancing girls.

The sixty-piece orchestra played "Hail to the Chief" for President Ronald Reagan, who seemed right at home in the show business ambience, and eighty-four grand pianos played *Rhapsody in Blue* (prerecorded). There was hoedown music, Dixieland, swing, Gershwin, and songs from Hollywood musicals.

Cecil B. DeMille would have been proud of David Wolper, who produced the show.

There were two notable absences. The Soviets didn't show up, giving us tit for tat since we had boycotted their games four years before—sort of like a child saying, "You didn't come to my party, so I won't come to yours."

The other absence was traffic. Pre-Olympics predictions had been portentous. The freeways, bad enough in the normal rush hours, would become mammoth parking lots, it was said, filled with smog-belching cars and drivers cursing in the many languages of the 140 participating nations.

That didn't happen. Many Angelenos just moved out of town for the duration, and visitors to the Games heeded the pleas of the organizing committee to take buses, not rental cars. As a result, day after day, I went disbelievingly from our hotel to the studio on virtually empty highways. It was one of the great triumphs of the Games.

Appropriately, it was in the United States that the first commercially sponsored Olympics took place. That was the work of a former travel agent named Peter Ueberroth. Urged on by L.A. mayor Tom Bradley, Ueberroth raised half a billion dollars from some thirty companies. Combined with the $225 million paid by ABC for the TV rights, the new approach made the Games a roaring financial success. The commercial influence foretold a flood of company logos that would spread over the American sports landscape in the years to come. Sports events and stadiums would be named after sponsors (giving birth to such strange appellations as the Poulan Weed Eater Independence Bowl), and the emblem of the Nike running shoe company would become as widespread as that of Coca-Cola.

Despite the Soviet boycott, and partly because of it, the Games were also a success competitively, at least for the host country. Carl Lewis mirrored the achievements of the legendary Jesse Owens by winning gold medals in the same events as Owens had in Berlin long ago—the 100 meters, the 200, the long jump, and as anchor of the 4 × 100 relay team.

The swimmer Mary T. Meagher won three gold medals.

In the heat of a stifling Southern California summer day, a New England girl, Joan Benoit, won the first women's marathon in Olympics history.

The gymnasts stirred Americans' national pride. The men upset the favored Chinese in the team competition, while a tiny West Virginian named Mary Lou Retton became the most acclaimed star of the Games when she scored a perfect 10 on the last event in the individual all-around to defeat the Rumanian, Ecaterina Szabó.

On TV, the audience saw and heard Mary Lou's coach, the Rumanian Bela Karolyi, shouting encouragement to her, much as he had eight years before to his previous student, Nadia Comaneci, before he defected to America.

If some of the Americans' success was due to the Soviet boycott, it didn't dim the glow from these Olympics. Sports, show business, and big business had combined to create a glittering Games.

And if the Soviets chose to stay home, the living room spectators thought, that was their loss.

CALGARY—1988

One day during the Winter Games of Calgary, Canada, the temperature was 72 degrees—warmer than it was on the same day in Miami Beach. We learned that day about a "Chinook," an unseasonably warm wind that sometimes comes over the Rockies into Calgary in the winter months. Water sloshed down the bobsled run and visitors rooted in their suitcases for something cooler to wear than a parka.

Fortunately, the heat wave didn't last, but the warm spirit of the Games did.

The Calgary Games were the Olympics of the Western plains. Cowboy hats rather than woolen caps were the order of the day, and the hosts displayed a warm openness reminiscent of American Westerners in the States, just below the border.

The glamour king of Calgary was the wealthy young Italian playboy Alberto Tomba, flying down the hill to gold medals in the slalom and giant slalom, hatless, his curly hair blowing in the wind, his bronze skin glistening in the sun, blowing kisses to the world after he crossed the finish line. The queen of the month was East Germany's beautiful Katarina Witt, becoming the first to repeat an Olympics figure skating victory since Sonja Henie.

Men's figure skating provided a memorable battle between the host country's pride, Brian Orser, and the classically styled American, Brian Boitano. Boitano was the winner in a tense, emotion-filled final.

But the most emotional drama occurred in speed skating, traditionally a family-oriented sport for the Americans. For many Winter Games, American skaters had been successful, despite the fact that they were true amateurs and came mostly from a small area of the country in Illinois and Wisconsin.

In Calgary, Dan Jansen, a Wisconsin man, was scheduled to skate in his first race, the 500 meters, at five o'clock on February 14th. At the urging of the American team, he decided to compete in the memory of his sister Jane, who had died of leukemia earlier that day.

There was cheering in households across the country as he burst from the start and flew down the straightaway. Then there were tears as Dan slipped and fell to the ice in the first turn, putting him out of the race. Four days later, he returned in the 1000 meters, and was on a world-record pace until he inexplicably slipped and fell on a straightaway.

He came up short again four years later in Albertville, France, finishing fourth in the 500.

Surely, the world felt, he would be vindicated at Lillehammer, Norway, in 1996. But a momentary stumble in the third curve dropped him to eighth place in the 500. It took great courage for Dan to try again in the 1000, but he did, and at long last, he won that Olympic gold medal for his sister.

When I think of the Calgary Games—my last—I always think with affection of two entrants who didn't even come close to winning medals.

One was the bobsled team from the Caribbean island of Jamaica. These young dreamers somehow got it into their heads that they would like to participate in the Winter Olympics. So they made a sled and put it on wheels and practiced under the tropical sun in the parking lot of a shopping mall in Jamaica. Pressed for funds in Calgary, they had "Jamaica Bobsled Team" T-shirts made, having no idea that they would become the "in" T-shirt of the Games. They sold fourteen thousand of them, became solvent, and, although they turned over and crashed their sled once, gave a respectable account of themselves in the competition.

The other noncompetitive, but memorable contestant was an English plasterer known rather derisively as Eddie the Eagle. His practice jumps were far short of all the other ski jumpers'. From the start, it was clear that he had absolutely no chance of winning a medal.

But he wanted to compete.

When he was brought into our studio for an interview after the competition, I expected to meet a smiling, ironic sort of personality, having a good time with his unrealistic bid. I greeted him with that attitude.

"Eddie," I said, smiling, "nice job. Are you having fun?"

He didn't smile back, and I realized that he wasn't playing an Olympic-sized joke. He was deadly serious about this.

"Well," he said, "I've accomplished what I came here to do—to compete and to land all my jumps."

Baron Pierre de Coubertin, founder of the modern Olympics, would have approved. The baron had emphasized that the most important thing in the Olympics was not to win, but to take part.

Eddie had done that.

And I was embarrassed. I, who had quoted de Coubertin so many times on the air, had missed the point. Eddie the Eagle wasn't flying for the crowd or TV or a fleeting moment in the sun—he was flying for himself. By landing his jumps, he had shown, in one of the most dangerous sports, that he was not foolhardy, but courageous.

I am afraid that the members of the International Olympic Committee may also have missed Eddie's point and forgotten the baron's words: Since Calgary, they have been making it more difficult for people like Eddie to participate in the Games.

☆

The closing ceremony in Calgary was my Olympics swan song. All the Games since have been shared by NBC and CBS, and since NBC has the rights to all the Games through 2008 it looks like I won't work on another.

But that closing night in Calgary was a special experience for me, and even more so for Peter Jennings, who was sharing the commentary chores with me that evening. He is extremely proud of his Canadian roots, and on that night, he was a wandering son experiencing a sentimental journey home as he watched the simple, but moving, closing moments of the Games. There were tears in the eyes of the famous news anchorman as he watched, and we both thought back to the first time we had worked together on the day of the Israeli tragedy in Munich, sixteen years before.

Later, back in ABC headquarters, there were the usual mixed emotions at the closing of an Olympics telecast. For the better part of a month, it had been a way of life. The people involved—producers, directors, commentators, associate directors, production assistants, and the technical crew—had shared an intense, physically and mentally draining time.

When it ended, there was a sense of tremendous relief, but at the same time, a feeling of emptiness, of "What do we do now?" I have had viewers tell me they had the same feeling, husbands and wives asking their mates when an Olympics is over, "What in the world will we do tomorrow night?"

As the champagne corks popped in the studios and control rooms, there was much laughter and tears.

Roone Arledge, who as always had personally produced the Games, drew me aside. Twenty-seven years before, he had made the phone call to me in Augusta asking me if I would be available for "a summer replacement show" lasting "twenty weeks" that would "require a certain amount of traveling." The "twenty weeks" of *Wide World of Sports* have stretched into the greater part of a lifetime.

Roone and I had worked together since the first telecast of *Wide World of Sports* in 1961. We had shared good meals, good wines, good times, fascinating trips, endless plane rides in tourist class (somehow I always got squeezed into the middle seat between him and Chuck Howard), and exhausting nights in editing rooms from New York to London to Prague to Moscow to Tokyo, with many way stations in between. We had gotten angry with each other more than once.

The best of times were when I sat in my position and Roone spoke to me through that little speaker in my ear called an IFB. He was always a calming influence, the only friend you have when you are all alone in an ad-lib situation, facing the nation with not much to say.

As he did in Fuchs's car, he always called me by my real name when we were on the air. "McManus," he might say, "this show is dying. Say something funny." Or, during a lull in competition in an Olympics: "McManus, we have no place to go. Just keep talking." Or he might give me a niblet of information I could talk about. Or, on one terrible night: "Jim, all the hostages were killed at the airport."

Now, standing in a corner of that crowded, noisy Calgary studio, he said, "McManus, I just want to say it's been a great experience working with you through the years." I nodded and said something inadequate like, "Me too."

Then we shook hands, patted each other on the shoulder, turned away, and joined the celebration.

THE McKAY RATINGS

In the case of Olympians I have covered, I have considered character and positive influence even more than I have in other sports. Baron Pierre de Coubertin, the Olympics' founder, saw the Games as much more than simply an athletic competition—he saw them as an inspiration to the youth of the world.

1. The U.S. Hockey Team—1980

They must be considered as a group, of course. To every kid who has ever been told that he is outclassed, or that he is too small, or too awkward, or that his opponent is unbeatable, they showed that the impossible dream can come true. The long, hard, boring practices during months away from home; the willingness to sacrifice personal ambition for team spirit; the love of country and love of one another—all these can make up in great part for lack of talent.

But a touch of realism was necessary, too. That was supplied by their laconic coach, Herb Brooks.

Captain Mike Eruzione described for me the scene in the American locker room before the gold medal game against Finland.

"Jim," he said, "just before the game, the biggest game of our lives, we wondered where in the hell Herb was. We were sitting there, all by ourselves, and he hadn't showed up. Then he walked in, stood for a moment, and said, 'Gentlemen, you were born to play this hockey game. This moment is yours.'

"Then," Mike continued, "he walked to the door, opened it, and turned back to us. He pointed his finger and said, 'And remember this: If you lose today, you'll carry it with you to your [expletive deleted] graves!'

"He went out, slamming the door behind him, and left us with our thoughts."

2. Jean-Claude Killy—1968

The Irish could take some satisfaction in the performance of this remarkable Frenchman. His ancestor, whose name was Kelly, came to France from Ireland as a volunteer in Napoleon's army.

But the Jean-Claude we saw in Grenoble was French in every way: good-looking, with a flair for clothes and a winning smile. His English was just accented enough to charm Americans—Maurice Chevalier on skis.

As he won all three Alpine skiing gold medals in Grenoble, and later, skiing as a professional in America, making a movie, and endorsing products around the world, he kept his head on straight and remained very much the same Jean-Claude we had started covering on *Wide World of Sports* when he was just a teenager.

A few years after the 1968 Olympics, Margaret and I were riding on the same plane with Jean-Claude. He came over to our seats and bent down in the skiing position (knees and hips bent) so he could talk to us. Only baseball catchers and skiers can stay in that position very long, as Killy did for about a half hour.

At one point, I told him that we had admired his poise and intelligence in accepting fame—making the most of it, but not being carried away and changed by it.

"Well, Jim, thank you," he said. "I just think that when these things happen to you, you must remember that you came from someplace else."

Jean-Claude came from a tiny Alpine village called Val d'Isére.

"For example," he went on, "a few months ago, I was back home in my father's sporting goods shop. It was very busy, so I was helping out, trying a pair of ski boots on a customer. A friend walked in, looked over at me, and said, 'Aha, Jean-Claude, have things gotten so bad?'

" 'What is so bad?' I said. 'This is my father's shop.' "

As always, I was struck by the man's priorities.

Later in life, he paid back to his sport, his hometown, and the Olympic movement by organizing and becoming president of the Albertville Winter Games.

The Alpine skiing events were held in Val d'Isére.

3. Mary Lou Retton—1984

The Olympics are different from any other sports event in this regard: For most of the competitors, it is a once-in-a-lifetime opportunity. And unlike a sport where you are judged over the course of a season, or where you have a number of opportunities each year to win a major championship, in the Olympics you must be prepared physically, mentally, and emotionally, at a specified time on a certain day, to make the greatest effort of which you are capable.

Wake up feeling sick that morning, or lose your concentration, or freeze at the thought of the moment's significance, and the opportunity is gone—not for the day or month, but forever.

No athlete has ever been more on the spot than Mary Lou Retton was in the Los Angeles gymnastics competition.

Just a couple of years out of her West Virginia country home, she found herself fighting for a gold medal in the Olympics individual all-around competition with the amazing little Rumanian Ecaterina Szabó.

Mary Lou had just one event to complete, the vault, and she knew exactly what she had to do: She had to get a perfect mark of 10 to win.

For her, this was that Olympic moment of a lifetime.

Her coach, the same Bela Karolyi who had coached Nadia Comaneci, shouted encouragement from the sidelines. A nation held its collective breath as she stood awaiting the signal to go, determination etched into every facial muscle. Then she accelerated down the runway, leaped, touching the vaulting horse with her down-stretched hands as she flew, and made a perfect landing. For a perfect 10.

On another night, she might not have been able to put everything together, but she did at the appointed moment, the only one that mattered.

For that—for the poise, the determination, and the inspiration she provided for children and adults alike—she makes my list.

4. Bob Beamon—1968

If Bob Beamon did today what he did that dreary morning in Mexico City, he would make a fortune, both in the stadium

I believe I am the first one in the history of the world
to hit a golf ball over the Great Wall of China.
I did take three tries. (*Courtesy Jim McKay*)

On September 4, 1972, Mark Spitz (top right) won his unprecedented seventh gold medal in the swimming competition. A day later the terrorists struck the Israeli team, and Spitz, himself a Jew, was whisked out of Munich. That hostage crisis in '72 has never been out of my mind. I remember watching the desperate efforts to rescue the hostages, like the West German sharpshooters (left) who tried to get in position to confront the Palestinian guerrillas (bottom right). Twenty-three hours it went on, and then I had to tell our viewers, "They're all gone." (*Associated Press/Wide World Photos*)

The newlyweds, Margaret and Jim McManus (yes, that's my real name), in 1948, when we were co-hosting a television show in Baltimore. (*Courtesy Jim McKay*)

The McKay family in 1961—Mary was eight, Sean, six. (*Courtesy Jim McKay*)

The first "scoop" of my career, beating everyone in the United States to an interview with Roger Bannister in New York a few days after he broke the four-minute mile. (*Associated Press/Wide World Photos*)

My first international event, the United States-Russia track-and-field meet in Moscow, 1961. Valery Brumel here is setting a new world's record in the high jump. (*Associated Press/Wide World Photos*)

That's one of my all-time racing driver champs, A. J. Foyt, being kissed by his wife after winning the 1964 Indy race. (*Associated Press/Wide World Photos*)

An exotic *Wide World of Sports* event, the World Barrel-Jumping Championship at Grossinger's, New York, in 1963. That's son, Sean, comforting me. (*Courtesy Jim McKay*)

Three golfing immortals all in one picture, Gary Player (left), Arnold Palmer, and Jack Nicklaus hitting away, 1962 World Series of Golf. Another of my golfing heroes is Lee Trevino (right). (*Associated Press/Wide World Photos*) (*ABC/Wide World of Sports*)

Here I am at Pebble Beach in 1974 with fellow golfers Kathy and Bing Crosby, and President Ford. (*Courtesy Jim McKay*)

My longtime colleague and friend, Roone Arledge, helping me
to hold on to a 1967 Emmy Award. (*ABC/Wide World of Sports*)

The 1980 U.S. Olympic hockey team—the impossible dream
had come true. I was cheering the team on from the studio.
(*ABC/Wide World of Sports*)

Here I'm interviewing an amazing athlete, Jean-Claude Killy, who won all three gold medals in Alpine skiing at the Winter Games of 1968 in Grenoble, France. (*ABC/Wide World of Sports*)

I was filling in for ABC's regular radio announcer when U.S. speed skater Terry McDermott won the gold in the 500 meter sprint, shown here. He was the only U.S. medal winner at the 1964 Innsbruck games. (*Associated Press/Wide World Photos*)

At the 1968 Summer Games, long-jumper Bob Beamon soared two feet farther than anyone ever had, setting a record that stood for more than twenty years. He's dedicated his life since then to helping young people, and to me that makes him a true hero. (*Associated Press/Wide World Photos*)

Jim Ryun clenches his fists in frustration after falling in a quarterfinal heat in the 1,500 meter race in Munich. Ryun only had to finish in the top four to advance to the semifinals, but by the time he rejoined the race, it was too late. But because he handled his misfortune with such grace, he's one of my all-time Olympic champions. (*Associated Press/Wide World Photos*)

Frank Shorter crosses the finish line of the Olympic Marathon in Munich, his hair still in place, his neatly trimmed mustache unwilted, as befitted a Yale man. (*Associated Press/ Wide World Photos*)

In her final vault of the 1984 Summer Games, Mary Lou Retton flew through the air and made a perfect landing for a perfect 10. She makes my list as one of the all-time greats because of her poise, determination, and the way she inspired us all. (*Associated Press/Wide World Photos*)

Fourteen-year-old Nadia Comaneci reminded me so much of Olga Korbut, the darling of the 1972 Games, as she scored seven perfect 10's and won three gold medals at the Summer Games in Montreal, 1976. (*ABC/Wide World of Sports*)

Also in 1984, Carl Lewis won gold medals in the 100 meters, the 200, the long jump, and anchoring the 4 x 100 meter relay team, mirroring the achievements of the legendary Jesse Owens. (*Associated Press/Wide World Photos*)

I'll never forget the courage of Scott Hamilton, who nearly died of a growth-stunting disease as a child, and won the gold medal in men's figure skating in the 1984 Winter Games at Sarajevo. (*ABC/Wide World of Sports*)

Dan Jansen, skating for the memory of his late sister, Jane, fell in both of his races at the 1988 Calgary Olympics. But he courageously returned to the Games at Lillehammer, Norway, in 1994, where he finally won a gold medal in the 1,000 meter race. (*Capital Cities/ABC, Inc. Photo by Peter Haase*)

Here I'm talking to Bill Shoemaker after his last race at Santa Anita Park, California, in 1990. I consider him the greatest jockey of my time in television. (*Photo by Robert Riger*)

Sunday Silence and Easy Goer were mirror images of each other as they dashed toward the finish line at the 1989 Preakness. Sunday Silence won by a nose. It was the greatest horse race I've ever seen. (*Associated Press/Wide World Photos*)

My son, Sean, and I are at our farm in Maryland, just after Sean was named President of CBS Sports.
(*Courtesy of Jim McKay*)

My daughter, Mary, and I enjoyed the spectacular view of the Coliseum in Rome, Italy, in 1995.
(*Courtesy of Jim McKay*)

On July 22, 1997, my fifteen-year-old grandson, James, and I stand in front of the clubhouse at the famed Old Course at St. Andrews, after he shot a round of 88. It was a wonderful day we'll both remember for the rest of our lives.
(*Courtesy of Jim McKay*)

Margaret and I at Bellefield Farm in Monkton, Maryland.
(*Courtesy of Jim McKay*)

and in the commercial world. When he made his great leap, the world was in awe—but just briefly. His fame was fleeting, his financial reward next to nothing.

For some unfathomable reason, he never received the amount of adulation that he should have.

Bob virtually disappeared from the spotlight, but he took it and went on with his life. He has used that life to work with young people—out of the spotlight, without fanfare or great financial reward. He is a neglected American sports hero, but he has never groaned or complained or declared himself to be a victim.

5. Jim Ryun—U.S.A.

In Mexico City, Jim Ryun, America's greatest mile runner, had suffered a deep disappointment, losing the 1500 meters to the Kenyan, Kipchoge Keino. Many thought that the loss was due to Keino's upbringing in the high mountains of Africa, while Ryun had grown up on the flat plains of Kansas. Keino, it was believed, had the advantage in the 7,300-foot altitude of Mexico City.

Ryun made no excuses, just went back into training, anticipating the rematch four years later in Munich. Jim was, and is, a very private, very religious person, but there was a competitive fire inside him, and he carried it with him to Munich, anticipating a final showdown with the African.

Had he lost to Keino in the final, that would have been one thing. But he and Billy Fordjour of Ghana clipped heels in a quarterfinal heat, a race in which Ryun had only to finish in the top four to move on to the semifinals. It was little more than a workout for him.

Until he and Fordjour tumbled to the track.

By the time Jim got up and rejoined the race, it was too late. His greatest challenge never took place.

It was another example of the special demands the Olympics puts on an athlete: Be ready on the assigned day and time or go home. For Jim, it was "go home," but not before he came to our studio that night and described the incident for us, not calling for a rerun, or cursing his luck, or blaming Billy Ford-jour, but taking it manfully and with a rueful smile.

Outside our studio that night, I shook his hand and said good-bye. His Olympics career was over.

☆

Since my first Olympics assignment in 1960, I have seen the Games grow tremendously in number of nations entered, number of competitors, number of on-the-scene spectators and television viewers, number of sports on the calendar—and the amount of commercialism.

The "shamateurism" days of the sixties, the under-the-table payments that embarrassed and degraded the athletes, are gone, replaced by a more honest professionalism that has brought its own share of problems.

In basketball, for example, the U.S.A. college all-America teams of yesteryear have been replaced by "the Dream Team," the cream of NBA pros, which has removed all sense of competition while drawing more spectators and adding to the Games' commercial value. No one admires the talents of those men more than I do, but pitting them against the under-manned teams they meet in the Games seems to me to miss the spirit of the Olympics.

The "bottom line" has just as magnetic a hold on the International Olympic Committee as it does on the most hard-driven CEO. It need not be so, because the IOC doesn't have to answer to stockholders, or anybody else.

There has long been a misconception abroad that the IOC is some sort of semigovernmental body, or an athletic United Nations. It is not. It is simply a group of men (and now a few women), a self-perpetuating club really, who report to no one but themselves. Most of them are wealthy, some are titled, and a few are a bit vague in their knowledge of geography.

Billy Payne, the man who sparked the unexpected winning bid of Atlanta for the 1996 Summer Games, told me of an IOC member who came to him, smiling, after Atlanta had won the Games.

"Congratulations, Mr. Payne," the man said. "I am very much looking forward to coming to Atlanta, and especially to visiting your casinos." The man was confusing Atlanta with Atlantic City!

My ultimate fear is that one day, the spread of logos and sponsorships may go all the way, and we will be viewing the Tylenol or Federal Express Olympics. (Please God, let it not be the Poulan Weed Eater Olympics.)

Having voiced these fears, let me assure you that I will be among the several billion viewers watching the 2000 Summer Games from Australia, and will be wishing that I were still sitting in the anchorman's chair.

Golf: The Game for a Lifetime

Why we took it into our heads to do it on Good Friday, the most somber of Christian holy days, I have no idea, but that was the day in 1935 that my cousin Frank Callahan and I chose to play golf at the Cobbs Creek Municipal Course in Philadelphia. God's disapproval was obvious to us as we hacked our way around and our scores swiftly mounted into triple figures. Frank won the fifty cents we had bet on the match. I told him I would definitely pay him when I got the usual five-dollar gold piece from my uncle as an Easter present.

Walking down Lancaster Avenue toward home, we felt pangs of guilt and decided that we should go to church, to the service called Three Hours Agony, which was well into its second hour. There we were, two early teenage kids in corduroy knickers carrying their golf bags into church. At least we were civilized enough to park our clubs in the vestibule before stealing into the back row. As we sat, ready to cleanse our guilt-ridden souls, heads swiveled toward the back of the church. One of the bags had fallen over with a loud clatter.

That is my first memory of golf, and I should have known then that I would be a slave to the game forevermore.

In the years since, golf has taken me to the sand dunes of Scotland, the spectacular Pacific shore of Pebble Beach, the Main Line elegance of Merion, the Rocky Mountain high of Cherry Hills outside Denver, and at least thirty-five other fabulous American courses, plus a few islands in the sun.

As a player, I have never come close to mastering the

sport, but I still and will always feel that it is the best game anyone has created yet for the average person to play for a lifetime. It is played amid beauty with the time and the ambience for contemplation, even while the golfer is getting a reasonable amount of exercise and learning a few lessons about life. Where else in sport can you find such a combination?

The other wonderful element of golf is that at all levels, from the weekend duffer to the most famous professional, the player polices himself—no umpires, no head linesmen, no referees. Even in this day of "in your face" and "image is everything," the pros still act as their own officials. They leave the ball in a terrible lie even if no one is looking; they call penalties on themselves that no one else has noticed.

Long years ago, Dow Finsterwald, the 1958 PGA champion, cost himself a chance at the Masters championship by realizing that he had practice-putted on a green after finishing play on that hole and thereby violated a rule that only the Masters observed (it wasn't a USGA rule). He called the penalty on himself after he finished his round, and it cost him the title.

Another time, I was doing the commentary at the British Open when Hale Irwin, the onetime University of Colorado football star and three-time U.S. Open champion, casually, with one hand, went to tap in a three-inch putt and missed the ball completely! He called it to the attention of his playing companion, added the stroke to his score, and eventually lost the championship by that single stroke.

In a day when some tennis players dress like derelicts and Olympic swimmers and runners compete in bikini-like swatches of polyester, golfers still dress like ladies and gentlemen and behave the same way—no screaming at the official, no throwing of clubs.

I believe these important social graces to be largely the heritage of one man, Robert Tyre Jones Jr. of Atlanta. It was Bobby Jones who set the tone of the modern game with his play and his behavior. As a golfer, the only one ever to win the fabled Grand Slam (U.S. Open and British Open, U.S. and

British Amateurs in the same year), he won four U.S. Opens and three British Opens in the short span of eight years. He was a marvel, one of the golden heroes of the 1920s, in the so-called Golden Age of Sport. And he was a true amateur, a law student who stored his clubs away from November until April.

The tradition of honesty and suitable dress had existed before Bobby Jones, but it was he who made these qualities the hallmark of a proper golfer.

Talk about lucky. In my career at CBS and ABC, I've been privileged to cover nearly a hundred major golf championships—twenty-eight U.S. Opens, twenty British Opens, twenty-eight PGAs, six Masters, and fifteen U.S. Amateurs. I have also been involved in Ryder Cups, Walker Cups, World Cups, and a gaggle of regular-tour tournaments.

I even met Bobby Jones, although he was confined to a wheelchair, long years after his glory days. The meeting was memorable only to me. We were introduced as he made his slow and painful way around the course at Augusta, I said something flattering about the Masters, he thanked me, and that was all.

The first major championship I covered was the Masters back in 1956, when I was with CBS. Considering the international standing of the Masters today, it is interesting to recall that the tournament had trouble getting on TV at all at that time, even though it had provided many thrilling finishes since its creation by Bobby Jones and Clifford Roberts back in 1934. It was only because of a friendship between Roberts and William S. Paley, the chairman of CBS, that we found ourselves on our way to Augusta, Georgia.

We took an overnight train from New York to Augusta. We could have flown, but Judson Bailey, who was producing the show for CBS, liked to travel the way the old-time sportswriters did, by train, playing cards and drinking whiskey through the night. Actually, it was fun to travel the old way, except for one thing. As everyone else, one by one, sneaked off to sleep, I was nailed by Jud. I would be his companion until he decided to go to bed, which was never.

We didn't play cards, but through the long night, as the train flew past one darkened small-town railroad station after another, while Jud told stories and the level of the whiskey bottle descended, I listened, fighting off sleep as best I could. Finally, about an hour out of Augusta, the producer dropped off. And so did I, only to be awakened by the squeals and bumps of the train arriving at the Augusta station. The rays of brilliant Southern spring sun slanted into my eyes as I disembarked. My stomach was sour, my brain fuzzy. It was a hell of a way to begin my career as a golf commentator.

I did the radio commentary that year, and I believe started the custom whereby golf announcers talk in hushed whispers. I didn't do it for dramatic effect, but simply because our radio commentary tower was located only about ten feet to the left of the eighteenth green and was no more than fifteen feet high. As a result, golfers playing on the eighteenth green could hear me unless I kept my voice very low. For years after, it became the vogue for all golf commentators to whisper, no matter how far from the action their position might be.

Jack Burke Jr. won the tournament that year, but the most dramatic story was that of a young amateur named Ken Venturi, who led the championship for four strokes until his game collapsed on the final day. He shot 80 and lost to Burke by a single stroke.

The next year I became the network's TV anchorman, the biggest thrill of my career at that point.

And I immediately found myself on the spot.

The custom of covering only the final three holes with no tape replays ignored the possibility of an early starter shooting a great round and winning the tournament before the telecast had even begun. Doug Ford, the fastest player on the PGA tour at that time, did us in. On that final round in 1957, Doug, who was not among the leaders when the day began, whooshed around the course. On the eighteenth, he holed out from a bunker for a birdie three and a virtually unbeatable lead.

By the time we went on the air, Ford had concluded his

press conference, had showered, and was having a celebratory drink while waiting for the other players to finish the course. Then he would be fitted with the traditional green jacket of the champion. And that would be the only time we would see him on our telecast that afternoon.

It was a hopeless situation for me. I had to say that Doug Ford had shot a sensational round and was being congratulated in the clubhouse, then resort to the cliché "You never know what's going to happen on a golf course," etc., etc., etc. Our young director, Frank Chirkinian (who would direct the Masters for the next forty years), kept urging me through the little speaker in my ear to *say something* to make it exciting. Like what? Nobody was even close.

All I could do was tell Doug Ford's life story several times, including the fact that he credited his excellent putting to his early years of shooting pool, while continuing to describe the dreary lack of action on the screen. I have been told that the events of that afternoon speeded up the development of videotape, which appeared before the end of the decade.

Since then, for more than forty years, I have walked the fairways of the world behind the game's greatest artists, playing in the most famous championships on the planet's most storied courses. During that time, golf has exploded, both as a spectator and a participant sport. Why? Some say it has been the combination of television and the work of former commissioner Deane Beman, who scouted up sponsors willing to put up tens of millions of dollars in prize money. Others credit the player-agent combination of Arnold Palmer and Mark McCormack.

All of these have played prominent roles in golf's ascendancy, but to me, it has principally been the result of the sterling careers of certain players, and not Arnold Palmer alone. I'll be audacious enough now to list my top ten players, whose achievements I have described on ABC and CBS during the past forty years. I rank them not on their performance alone, but for their impact on the game through behavior on and off the course, and on their endurance and charisma.

THE McKAY RATINGS

1. Jack Nicklaus

When Jack Nicklaus first came upon the scene, it was difficult to see him as a hero. He was, after all, from the frozen fields of Ohio, not the Sun Belt; he went to Ohio State, not Wake Forest or the University of Houston; he was—well, he was a fat kid in baggy pants whose shirttail tended to hang out and whose golf cap never seemed to sit quite right on his crew-cut head. He was not up from the caddy corps in the approved manner of those days, but the son of a successful pharmacy owner and country club member. He seldom smiled.

Worse than that, after winning the U.S. Amateur twice, in 1959 and 1961 (the first at the age of nineteen), he appeared on the professional tour and in his first year as a pro won the U.S. Open championship, defeating Arnold Palmer in a playoff at Oakmont, outside Pittsburgh, which was virtually Palmer's home course.

After Nicklaus played safely on the final playoff hole and won, an announcer assigned by NBC to interview him had the temerity to ask, "Jack, why did you choke on the last hole?" It was not the last stupid and unfriendly question the new champion would hear in his career.

"How dare he beat Arnold Palmer?!" seemed to be the golf world's reaction. Palmer was the game's demigod. To be beaten by the kid whom the golf press had quickly dubbed Ohio Fats was too much for "Arnie's Army." In those early years Nicklaus was the only player I have ever heard booed on a golf course.

That all changed quickly enough.

No one realized it at the time, but the final battle for supremacy between Nicklaus and Palmer took place at the Baltusrol Golf Club in New Jersey in the 1967 U.S. Open. At the age of twenty-seven, Nicklaus was after his second Open and ninth major championship win. Palmer, ten years older, was also in pursuit of his second and ninth, and they were paired on the final day.

By this time, Nicklaus had undergone a physical and sartorial makeover. He had taken off weight, had let his hair grow, and was as neatly dressed as anyone in the sport. He was no longer the usurper, but Palmer's equal, battling for recognition as the game's top player.

And he wasn't being booed anymore.

On the seventh hole of that final round, Jack made a long putt, Arnie missed a shorter one, and Nicklaus led by two. By the eighteenth, Nicklaus's lead was four strokes and it appeared to be over. As they teed off on the final hole, I was coming in from my tower at the fifteenth, driving a golf cart, with Denny Lewin, then a production assistant, sitting beside me and my twelve-year-old son, Sean, standing on the back.

Jack pushed his tee shot into the right rough under one of our cables. After a free drop, he hit a fat eight-iron and left himself with a 238-yard uphill shot to the green. One more bad shot and he might have trouble.

It was just then that our golf cart ran out of juice. Denny, Sean, and I began pushing the thing, while a marshal called, "Quiet, please!" and Nicklaus prepared to hit his all-important shot. Pushing and trying to steer at the same time, I watched Nicklaus select a one-iron, then hit a shot for the golf history books, right onto the green, assuring his victory with two putts for a par five. A few minutes later, still a bit short of breath and with my dignity only partially restored, I was interviewing Nicklaus as the winner.

Palmer would never win another major championship; Jack would win eleven more. To me, looking back, that was the day, and the one-iron shot was the moment, when Nicklaus became the new king of golf.

☆

Fast-forward thirteen years, to the U.S. Open of 1980, again at Baltusrol. Nicklaus is now a forty-year-old veteran. The number of his major championships is at seventeen, but the last one was five years ago. He has not won any tournament in almost two years, and in his last appearance before the Open, he missed the cut.

They were beginning to write about his unequaled career in the past tense, not critically, but assuming that the glory days were all behind him.

But on that hot June weekend in New Jersey, it was as if the years melted off Nicklaus and he was back vying with Palmer to be King of the Hill. Except that this time Palmer was replaced by a solemn Japanese named Isao Aoki, and the decisive blow would come not on the final hole, but on the one before, Baltusrol's famous seventeenth, at more than six hundred yards, the longest ever played in the U.S. Open.

By the luck of the draw, Nicklaus and Aoki had been paired together all four days of the championship. Jack was outdriving the Japanese by thirty or forty yards, but Aoki was working wonders on the green with his unorthodox putting address, the toe of the club pointed toward the sky. Now, here was the penultimate hole. Jack led by two strokes.

Both were on the green in three on the par five hole. But Aoki was in birdie territory, only five feet from the cup, while Jack was twenty feet away. A birdie by Aoki and a three-putt by Nicklaus, both very possible, and they would have been tied.

The old champion stared at the putt until he was satisfied with his reading, then knocked it into the hole for a birdie. Our greenside camera caught a tight close-up of Jack's face with a huge, boyish smile that seemed to announce, "The career isn't over yet!"

He spread his arms then to quiet the crowd as Aoki putted. Isao made it and the lead was two strokes going into the eighteenth. Isao still had a chance, but an eagle three would be needed, assuming Jack made par. (Both finishing holes at Baltusrol are par fives, an unusual arrangement.)

As they approached the final green I watched them from our tower and witnessed a near-miracle shot. Aoki's third, a pitching wedge, landed on the green and rolled toward the cup—closer and closer, finally sliding past the cup by only a few inches. If it had dropped . . . but it didn't. Both men finished the hole in grand style, with birdies, and both broke the previous U.S. Open scoring record.

So there was Jack, triumphant once more, and a group of young fans, marveling that a man of forty could accomplish such a thing, gathered around the scorer's tent, chanting, "Jack is back, Jack is back!" The scoreboard operator joined in the fun, posting the same message on the big board.

Nicklaus joined in, too, smiling and waving to the young people in an uncharacteristic fashion. It was obvious that this moment was special to him. It had taken a long time to win the fans over, to attain their respect for his achievements, to get out from under Arnie's long shadow.

I remember that championship as the self-fulfilling climax of his career, even though, two months later, he won his fifth PGA.

Even though, six years later, he won his sixth Masters.

Even though, sixteen years later, he was only one stroke off the lead in the British Open at the halfway mark.

Read the roll call of his achievements:

Six Masters championships (no one else has won as many);

Five PGAs (equaling Walter Hagen's record);

Four U.S. Opens (only Ben Hogan, Bobby Jones, and the turn-of-the-century star Willie Anderson have won as many); and

Three British Open titles, two won at St. Andrews, the world's most famous course, the other at Muirfield, considered the most difficult in the British Open rota. He finished second a remarkable seven times in the British classic.

Twenty majors in all. Will anyone ever equal that? (In recent years, some reporters have started to claim that he has only eighteen majors, discounting his two U.S. Amateur titles. To me, this is rewriting history. The Amateur was counted as a major at the time he won his pair, and I still count them.)

Tack on a total of seventy wins on the PGA Tour, two

Walker Cup teams, six Ryder Cup teams (twice captain), two U.S. Senior Open titles, and a Senior PGA.

He intimidated his peers like no one since Bobby Jones.

Nicklaus was not, however, without his crushing defeats or his personal insecurities. His toughest loss came at Pebble Beach in the 1982 U.S. Open. At the age of forty-two, he had finished his final round of the championship and was standing beside the scorer's tent waiting to be interviewed as the first player ever to win five U.S. Opens, if Tom Watson bogied either of the last two holes. And Watson was in trouble, his ball sitting in long grass behind the green of the par three seventeenth. From our tower at eighteen, I looked down on Nicklaus. He was staring at a monitor showing Watson lining up his shot. From the difficult lie in the long grass, it might well run far across the green, leaving him a likely bogie on the hole and setting up victory for Jack.

But Watson made "the shot heard round the world," knocking the ball into the hole for a birdie, running after the ball as it hit the flagstick and dropped, smiling and staring up to the heavens, as if thanking the deity. In that instant, as he stood just below me, Jack's expression was not his usual ironic half-smile of defeat, but a look of total shock and deep disappointment, the face of a stricken youngster, not of the most famous golfer in the world.

Insecurity? Once, while watching him hit practice balls, I asked him if he ever dreamed about golf. He smiled. "Yes, I do," he said. "Actually, I have a recurrent dream. I am walking up the eighteenth fairway of the U.S. Open with a one-stroke lead, when suddenly I realize that I am far over the fourteen-club limit of allowable clubs in my bag; I must have twenty or more. In the dream, I walk along, trying to surreptitiously discard one club at a time. An official walks toward me—then I wake up in a sweat!"

Intense as he is on and off the course, he does have an occasional sense of impishness. Once, our commentator Bill Flemming and I decided to play tennis after a round of the Hawaiian Open. As we were warming up, Jack came by. He watched for a moment, then said, "You two thieves can't be trusted to make calls on each other. You need an umpire!" With that, he climbed up into the umpire's chair and proceeded to call the match, complete with needling comments to both of us.

His not-so-secret weapon all through his career has been his wife, Barbara, a one-woman PR firm for Jack as he concentrates on business. She follows him every step of the way on the golf course, talking pleasantly with spectators. Often, as she passes under the tower at eighteen, she will look up at us, smile, and wave, if Jack is playing well. If he is not, she still smiles, but shrugs her shoulders.

Nicklaus was once asked if he ever played golf for fun, and he replied that he always does. "But you have to understand," he said. "Fun to me is walking up the eighteenth fairway on the final day of the Masters with a one-stroke lead."

To my mind, by any measurement of achievement, Jack W. Nicklaus is the greatest golfer of all time.

2. Arnold Palmer

The final match for the 1954 U.S. Amateur championship featured an unlikely but attractive pairing. Robert Sweeney, international socialite, resident of London and Palm Beach, was facing a twenty-four-year-old youngster from western Pennsylvania whose knowledge of major cities was basically limited to Pittsburgh. Sweeney was handsome and elegant, both in appearance and in manner of playing. He moved among the world's most beautiful people in the days before they were called that, and the country clubs of England and America were his playgrounds.

The kid from Pennsylvania couldn't have looked more different. He resembled a college halfback rather than a champion golfer. Growing up as the son of a club pro and greenkeeper, he had not even been allowed in the country club pool. He strode the course as if on a mission, following the ball in flight and whispering to it as if, by doing so, he might control its destination.

By nightfall of that long-ago day, Latrobe, Pennsylvania, had bested London and Palm Beach, and Arnold Palmer was the new national amateur champ.

Many years later, I sat with Arnie by the backyard pool at his home in Latrobe—we were doing a TV special on him—and asked him what was the most satisfying moment of his legendary career.

"It probably will surprise you," he said, "but it was beating Bob Sweeney for the national amateur championship. By the way, he was a great guy; I liked him a lot. At the time, I just couldn't believe I had gotten to the final, and then to win, and to beat him—well, as I say, it sticks in my mind to this day as my greatest thrill."

This from the man who would lead golf's greatest renaissance, who would transform the British Open, singlehandedly, from a fading anachronism—its greatest years long past—to the most glittering prize in the game, the unofficial world championship.

This from the man whose following would be described not as a gallery, but an army; who would become a spokesman for more than two hundred companies around the world; who would golf with presidents and kings, declining the urging of friends to run for the U.S. Senate; who would design golf courses from Orlando to Malaysia; who could demand the price of a briefcaseful of country club memberships simply to visit a course and play for a one-day corporate outing; and who would amass a fortune larger than the gross annual product of his old hometown.

To understand Arnold Palmer and his endless appeal to Everyman, it helps to sit with him as I did that day at the home he and his wife, Winnie, have lived in for more than thirty-five years and understand that he *is* Everyman. Despite all the things that have happened to him in the past four decades and more, he still loves to sit by the pool, looking down toward the course he grew up on, just at the bottom of the hill.

That day some four or five years ago, he smiled and told me how his first memory of "big money" was the time a member gave him fifty cents for caddying nine holes—thirty-five cents over the regular fee. And how he used to lie outside his family's house on the edge of the course and wait for the woman to come by the sixth hole—the woman who always gave him a nickel if he would hit her ball over the water hazard for her.

"I can see myself now when I was really small," he said. "Making sure my dad couldn't see me because I wasn't allowed on the course, I would sneak out to the third fairway with a toy gun strapped to each hip and a cut-down golf club in my hand."

Our TV crew broke for lunch and Arnold said, "Let's go."

"Where?"

"Where I like to go most days for lunch when I'm home."

We got into his Cadillac and took the short drive down the hill to the Latrobe Country Club. He has no trouble getting in the clubhouse these days—Arnie owns the place, literally. Our destination was a big round table in the Nineteenth Hole, where five or six club members were gathered, waiting for their man. For almost an hour, I sat, had lunch, and listened to them all talk about the condition of the course, recent notable rounds turned in, and the latest gossip of Latrobe.

It was obvious that this was not a pose with Arnie.

This was the real Arnold Palmer, who loves to sit, have a beer and a sandwich, and talk golf, whether it's home in Latrobe, in the clubhouse at Augusta, or in the residents' lounge at Rusack's Hotel, just off the eighteenth fairway of the Old Course at St. Andrews, Scotland.

I have followed Arnold Palmer around golf courses since I first went to Augusta in 1956. I was there for his first two Masters wins, as his army began to mobilize. I was there at Royal Troon when he won his second straight British Open in 1962, setting a record score for the championship and gathering a

British Foreign Legion branch of his army in the process. They swarmed around him at the final green, almost crushing him with affection. Windows in the clubhouse were shattered in the confusion. Troon, in all its storied and dignified history, had never seen anything like it.

My personal memory of that week is one of exhaustion. Producer Bill Seaman and I were assigned rooms at the American Air Base in nearby Prestwick. Our quarters, it developed, had previously been a stairwell, with a skylight, before being converted on an emergency basis during World War II. Now, as Bill and I tried to sleep, the sun streamed through the skylight straight into our eyes until 11:00 P.M. and again when it rose about 3:30 A.M. Scotland, like Norway, is the land of the midnight sun in the month of July.

We should have known something was amiss when we noticed that there was an exit sign over the door to our room. We could hardly complain, though. There were no other rooms available in the area, and the room charge was 2 pounds a night, the equivalent then of about $5.50.

Palmer's 1964 Masters win, in the year that Lyndon Johnson was elected president and the Beatles first came to America to appear on *The Ed Sullivan Show*, would remain, for all time, his last major championship.

I was there at the Olympic Club in San Francisco on the day Arnold's career started its descent. For the 1966 U.S. Open. I was stationed at the fifteenth hole for the fourth round. As Palmer and his closest pursuer, Bill Casper, teed off on the short par three, Palmer had a five-shot lead. How could he lose? The only question was whether he would break Ben Hogan's record 72-hole score for the championship.

What happened next was unpredictable and shattering.

With the hole cut into the right side of the green and a sand bunker right beside it, Palmer went for the hole in typical aggressive fashion. The ball faded into the bunker. Casper played safely into the middle of the green, then made his putt for a two. Arnold blasted out, took two putts, and had lost two strokes of his lead.

On the next hole, a par five, Arnold took a powerful swing and hooked his tee shot into the woods. By the time they finished the hole, he had lost another two shots. He lost yet another on seventeen, and had to make a testing four-foot putt on eighteen to remain even and force a playoff. But the next day, Casper, not Palmer, won the playoff.

Palmer has played on for decades more, but his last win on the regular PGA Tour was in 1973, his last victory on the Senior Tour in 1988. In the PGA Tour information book, you will not find him listed in the hundred all-time career money winners. He lies well behind Cal Peete, Steve Stricker, and Fulton Allem. This, of course, is a function of the skyrocketing purses available on the tour since Arnold was winning—purses that his fame and influence made possible.

My most lasting memory of Palmer came in 1990 at St. Andrews, in what he announced would be his last British Open, exactly thirty years after his first, when he lost to Kel Nagle of Australia by a single stroke on the same course.

He and some friends in Rusack's recalled other days and other victories. As we talked, Arnold's longtime caddy, Tip Anderson, quietly approached our table, holding his cap in his hand. Arnold has said of Tip that in his first British Open at St. Andrews, "He led me around the course like a man leading his dog."

Now, the aging caddy, his face weathered through three decades of carrying Arnold's bag, stood with tears in his eyes and looked down at his man. "Arnie," he said. "It's all my fault that we didn't make the cut. I'm sorry." Conversation at the table stopped.

Palmer stood up, put his arm around Tip's shoulders, and told him quietly that the player is always responsible—that he, Tip, had done a great job, and had nothing to feel sorry for. Tip walked away, and it was Arnold's turn to have tears in his eyes. As did we.

☆

Like an old thespian making yet another farewell tour, Arnold reconsidered his resolve and returned to St. Andrews when the championship returned there in 1995. Again, he failed to make the cut.

But the galleries have never tired of the man from Latrobe. They still follow him as his hair has turned from blond to silver, his waistline has thickened, and his tee shots have grown shorter and less precise. And they will follow him as long as he—and they—can walk eighteen holes.

I once asked Arnold Palmer how he has kept such a hold on his fans. He looked at me, a faint smile on his face.

"Jim," he said, "maybe it's because they understand who I am. I think I am an honestly sensitive and sentimental person. Maybe they sense that I care a great deal about what I do and that their encouragement means a lot to me."

I suggested that perhaps he has the elusive quality that the Spaniards call *duende*. I couldn't define it for him, except to quote someone who said that Ted Williams had duende while striking out, while others didn't have it when hitting a grand slam.

Arnie smiled.

3. Lee Trevino

Back in the early sixties, the Tennyson Park public golf course in Dallas was a hustler's haven, a place where what you saw in your newfound playing partner on the first tee was not always what you got by the end of the day. Your opponent might be young or old, fat or slim.

He might be the postman named Kennedy, who played you only under his own rules—or rule. There was just one: Move the ball anytime you want, but under penalty of one stroke. Somehow, the single rule always worked out to his advantage.

Your opponent in those days might have been a friendly young Mexican-American named Lee Trevino, a chunky five feet, seven inches tall, a self-taught golfer just out of a four-year hitch in the marines. He talked and laughed his way around the courses, entertaining his partner of the day while taking his money. Lee played all the hustler's games well. His specialty was betting he could beat you playing with a taped-up Dr Pepper bottle. Or he might say he could use fewer strokes than you going down the first fairway, through a tunnel under a railroad track, across to another tunnel, through that tunnel, and up the eighteenth fairway and into the hole. Lee was the champ hustler of Tennyson. Nothing dishonest. He was just a lot better than he looked.

And he might be hustling still had not his wife of the time sent in his entry for the 1967 U.S. Open championship at Baltusrol, the very tournamant in which Nicklaus asserted his mastery of Palmer.

My commentary position at that tournament was at the fifteenth hole. From there, I could also see the fourteenth fairway. During a commercial break on the final day, I noticed a stocky young man with a cocky, aggressive walk, striding down fourteen. He was talking to the people in his very small gallery and laughing. Unusual behavior in the U.S. Open. Wondering who he was, I looked down my notes and found that his name was Lee Trevino. I had never heard of him. Then I looked at my scorer's sheet and saw that Lee Trevino was only two strokes out of the lead!

Scoring systems were still rather primitive in 1967, so I tried to reach our producer, Chuck Howard, to suggest to him that we cover this guy. Unfortunately, I couldn't get through the chaos of the TV truck. Fortunately for ABC Sports, Trevino stumbled over the final holes. If he hadn't, we would have missed a very big story. Still, he finished fifth in his first major championship.

The media took to him immediately as a refreshing and entertaining new member of the golf tour. He told them of his childhood, growing up in the humble home of his grandfather, a Mexican grave digger. Asked it they ate beans every night, he told them, "Hell, no! Beans were a Sunday treat!" He had a snappy answer for everything, and all of his lines were original.

In January of 1968, Trevino won the Hawaiian Open. None of us, however, was ready for what he did that summer at Oak Hill, the wonderful old Donald Ross–designed course in Rochester, New York. In only his second U.S. Open, he won the title and suddenly was the champion of American golf, and the first champion ever to play all four rounds of the Open under 70. Jack Nicklaus finished second, and a new golf rivalry was born.

From Rochester, Lee went to the PGA championship in San Antonio. Upon arrival, he was asked if he had brought his wife. Looking around at the pretty Mexican-American girls who were assigned to greet the golfers at the airport, and with the usual Trevino grin, he answered, "Of course not. When I go to the Milwaukee Open, do I take along a six-pack?"

One day during that tournament, he was hitting practice balls and a woman spectator kept oohing and aahing and saying "Marvelous!" after every shot. Finally Lee turned and said, "Lady, I'm the U.S. Open champion. What do you expect, ground balls?"

He didn't win that PGA, but he won two of them later on (the second at age forty-four), to go with another U.S. Open and back-to-back British Opens. Of the four major professional championships, only the Masters has escaped his grasp. He has been a star of the Senior Tour, despite recurring back and knee injuries, winning more than a million dollars in three different years. He has won tournaments from Mexico to Morocco.

Married twice, he has fathered six children, most recently at the age of fifty-three. Both of his wives have been named Claudia, prompting him to say, on the occasion of his second marriage, "It's great—I don't even have to change the monogrammed towels!"

What Nicklaus vs. Palmer had been in the sixties, Nicklaus vs. Trevino became in the early seventies. In the U.S. Open, it was Trevino winning in a playoff with Nicklaus at Merion in

1971. (It was also there that Lee tested Jack's sense of humor by tossing a rubber snake at the great man's feet as they prepared to tee off on the first playoff hole. Nicklaus jumped, then laughed. Although Jack never liked playing with opponents who talked a lot—Hubert Green is one such—somehow he didn't mind Trevino. He seemed to enjoy his chatter, actually.)

Nicklaus came back to win the Open the next year at Pebble Beach.

In the British Open, Nicklaus won in 1970; Trevino won the next two years in a row.

In the PGA, it was Nicklaus in 1971 and 1973, Trevino in 1974, and Nicklaus again in 1975.

My most vivid memory of Trevino in his heyday is at the 1972 British Open on the Muirfield links in Scotland. As the defending champion, he was greeted by a huge gallery on the first tee of the first round. I had acquired a credential that allowed me inside the gallery ropes so that I could see and hear Lee close-up as he made his way around the difficult Muirfield layout.

It could have been the Pro-Am preceding the Quad Cities Open as far as his attitude was concerned. He kept up a running conversation, or more properly a monologue, with the Scottish gallery all the way around. Standing on one tee, he turned to the crowd and said, "They took me to an old castle for dinner last night. We had food like they ate back in the old days, and we ate like they did—with our fingers. Hell, back home in Texas I even have a cat I taught to eat with a fork!"

Then he laughed and knocked his tee shot in his usual left-to-right arc into the middle of the fairway.

At another point, Trevino walked over to me, put his arm around my shoulders, and called to his followers, "Hey, you should know this guy. This is Jim McKay, the famous golf announcer from America!" Some of the crowd applauded, others laughed, and I think one guy booed. He must have been from New York.

Casual and insouciant though he seemed, Trevino's attitude has been his way of keeping himself relaxed during a round, just as it was at Tennyson Park long ago.

That 1972 championship turned out to be one of the most exciting I have ever seen. On the final round, Trevino and Tony Jacklin, the Englishman, playing together, fought for the lead. Nicklaus, six shots behind when the day began, was tied with them for first place by the end of nine holes. All through the back nine, shouts echoed across the sand dunes by the Firth of Forth, from the gallery of Nicklaus, playing ahead, and the crowd following Trevino and Jacklin.

As Lee and Tony played the par five seventeenth, Nicklaus finished his round and could only wait. Jacklin, the hero of the U.K., was on the green in two shots. Trevino was off the green, in a difficult sidehill lie, in three. It was Tony's championship to win—until Lee, using a ladies' Helen Hicks model wedge he had salvaged from a pro shop barrel and christened "Miss Helen," almost resignedly pitched onto the green—and into the hole for a birdie! Whereupon Jacklin three-putted for a par. He had lost his concentration. Tony staggered through the eighteenth and Trevino had won his second British title in a row. Jacklin later said that the crushing blow on seventeen had ended his career as a major force in international golf.

Nicklaus, Palmer, and Trevino are my top three, because of their achievements, the influence they have had in popularizing the game, and the remarkable length of their careers (as of 1997, Trevino has been playing championship professional golf for thirty years, Nicklaus for thirty-five, and Palmer for an astonishing forty-two). Part of the reason for their longevity has been the emergence of the Senior Tour, but without their great and well-earned popularity, there might never have been a Senior Tour.

Each of them is a unique personality, cut from no mold, creature of no guru.

Nicklaus's power has long since been eclipsed by the John Dalys and Tiger Woodses; Palmer's all-pervasive influence has, for the past twenty years and more, been based mostly on reputation and behavior; Trevino's swing is one of the least fashionable of his time. But they will be remembered with awe and affection as long as Old Tom Morris, or Bobby Jones, Walter Hagen, Ben Hogan, Byron Nelson, and Sam Snead.

4. Tom Watson

It is still something of a mystery that Tom Watson, Huck Finn revisited, the red-haired, smiling, gap-toothed, boyish pride of Kansas City, U.S.A., should find his greatest golfing glory on the windswept, whins-ridden fairways of Scotland.

For any golfer, regardless of nationality, to win five British Opens is a monumental task, achieved only by the hallowed triumvirate of J. H. Taylor, James Braid, and Harry Vardon in the early years of the century (Vardon actually won six), and by the Australian Peter Thomson in the fallow days after World War II when there was little or no American challenge.

Tom Watson has won five British Opens—and he did it in the short span of nine years.

To my mind, his signal achievement was not chipping into the hole at Pebble Beach to win the U.S. Open in 1982, but his stirring head-to-head win over Nicklaus in the British Open at Turnberry in 1977. Paired together, each shot 65 in the third round. On the final day, again playing together, it was neck and neck.

On the eighteenth green, Watson appeared to have victory assured. He was only about four feet from the hole with his approach shot, while Nicklaus had left himself with a long, curling putt. However, when Nicklaus, in characteristic fashion, made the putt, Watson's four-footer suddenly looked a lot longer. But he made it without hesitation, and again was the "champion golfer," as the Open winner is known in Britain.

There is another mystery about Tom Watson. After winning the Nabisco Championship of Golf in 1987, he was, at the age of thirty-seven, the heir apparent to Palmer and

Nicklaus as the king of golf, ten years younger than Nicklaus, twenty younger than Arnold. Then he went nine years without winning an American tournament (only the 1992 Hong Kong Open appears on his victory list during that time). He had always been one of the boldest and the best of putters, but suddenly his touch deserted him. He had always believed that if you putt the ball hard enough to go past the cup, it always had a chance of going in. Now, even short putts were falling short.

But the quality I most admire in Tom Watson is his tenacity.

I am thinking not only of the admiration all golf fans share for his behavior (during those long years of winless frustration on the American tour) but of the manner in which he won his eight major championships. In each of his two Masters victories, and in his only U.S. Open, he edged out Jack Nicklaus, in his prime, by just two shots. It was appropriate that when he finally did win again in the United States, it would be in Nicklaus's own Memorial Tournament at Muirfield Village in Dublin, Ohio, in 1996.

Of his remarkable five British Open victories, four of them were won by a single shot, one in a playoff.

If Nicklaus was the greatest and Palmer the most charismatic of championship golfers, certainly Tom Watson, as he plays on in his late forties, still convinced that he will win another major, is the most tenacious.

5. Gary Player

In July of 1954, at the age of eighteen, Gary Player stepped off a train at a small town in Scotland, carrying a cardboard suitcase held together with a piece of rope. The suitcase, and the smallish youngster, had traveled hard, all the way from Player's home in South Africa, as he made his way to the British Open championship.

Since that day, while staying home in South Africa long

enough each year to win its national golf title thirteen times, father six children, and build a stable of race horses, he has become the world's most traveled athlete, flying around the globe year after year, winning the national championships of the United States, Great Britain, Australia, Chile, and Brazil, among others.

He has won more major championships than Arnold Palmer.

He is one of only four men to have won all four professional major championships in a career, the others being Ben Hogan, Jack Nicklaus, and Gene Sarazen.

He is the only golfer in this century to win the British Open in three separate decades.

Somehow, he has managed to continue his career through the years while other South African athletes were being barred from international sport because of their country's apartheid policy.

And at the age of sixty-one, Gary Player is still at it, winning half a million dollars on the U.S. Senior Tour in 1996.

He is one of the smallest great golfers in the game's history—five feet seven inches tall, 147 pounds. His dedication to fitness and proper diet borders on the fanatical, and some of his beliefs approach the mystical.

In the earlier days of his prominence in the sixties, when he, Nicklaus, and Palmer were called the Big Three, he would usually dress totally in black on the course. "Why?" he was asked. "It must be terribly hot, isn't it?"

"Yes," he replied, "but it makes me feel strong."

Once, when he was playing particularly well, I approached him and put out my hand. Instead of shaking it, he grasped my wrist. "Excuse me for not shaking your hand, Jim," he said, "but I greet so many people that I'm afraid of injuring my hand. Playing as well as I am now, that could cost me a lot of money." Others whisper that he actually fears, when on a hot streak, that the power will pass from his hand to yours.

One year, Gary agreed to play in a minor tournament at the Hillendale Country Club outside Baltimore on the condition that the organizers also invite his son, Wayne, to play. Margaret and I invited them both to dinner at our farm. We noticed that Gary ate his meal very selectively and at the end produced a small packet of a tea unfamiliar to us. Would Margaret mind brewing it for him? It was a special brand, decaffeinated.

The only exception to his routine that weekend came when I took him to the nearby breeding and training farm of our friend and trainer, Billy Boniface. On the way up, he asked me to be sure to keep him posted on the time, because he unfailingly hit practice balls for a half hour before sunset.

He was fascinated by the farm's beauty and by Billy's training methods, peppering him with questions until the sun began to descend. I reminded him on several occasions about his request regarding the time.

Finally, as we were driving back in the twilight, I said, "Looks like you're going to miss your practice session, Gary."

"Oh, well," he said, smiling, "I guess there is an exception to every rule."

On the golf course, however, his dedication remained total. Coming to the final hole of the second round of that tournament, a par five, he knew that he almost certainly needed a birdie to make the cut. He hit a good drive, then faced a long, uphill second shot to the green. If he parred the hole and missed the cut, he would have the weekend off to enjoy himself. Instead, he took out his driver and drilled the ball onto the putting surface. Two putts gave him a birdie and the obligation to stick around for the rest of the minor, low-paying competition.

He won't say so, but I think his endless tour of the globe—he likes being billed as "Gary Player, World Golfer," and that he is—must often be a lonely one. Since joining the PGA Tour forty years ago, he has been *on* the tour but not *of* it, always considered a stranger in our midst. But for his many accomplishments on the course, and for his role in popularizing the game of golf, he must be included in my top five, a cut above all the others.

6. Greg Norman

I feel uncomfortable not placing Greg Norman in my top bracket. Today, he is probably the best-known golfer in the world, having won fifty-five tournaments internationally, as well as sixteen on the American tour. He is the leading money winner of all time—more than $10 million in all.

His face is familiar everywhere, his manner charismatic, his swing one of the very best.

But . . .

He has won just two majors, both British Opens. His first, at Turnberry in 1986, was a bravura performance, as he battled rain that blurred our camera coverage, and wind that blew his umbrella inside out, and still won by five strokes.

He has been runner-up in eight other major championships, several times in heartbreaking fashion.

At the Inverness Club in Toledo in 1986, he seemed to have the PGA championship in hand on the final hole. Tied with young Bob Tway, who was playing in his first PGA, Norman was on the green in two and Tway was in a greenside bunker as we went to a commercial. I remember watching nervously as the commercial break seemed to go on endlessly and Tway prepared to hit his shot. I thought, "Suppose he . . ." We came out of the commercial no more than one second before he hit, just long enough for me to say, "Here's Tway's shot." We were luckier than Norman was. Tway blasted the ball into the hole, Norman three-putted, and Tway won.

The next year in the Masters, Norman was on the green on the second playoff hole. Larry Mize, playing in his birthplace, Augusta, was to the right of the green, thirty-five yards away. Mize flipped a sand wedge shot onto the green and into the hole for the win. After that, ill fortune seemed to follow Greg everywhere, in tournaments major and minor.

Close followers of the game began to think that he was "hearing footsteps," dreading the final holes of every tournament he led. Finally came the historic collapse in the 1996

Masters, when he blew a six-shot lead in the final eighteen holes.

Every great player has performances he would rather forget, but Greg's have come in the spotlight of major championships and have come in such dramatic fashion that they dominate his image, despite all his achievements.

For that reason only, and regretfully, I leave him out of my big five.

7. Seve Ballesteros

His emergence was sudden, his impact enormous, his downfall unforeseen and shocking.

He was just twenty-two years old when he won the British Open in 1979, a tall, dark, and handsome caballero from a small town in Spain, striding along the fairways of England's Royal Lytham as if he owned them, reminding me of the young Arnold Palmer in the way he moved.

There was Seve in victory again, at St. Andrews in 1984, holing out in the shadow of the Royal and Ancient clubhouse, then pumping his fist to the sky, his teeth clenched behind a defiant smile.

And there was Seve at Lytham again in 1988. He had put his second shot on a par five hole far to the right, into an area that was in bounds, but where some people had illegally parked their cars. I sat with my longtime colleague and friend Dave Marr in the commentary booth. When Ballesteros put the shot into the hole for an eagle three, Dave laughed and said, "I've heard people *kid* about making a three from the parking lot, but this guy just did it!"

In between his British Open wins, he had built an American following with two Masters triumphs, in 1980 and 1983. He also won the national championships of France, Switzerland, Great Britain, Spain, Ireland, Germany, Japan, Kenya, and the Netherlands.

After winning his third British title with that shot from the car park, Seve was King of the Hill. He has slid slowly but inevitably downhill ever since, finishing 69th on the European money list in 1996 and 280th in the U.S. There have been no more major titles.

What happened? No one knows, although some theorists blame imperfections in his swing, others the explosive nature of his character. But it seems to be over for Seve at age forty, unless he can pull some middle-aged miracles as he creeps toward fifty and the Senior Tour.

His impact on the game remains, however.

It was he who made golf a European game, who brought money to the European tour. Perhaps most important, it was his play that forced expansion of the Ryder Cup matches from the U.S. vs. Great Britain and Ireland to the U.S. vs. all of Europe. As a result, the matches, which had attracted minor attention in the United States until that point, have become an increasingly competitive and major event.

His place in golf history is secure.

8. Nick Faldo

I rank Nick Faldo behind Ballesteros only because of Seve's great influence in bringing Europe into the international golf community. As Ballesteros brought golfing fame to the Continent, so Faldo restored the good name of England in international golf.

With the single brief exception of Tony Jacklin, British prominence had been dormant since the glory days of Henry Cotton, before and just after World War II. When the young Faldo appeared, all of Britain pinned its hopes on him. But he flashed, then faded, on and off, to the point where the unrelenting English tabloids started referring to him in headlines as El Foldo.

Then, in 1987, he won the British Open, and his country's thirst for glory was reflected in the Queen's decision to immediately place him among those princes and dukes and field marshals of old as an MBE—a member of the Order of the British Empire.

The following year he tied for first in the U.S. Open, but lost the playoff to Curtis Strange at the Country Club in Brookline, Massachusetts. Since then, he has won two more British Opens and a trio of Masters. In 1990, he became the first foreign player to be named American PGA Player of the Year.

He has not yet joined the pantheon of the game, partly because of his rather phlegmatic personality and, in the minds of some people, because of his reliance on a golfing guru named David Leadbetter, who completely rebuilt Nick's swing and follows him around the course and to the practice tee as if Faldo were still a student, not a champion.

At times, I have found myself thinking, "Can you imagine Ben Hogan being followed every step of his career by a coach?"

And yet, it really should be to his credit that Faldo, at age forty, is still intent on improving his game. He has withstood the slings and arrows of the British yellow press, which has spent more time on his marital problems and his lack of charisma than it has on his achievements, and that spot in the pantheon may still one day be his.

9. Ray Floyd

How's this for career longevity? He was only eighteen when he turned pro thirty-five years ago. Now, as he nears his mid-fifties, he is still winning on the Senior Tour and occasionally returning to the regular tour to instruct his juniors by example on how to play the game with skill and dignity.

He was considered quite a mischievous kid in his early years, but then he met Maria, they were married, and his life was changed forevermore—for the better.

He won his first tour tournament in his twentieth year. His first victory in a major was the PGA, at age twenty-seven, and his last, the U.S. Open, came at age forty-three. He won a regular tour title at age forty-nine, and later that year, after his birthday, he won his first Senior Tour event. He has joined Sam Snead as the only golfers to win tour events in four decades.

The onetime youthful carouser is now one of golf's elder statesmen, with a life outside the PGA Tour. Every August, for example, you'll find him and Maria sitting in the number one box at the racetrack in upstate Saratoga, New York, with their good friend Ogden Mills "Dinny" Phipps of the famous thoroughbred racing family.

To round out my top ten, I'll have to resort to that old cop-out, a tie. In this case, a three-way tie, among . . .

10. Ben Crenshaw, Tom Kite, and Hale Irwin

There is something about Ben Crenshaw that still reminds me more of the young hero of a boys' book than a forty-five-year-old veteran who played in his first U.S. Open back in 1970. He is still much more likely to exclaim "Goll-EE!" than something stronger when he misses an important putt. And the history and lore of golf haven't lost any of their luster for him after twenty-four years as a touring pro.

His most dramatic victory came at the 1995 Masters, and it came not as a personal triumph but, he said, as a memorial to his old golf teacher, Harvey Penick, whose funeral he had attended in Texas instead of playing a practice round for the championship earlier in the week. Harvey, Ben had said, had been in his mind every step of the seventy-two holes, and his mentor's spirit had guided him to victory.

Tom Kite played in Crenshaw's shadow as his teammate at the University of Texas. They shared the 1972 NCAA title, but Ben won that championship by himself in 1971 and 1973.

Crenshaw won the first tournament he played in as a pro, in 1973. Kite had to wait until three years later for his first win.

But in most ways their careers have nearly mirrored each other's. Each has won nineteen tournaments on the American tour. Ben has taken two majors, both Masters; but Tom has a U.S. Open to his credit and Ben doesn't. Kite is second on the all-time money winning list; Ben is tenth. So there is little to choose between them, and both certainly belong in my top ten.

And so does Hale Irwin.

For more than a quarter of a century, he has been one of the more prominent, if not flamboyant, players in golf, quietly going about his business but not exuding that elusive quality called charisma. Despite two U.S. Open wins, he has seldom attracted the galleries of the other top stars. While anecdotes abound regarding Nicklaus, Palmer, Trevino, Watson, et al., the usual descriptive line about Hale is: "former All-Big Eight defensive back at University of Colorado." Sometimes it is mentioned that he once carelessly whiffed a three-inch putt in the British Open to lose the title by that single stroke.

Then one day at the Medinah club outside Chicago, he put himself among the game's legends by sinking a forty-five-foot putt on the final green to tie Mike Donald for the U.S. Open championship, after which he circled the green with a huge smile on his face, high-fiving every spectator he could get his hands on. The next day, he won a dramatic nineteen-hole playoff for his third Open win.

He has had to wait for everything. His best finish on the regular-tour money list was third, but that was twenty years ago. Then, in his second season on the Senior Tour, he won over $1.5 million, more than twice what he had ever won in a single year in his career. Ironically, that was still only good enough for second place, $12,000 behind Jim Colbert. But in 1997 he topped them all, with $2 million winnings.

Now what shall I do about Tiger Woods and Ernie Els?

Els, the twenty-seven-year-old South African, has already won two U.S. Opens and tied for second in the British Open. He seems certain to at least challenge the achievements of his countryman Gary Player, one of only four golfers to have won the four major championships in a career.

Woods's achievement in winning the '97 Masters the way he did will place him in the game's mythology, even if he doesn't become golf's dominant player for years to come.

Woods and Els are actually the leaders of a youthful pack who served notice in the '97 British Open that a new day has dawned in golf. Twenty-five-year-old Justin Leonard of Texas was the winner, and twenty-eight-year-old Darren Clarke of Northern Ireland tied for second. Woods challenged briefly with a third-round 64, tying the course record. And there are others on the way, like England's Lee Westwood.

In fact, all three of the world's most famous championships were won in '97 by men in their twenties; Woods, twenty-one, the Masters; Els, twenty-seven, the U.S. Open; and Leonard, twenty-five, the British Open.

Might one of them be the new Nicklaus or Palmer?

Possibly.

But as far as ranking any of them or any of the others I've discussed, I can only echo the comment made long ago by Red Smith. After Willie Mays had turned in his second great season in the majors, someone asked Red if he thought Mays was as good as Joe DiMaggio.

"Come back and ask me that in twenty years," he said, "and I'll tell you."

I must mention my dear friend, the late Dave Marr. He won a single major championship, the PGA at Laurel Valley in Ligonier, Pennsylvania, in 1965. But he was one of the best-known and best-liked players in the game until he died of cancer, at age sixty-three, in 1997.

His famous wit was often self-deprecating and always kind. His criticisms of other players while serving as commentator for ABC with me for many years were honest, but couched in soft words. When I asked him once on the air why a certain player might be collapsing, as he was, on the final round of this national championship, Dave said simply, "Three words, Jim, just three: United. States. Open."

His greatest thrill was playing on, and later captaining, the U.S. Ryder Cup team.

"Jim," he told me one morning while we were riding from St. Andrews to the Edinburgh airport after a British Open, "When you're picked for the Ryder Cup team, your first thought is, 'Wow, I made the all-star team!' But when you get to the scene of the competition, and they raise the American flag and play our anthem, you gulp and realize that it is much more than that.

"And when you stand on the first tee, and the man says, 'On the tee, Dave Marr, United States of America,' that club starts shaking in your hand and just won't stop."

Even in his final days in the hospital, Dave tried to lighten things up a bit for his family. His grown daughter, Elizabeth, began to cry while visiting him one day.

"What's the matter, honey?" Dave said.

"Oh, Daddy, I'm just so sad."

Dave managed a small chuckle, smiled wanly, then said, "Hey, you ought to see it from this side!"

I treasure a scorecard from the Old Course at St. Andrews. It shows that I won a British pound from Dave one lovely, cool Scottish evening long ago (he was, of course, giving me a stroke a hole). And written on the card in Dave's hand are the words, "Don't spend that pound just yet, Jim."

No way.

☆

As the years roll by, my personal fascination with golf only increases. And an adventure I shared with my fifteen-year-old grandson, James Fontelieu, just after the '97 British Open gave both of us a memory that will last all our lives.

It happened on the Old Course at St. Andrews, that legendary links on the Firth of Tay where Mary, Queen of Scots played golf, and where today's pilgrims play much the same course as their ancestors did more than five hundred years ago. When I first proposed a trip to the British Open for just us two, I was surprised when James immediately said the most important thing to do in Scotland was to play the Old Course. After all, at fifteen, nostalgia is not usually a priority.

But that was what he wanted, and so we found ourselves on the first tee on a gorgeous morning in July, two days after the '97 Open had concluded. Watching us was the usual gaggle of St. Andrews citizens, with babies in perambulators, older children staring solemnly at us, and dogs remaining obediently silent. In St. Andrews, even infants and dogs know that one does not make noise when golf is being celebrated.

James cupped his hand and whispered in my ear, "You go first, Pop." He was nervous, and I hoped it wouldn't show in his tee shot. In fact it was a bit weak, down the right side of the short par four. But his second shot was true, soaring high over the Swilken Burn, the narrow stream that flows just in front of the green, and ending up close enough for an easy two-putt par.

It was his tee shot on the second, another par four, 411 yards long, with out of bounds lurking left and right, that made me wonder if the gods of golf really do dwell in some ancient bunker on the Old Course. James has been showing promise for a year now, but the tee shot on two was in another dimension. It flew off his clubhead as if shot from a rifle, as straight as if pulled by some invisible string, climbing higher and higher into the azure Scottish sky, finally falling to earth and rolling to a stop some 290 yards from the tee. A sand wedge took him to the green, where he calmly stroked the ball into the hole for a birdie.

The short walk from the second green to the third tee is permanently printed in my mental memory book. Without even realizing it, he put an arm around my shoulders as we walked, and allowed me to put one of mine around his waist. Fifteen-year-old boys seldom let an adult get that cozy. We

smiled at each other in a way that only golfing partners understand.

That moment alone would have made the whole journey
worthwhile, but he parred the third hole, and continued to
play extremely well all through the front nine. He made the
turn in 41, and visions of—dared I even think it—a 79 danced
in both our heads, though not a word of such a dream was
spoken.

From the start, as we walked along under the warm sun, I
had been pointing out landmarks on the links to him. There
are two bunkers named Kruger and Mrs. Kruger (old man
Kruger of long ago had a terrible hook, so his is on the left
side; she was a slicer, so hers is on the right). And another
lady of the town, quite amply endowed, is immortalized by
two large humps called Mrs. Cheape's Bosom.

On the fourth hole, I showed him Cottage bunker, from
which Bobby Jones holed out a 160-yard shot in 1930. And
when we reached the eleventh, its green sitting high above the
River Eden, I cautioned him that the fairway gods do not always smile on even the best of us.

"Here," I said, pointing out the small bunker from which
Jones had emerged on his first British Open appearance, fum-
ing with rage, "here, the great Bobby Jones tore up his scorecard and stormed off the course, swearing that he would
never return. He did return, of course, won the Open here,
and later said that if he had to be put down in one place for
the rest of his life, to play golf on only one course, this would
be it."

As if to underline my caution, the wind freshened as we
walked onto the twelfth tee. It was dead against us, and had
that especially strong effect on the ball that only Scottish seaside winds seem to have. On the twelfth, James found a bunker for the first time. It was one of those little pot bunkers that
the British golf writer Bernard Darwin (nephew of the famous
naturalist Charles Darwin) once described as being only large
enough to accommodate "an angry man and his niblick."

James was learning that the Old Lady, as the locals call the course, does not bestow her favors easily for a complete round, even though she might welcome the newcomer as she had welcomed James on the front nine. I could see that my grandson's anger was rising, but he played on without cursing or club-throwing and made a six on the hole.

Quite suddenly, the air became chilly, as a frosty mist drifted in from the nearby beach. It wasn't a fog; more like a silvery, translucent patch of gauze, moving slowly across the fairway. I turned to my caddy, Gordon. "What the hell is that?" I asked.

"It's a haar, Jim," he said.

"A what?"

"A haar. *H-A-A-R.* On a warm day such as this, when the tide comes in, the cold water of the Firth washes over the hot sand of the beach and creates a kind of steam. Aye, it's a haar. Your grandson is experiencing just about everything the Old Course has to offer on his first time here."

So he was. And handling it very well.

It took all the self-control he could muster on the fourteenth, however. It is the longest hole at St. Andrews, and features one of the world's largest and most famous bunkers, named simply Hell. I told James how Arnold Palmer, when we were filming a head-to-head, winner-take-all match between him and Gary Player in 1961, drove into Hell, then put a large slice in his ball as he angrily hacked his way out. When Palmer took the ball out of play and tossed it aside, I furtively picked it up and slipped it into my bag, where it remains, a reminder that even Arnold Palmer, in his heyday, wasn't perfect.

The story gave little consolation to James when he, too, found his way into Hell, then hit a nice shot out, only to find that it had run into another almost invisible fairway bunker, a tiny one called, ominously, Grave. As the air continued to cool, and the haar obscured what lay ahead from view, my grandson was being tested, as many thousands before him, through the centuries, had been on the Old Course.

But he persevered, struggling manfully through fifteen

and sixteen. He tried to cut the corner on the renowned Road Hole, number seventeen, but instead hit a low hook that left him far from the green. When he finally reached the putting surface in three, my caddy murmured to me that he hoped James wouldn't putt into the bunker and eventually end up with an eleven, as the talented Japanese, Tommy Nakajima, had done some years before in the Open championship. Ever since, that bunker has been referred to as the Sands of Nakajima. The caddy was reminded of the incident because Nakajima, by coincidence, was playing a few groups behind us on this very day.

James avoided such a disaster and we moved to the final hole. As we did, the haar dissolved and the sun shone once again. We both knew, but didn't say, that he needed a par four or a bogie five to score under ninety, something he had not yet done on any course. I told him how Gary Player, on that day long ago of his match with Arnold Palmer, had hit a wild slice that caromed off Rusack's Hotel, where we were staying, and bounded back into the fairway.

James wasn't listening.

He hit a nice tee shot, far over the little footpath called Granny Clark's Wynd. We walked over the little stone footbridge that was built in Roman times, then stood and looked toward the green. The most important consideration for James was to put the ball over the deep depression in the front of the green called the Valley of Sin, yet not fly it over the green and out of bounds.

James selected his seven iron.

As on the first tee, he was conscious that a small group of spectators was gathered behind the green, watching each group play their final shots. This time, he blocked out the spectators and hit a solid shot to the middle of the putting surface. Two putts for a par gave him a round of 88, the best he had ever scored in his young life—and on the world's most famous course.

There were handshakes and smiles all around.

"What did you have, Pop?" James asked.

"Ninety-seven." I thought of that round I had played on the links thirty years before with Dave Marr. I had scored 88, the same as James's score this time.

Winning that pound from Dave was a career highlight, but not quite like this. Watching James mature as a golfer, and as a man, before my eyes made this the most exciting and rewarding day I had ever spent on a golf course.

As we walked off the green, carrying our bags back to the hotel, he said, "Pop, can't we play the Old Course again tomorrow?"

We couldn't. It had taken the intercession of Michael Bonallack himself, the secretary of the Royal and Ancient, to get us a tee time today.

At nine-thirty that evening, in the long Scottish twilight, he cajoled me into walking a half-mile to the town driving range, where we hit balls for an hour.

As we walked back to the hotel in the gathering darkness, my legs ached and I couldn't suppress a yawn. I was exhausted, but smiling.

Because I knew that we will return to the Old Course one day, James and I.

Maybe next time, I can shoot an 88.

The Thoroughbred

"They give their lives for our entertainment."
—Trainer Ron McAnally

On the first Saturday in May 1975, I stood awkwardly on the presentation stand in the infield at Churchill Downs. It was my first Kentucky Derby.

As the horses came on the track, the band struck up "My Old Kentucky Home" and the crowd of 113,324 began to sing. From my vantage point, I could take in the whole scene, from the head of the stretch to the clubhouse turn. Like everyone else, I choked up, unaccountably, as the singing swelled on the line, "Weep no more, my lady. Oh, weep no more today. We will sing one song for My Old Kentucky Home. . . ."

Through my binoculars, I looked up to the balcony where Margaret, Sean, and Mary stood, guests of John W. Galbreath, owner of two previous Kentucky Derby winners. I waved; they waved back and smiled. I noticed that Margaret was talking with Bing Crosby. I wondered if he was crooning along with everyone else. And then, I don't know, something came over me.

The colors of the jockeys' silks, the beauty of the thoroughbreds, the immense crowd, the singing, and the sight of the family up there enjoying themselves gave me a feeling that was at once exciting and, somehow, comforting.

"Life," I thought, "doesn't get any better than this."

At that moment, I became totally hooked on thoroughbred

racing, and hooked I have remained. I subscribe to what Red Smith, perhaps the greatest newspaper sportswriter of them all and my boyhood idol, once said about horse racing being his favorite sport.

"It's because there are more stories in horse racing than in any other sport."

And there are, as I found out over the years.

My interest in horse racing didn't actually start from scratch on that, my first Derby Day. Way back in 1947, my first TV assignment, as I've told you, had been a routine weekday race at Pimlico, the first program ever televised to the three or four hundred sets that existed in Baltimore. And H. L. Mencken had said I was awful. Well, I guess I was.

The following spring, I think I got a little better when I covered Citation's easy win in the Preakness. Having breezed to victory in the Kentucky Derby at odds of 2 to 5, he went off at 1 to 10 in the run for the black-eyed Susans, and justified those odds. Citation went on to win the Triple Crown, of course.

Years later, I sat with his jockey, Eddie Arcaro, and asked him how he ranked Citation. "Citation?" he said. "He was the greatest, that's all. At least, the greatest *I* ever rode."

And Eddie rode the best.

We did a local telecast of that 1948 Preakness while CBS covered the rest of the country. I have a sharp memory of the CBS announcer, purloined for the day from his job as racing columnist for the *New York Herald Tribune*. He was Joe H. Palmer, one of my personal newspaper idols. Joe had a rather forbidding look about him, so I didn't have the nerve to speak to him, but I did peek into his booth and see the tools he would use for the show. They sat on a small table with the microphone and a monitor—a beat-up pair of binoculars, a few scribbled notes, and a half-empty bottle of Jack Daniel's whiskey.

I covered racing at the New York tracks while at CBS in the 1950s, discovering Saratoga in the process. It was the same Joe Palmer who best described his love affair with that grand old place. Having discovered the upstate New York spa long before me, in 1936, he never got over his love affair with it:

"I rather think that the charm of Saratoga is that it represents, to those of us to whom racing is a way of life, something to which they may at need return. It is, of course, the oldest track in America, and its ways are old-fashioned ways. After eleven months of new-fashioned ways, it is as restful as old slippers, as quiet as real joy."

I kind of felt that way, too, when I visited the town. We had breakfast on the clubhouse lawn, and drove past the beautiful Victorian houses on upper Broadway. Our hotel was the famous, but fading, Grand Union, where we sat in the rockers on its immense porch overlooking Main Street. The Grand Union hotel is gone today, replaced, ironically, by a Grand Union supermarket.

Today, as we approach the millennium, race-goers still spread their camp chairs on the lawn, open their picnic baskets, and enjoy a day at the races, the way it used to be. They watch as the horses are saddled under the trees of the paddock area, townspeople of Saratoga and working guys up from the Big Apple rubbing shoulders with people named Phipps and Vanderbilt, Reynolds and Mellon.

These gentlemen of breeding and others of their ilk are still required to wear jackets and ties in the clubhouse. But there was an exception to that rule one sweltering August day. A few years ago, Alfred Gwynne Vanderbilt, one of the sport's most hallowed figures, actually took off his jacket, a silent signal that others might do the same. They did.

Saratoga endures, and the numbers tell why. Although it is a three-hour drive from New York City and the track has no air conditioning in the hottest month of summer, Saratoga outdraws in attendance, and has a larger total betting handle than, the New York City tracks, Aqueduct and Belmont.

And so, the old red and white wooden grandstands are still there, and the symbolic canoe floats in the infield lake, bearing the colors of the previous year's winner of the Travers Stakes, Saratoga's historic "Midsummer Derby."

But most of the time, I was covering horse racing in a much different environment.

One summer on *Wide World* in the 1960s, we did all the great races of Europe—the English Derby, the Grand National Steeplechase, Royal Ascot, the Irish Derby, and the Prix de L'Arc de Triomphe.

Royal Ascot, just a few miles from London, the most elegant of British race meetings, was literally a washout. Each morning, for the three days of the scheduled competition meeting, producer Barney Nagler, the one and only Eddie Arcaro, and I donned our formal clothes, complete with top hat. They were rented, as is the London custom, from a shop called Moss Brothers, known to Londoners as Moss Bross.

In the racing world, Arcaro is known simply as The Master. He won five Kentucky Derbies, six Preaknesses, and six Belmonts. He won the Wood Memorial, Aqueduct's traditional prep race for the Derby, eleven times. One year, because of the large number of entrants, the Wood was split into two divisions. Eddie won both. He is the only rider to have won the Triple Crown twice.

Each afternoon at Ascot, we stood in the royal enclosure in the pouring rain, waiting for some action. The only action we saw was Queen Elizabeth splashing down the track in her carriage, because the downpour was too much even for the English. The entire meeting was rained out.

I had expected Aintree, scene of the Grand National Steeplechase, to be a lovely sylvan retreat, sequestered on some nobleman's estate. Not so. It is a rather rundown ancient jumping course not far from the docks of Liverpool. In fact, we stayed in the Adelphi Hotel in Liverpool, the nearest decent lodgings.

Lurking in the near distance from the race course are two huge smokestacks, belching out a brownish haze much of the time. When we first went there, a Mrs. Topham, a former dancer on the London stage, had recently taken ownership upon the death of her wealthy husband. There were fears, unfulfilled in the long run, that she might turn the track into a housing development.

The Aintree course is the most difficult and dangerous in the steeplechasing world. Some of the jumps that are allowed at Aintree are disallowed at other courses because of their height, but still exist because of the race's fearful tradition.

One time, on the day before the Grand National, Arcaro and I stood at the famous jump called Becher's Brook, where the horses must clear a high hedge and a small stream before landing in an area six feet lower than their takeoff point.

Looking up at the hedge, Eddie said, "No sumbitch would ever get me to ride in this thing."

And then he told me of the time his daughter, attending an elegant private school in Virginia, kept begging him to come down and ride to the hounds with her. Eddie finally gave in, came to Virginia, put on the appropriate jacket and hard hat, and took off with his daughter. They were riding along nicely until Eddie spotted a stone wall just ahead.

Arcaro shouted, "Look out, honey, there's a stone wall ahead!"

She said, calmly, "I know, Daddy, that's what we're going to jump over."

"Maybe you," Eddie said, "but not me! I'll see you later."

The great Eddie Arcaro cantered briskly back to hunt headquarters for a calming Scotch.

Charlie Fenwick, a Marylander who rode to victory in the Grand National in the early eighties, told me, "Jim, I'm proud to have won it, but I would never have ridden in it a second time."

At Epsom Downs for the English Derby, we wandered through the common ground in what we would call the infield, sampling the jellied eels that are a tradition there and interviewing a famous tout, a large man of African descent who called himself Prince Monolulu and was garbed in the colorful robes of some kingdom he had invented for himself.

The Irish Derby that year was a particularly exciting race

because a horse owned by Bing Crosby won it. The Curragh, the famous race course in County Kildare, exploded into a riotous scene of adulation in the winner's circle. The Groaner, as Crosby liked to call himself, stood smiling, an Irish tweed hat on his head, a clay pipe in his mouth.

Someone in the crowd, in a loud voice, begged Crosby to sing a chorus of "Galway Bay."

Bing obliged, and there wasn't a dry Irish eye in the house. Nor a dry throat, either.

As for Paris and "The Arc," frankly, my clearest memory is of Margaret and me going to Mass at Sacré-Coeur on a beautiful, warm Sunday morning, and afterward buying a baguette, a chunk of cheese, and a bottle of red wine. We happily consumed them as we walked all the way down the hill, some two or three miles, from Montmartre to the Prince de Galles hotel downtown.

Longchamp, scene of the Arc de Triomphe race, would be in the top three for any competition to choose the world's most beautiful racetrack. (Hialeah, the lovely old Florida track, was consciously modeled after Longchamp.) The crowd is elegant, reminiscent of the racing scenes in *My Fair Lady* and *Gigi*.

But most of my favorite racetrack memories come out of homegrown soil. For example, the 1990 Kentucky Derby. That year, it was expected to be a battle between Summer Squall and Mister Frisky, the Puerto Rican wonder horse who was the spring's media darling. Instead, the most memorable scene of the day, and perhaps of the entire racing decade, was horse trainer Carl Nafzger describing the stretch run to his ninety-two-year-old owner, Frances Genter, whose vision was extremely limited. She was the widow of the man who invented the pop-up toaster, and had owned quality race horses for half a century, but had never had one even reach the starting gate in the Derby.

But here she was, at last, with a horse in America's biggest race, albeit a lightly regarded colt named Unbridled, who went off at odds of 11 to 1.

So the whole country was watching and listening as her colt, Unbridled, passed Summer Squall, second choice in the betting at 2 to 1, at the quarter pole, and Nafzger shouted in her ear (she was also quite deaf), "We've got the lead, Mrs. Genter, we've got the lead!" She stood, squeezing her hands together, then smiled as Nafzger, carried away with emotion, shouted, "We won, we won! Oh, I love you, Mrs. Genter!"

And he crushed her with a hug.

Somehow, the small, frail woman made her way to the presentation stand. I didn't realize until I watched the tape of the race later that I also gave her a hug when I was interviewing her.

The fact that trainer Nafzger was wearing a microphone was a tribute to the expertise and foresight of our producer, Curt Gowdy, Jr., and our associate producer, Steve Naples. Long shot though Unbridled was, Nafzger was the only trainer they had decided to put a mike on that day.

As I said, I have been stationed on that spot in the infield at Churchill Downs ever since 1975, watching every winning owner, trainer, and jockey make their way up those three small wooden steps to the platform. Only the governor of the state, track president Tom Meeker, and I know in advance that we will be in that special spot. Governors have come and gone, but I have been fortunate enough to keep my place.

Lucky newcomer or three-time champion, without exception the winning owners, trainers, and jockeys have a glazed, unbelieving look on their face as they mount the platform and face the crowd and cameras.

Jockey Chris McCarron told me that he had always thought winning the Derby would be the climax of his career and would be enough to savor for a lifetime. "But when I won on Alysheba in 1987," he said, "I thought, 'Gee, this is even more fun than I thought it would be. I want to do it again!' And when I won on Go for Gin in 1994, I still wasn't satisfied."

Another one who sought satisfaction at Churchill Downs was the legendary trainer Charlie Whittingham. He had been training horses since the 1930s, and had come to Louisville earlier in his career. But after a bad ninth-place finish with

Divine Comedy in 1960, he swore that he would never become involved in another Derby unless he thought he had a real, solid chance. And here he was, twenty-six years later, at the age of seventy-three, sure he had a chance to win the thing.

All week long in the mornings on the backstretch, Whittingham was telling the press with quiet conviction, "My horse, Ferdinand, will win the Derby. I tell you now, go to the windows." Apparently, neither the media crowd nor their readers believed him, because Ferdinand, in winning the Derby, paid the neat price of $37.40. And it made Whittingham the oldest trainer ever to win the Run for the Roses.

I saw the tears in his eyes now as he stood on the victory stand with his old friend and drinking pal, Bill Shoemaker, who had ridden Ferdinand and was now, at fifty-four, the oldest jockey ever to win the big one. Even after all Whittingham's triumphs and after three previous Derby winners for Shoemaker, this race had a special meaning for the two men.

It was a particularly notable comeback for Shoemaker, because the whispers on the West Coast were, "If you watch closely, you'll see he doesn't make the bold moves anymore." On this Derby Day, not only had the Shoe won, but he had seized the race with the boldest and most dangerous of moves in the stretch, darting through an opening that was only there for a second or two.

As for Charlie, I asked him, now that he had won the big one, when he would retire. He made the sign of the cross in the air with his hand as he answered, "When the man stands over me and says, 'Ashes to ashes and dust to dust . . .' "

As for Shoemaker, winner of more races than any other rider in history, he simply turned to me and, like an apprentice who has just won his first race, asked, "Jim, is it okay if I say hello to my little daughter?"

Today, Whittingham, who won the Derby again in 1989 with Sunday Silence, trains on at the age of eighty-four. Shoemaker, a quadriplegic since the automobile accident that paralyzed him, also became a trainer, appearing at the barn each morning in his wheelchair, hoping that one day he could say that he and Johnny Longden were the only men to ever win the Derby as both a jockey and a trainer. Didn't happen. Bill Shoemaker retired in 1997.

Ten years earlier, Jack Van Berg, the winningest major track trainer in history, was standing beside me with tears streaming down his tough racetrack face following Alysheba's victory. After some five thousand winners at tracks across America, he finally had *the* winner, and his thoughts were of his father, Marion. "He taught me everything I know," Jack said.

It almost seems that the more talented and successful the winners have been, the more humble they are in victory at Louisville. When Laffit Pincay Jr., the hardest-riding stretch driver of them all, won in 1984 on Swale, he confessed on the victory stand to having prayed before the race.

"Do you mind telling me what you prayed?" I asked him.

"Not at all," he said. "I said, 'God, I have told you before that I would never pray to you for winning a race. But if today, you could give me just one little push . . .' "

He smiled, and the world smiled with him.

If anyone seemed immune to the ecstatic moment of victory at the Kentucky Derby, it was the most successful trainer of his era, D. Wayne Lukas. He had won the great race in 1988 with the filly Winning Colors (becoming only the third of her sex to win in 114 runnings of the Derby) and again in 1995 with Thunder Gulch. Even on those exciting occasions, he was poised, rather cocky, and constantly aware of his personal public relations image.

But in the fall of 1993, his son and assistant, Jeff, was trampled and nearly killed by a two-year-old named Tabasco Cat, owned by a seventy-five-year-old businessman named W. T. "Bill" Young.

Wayne sat at his son's side while Jeff lay in a month-long coma. In time, the danger of death finally passed and Jeff began a slow and painful recovery.

When I saw Wayne early the following spring, he seemed a changed man. He was quieter, less quick to anger, more philosophical. And suddenly, tragedy turned to incredible success on the racetrack. Tabasco Cat, the very colt who had trampled Jeff, won the Preakness and the Belmont that spring.

The next year, Lukas took the Triple Crown with two different horses, Thunder Gulch in the Derby and Belmont, Timber Country in the Preakness.

In 1996, Wayne Lukas was going after his sixth Triple Crown victory in a row. His horse was a colt named Grindstone.

Ironically, both were owned by Bill Young. He started two colts, Editor's Note and Grindstone. The Kentuckian had been almost as stricken as Lukas three years earlier, because it was his colt, Tabasco Cat, who had trampled the trainer's son.

For a decade, Young had poured many millions into racing with the specific hope of one day winning the Derby in his home state. Despite a long string of Derby Day disappointments, he had stayed with his trainer. In fact, he told me that if he couldn't have Lukas for his trainer, he would drop out of the sport.

And here, in '96, came one of the closest finishes in Derby history.

Grindstone had been considered the lesser of Young's two-horse entry. With a half-mile to go, Grindstone was far behind, in fourteenth place out of the nineteen horses in the field. Then, jockey Jerry Bailey began to weave him skillfully through the crowd. By the top of the stretch, he had advanced to fourth place, but Cavonnier, under Chris McCarron, had put on his own charge, coming from fifth place at the half-mile pole to take the lead at this point.

As Grindstone charged on the outside, our race caller, Dave Johnson, the best in the business, shouted his trademark phrase with added conviction: "And down the stretch they come!!"

The race was a classic now. Two great jockeys were driving two indomitable colts, Grindstone and Cavonnier, as 135,000 voices reached a crescendo. And they hit the wire together.

"Too close to call!" Johnson said, sounding as exhausted as the horses, the jockeys, and the crowd all must have felt.

After what seemed an interminable wait, the photo showed Grindstone the winner by a nose, in the closest Derby finish since Tomy Lee had edged Sword Dancer thirty-seven years before.

On the victory stand, I asked Wayne Lukas for his comments, expecting his usual poised and calculated statements. Instead, he choked up and the tears came.

"This one is special, Jim," he said. "This one is for Mr. Young. He's given so much to this sport and been so patient waiting for this day. . . ."

Yes, the winner's circle at Churchill Downs seems to plumb the depths of people's emotions more than any other sporting moment that I know.

With rare exceptions.

Trainer Johnny Campo was something else. Campo, a rotund, tough-talking New Yorker, and the horse's owner, the patrician Thomas Mellon Evans, of Virginia, seemed an unlikely pair to be joined in victory. But there they stood together in 1981 with their winner, Pleasant Colony. Evans made a soft, sportsmanlike comment, then I turned to Campo and asked him how he accounted for the victory. Without a pause, he snarled from the corner of his mouth, "Because I'm a good horse trainer, pal, and don't you forget it!"

He laughed, and loud, but I don't think he was kidding.

In 1980, the filly Genuine Risk became only the second of her sex ever to win the Derby, and she caused her trainer to be the only person I've ever seen embarrassed by victory.

Owner Bert Firestone had been attending the yearling sales at Keeneland, the famous Kentucky horse sales venue, when his fifteen-year-old son, Matthew, came up, begging him to come look at a certain horse. Rather than continue to be distracted, the father finally said, "Matthew, you go bid on her yourself. But don't go any higher than thirty thousand." Matthew got the horse for the price, and it was, of course, Genuine Risk.

When the filly finished a fast-closing third running against males in New York's famous pre-Derby race, the Wood Memorial, I asked trainer LeRoy Jolley if he would have to consider running her against the boys in the Derby. "It's no problem for me, Jim," he said, emphatically. "We're not going to Louisville. Period."

Owner Firestone, however, thought differently, and so did young Matthew. Reluctantly, Jolley entered the horse in the Derby. The bettors seemed to agree with the trainer, sending Genuine Risk off at odds of 13 to 1, even though she had heavy support from women all over the country. After all, in the 105 previous Derbies, only one filly, Regret in 1915, had ever won the race.

But jockey Jacinto Vasquez believed in the filly, letting her coast along in the middle of the pack until the far turn. Then he turned her loose. She took the lead at the quarter-mile pole and held on as they flew down the stretch. Vasquez kept her mind on business with one stroke of the whip right-handed and another six from the left side. She easily staved off the late charge of Rumbo and made racing history.

On the winner's platform after she won, I reminded LeRoy of his statement that they wouldn't be here on Derby Day. He blushed slightly, smiled, and said, "Well, Jim, I guess I've learned that you have to keep an open mind on these things."

One of the odd and sort of splendid things about horsemen is that they never seem to retire. Jockeys ride into their fifties, trainers and owners go on until the end. In his nineties, the Maryland Hall of Fame trainer Henry Clark still has the same stalls in Barn AA at Pimlico that he has used for well over fifty years.

In 1984, Woody Stephens, then seventy-one years old, was in a Louisville hospital during Derby week. Prayers were being offered and obits prepared for the veteran trainer. But on the afternoon of the race, he shocked us all by appearing on the arm of his doctor to sit in the director's room to watch his colt Swale run, and win, the Derby. And there was Woody, hugging the doctor on national TV. He actually made it to the winner's circle, did a nice interview with me, then went back to his hospital bed.

The following year, still fighting illness, he won his fourth consecutive Belmont Stakes, and the year after that, his fifth straight, setting a record that may never be broken.

In the spring of 1997, at age eighty-four, he announced his retirement. But on the day before that year's Belmont Stakes, there was Woody, sending another horse to the post. In the fall of the year, he retired again. Or so he said.

Watching the horses work out early one morning at the farm of my trainer and friend, Billy Boniface, I asked him the $64 question.

"Billy, I've noticed that horse people seem to live to great ages. Why is that?"

He didn't hesitate in his answer.

"That's easy, Jim," he said. "You have to stick around until you get the *big* horse."

There's more truth than hyperbole in that statement.

Herman Cohen, co-owner of the Pimlico track with his younger brother Ben, said he was about to retire. I asked him what he was going to do with his time. "I'm going into breeding," he said. He was ninety-five years old.

☆

That feeling of eternal hope is strengthened by the fact that new stars emerge from nowhere almost every year, and race-trackers down on their luck suddenly come upon that one big horse of which Billy Boniface spoke.

In 1988, Louis Roussel III, then the owner of the Fair Grounds track in New Orleans, appeared in Louisville as the owner-trainer of a Kentucky Derby hopeful named Risen Star. When I saw him one morning on the backside, he took me into the horse's stall to get a good look at the animal, who was big, powerful, and beautiful. Trainers don't normally do that with Kentucky Derby contenders, but Louie was not your ordinary trainer.

I told Louie that I thought he was a track owner, not a trainer.

"You're right," he said. "I'm sure that if Risen Star could speak, he would say, 'Please, take me to Charlie Whittingham.'"

He told me that the horse's name had given him a religious feeling, and so he'd promised to give a share of its earnings to the Little Sisters of the Poor.

Another man leaning against the wall of the stall that morning was Ronnie Lamarque, a wealthy New Orleans automobile dealer, co-owner of the horse, and a frustrated singer.

"I've written a song about Risen Star," he said. "When we win the Derby, will you let me sing it on national TV?"

Of course, I said blithely.

All week long, Roussel, a slight, black-haired man with the pencil-line mustache of a Louisiana riverboat gambler, was pessimistic about his horse's chances. Several times, he said he thought he would scratch him from the Derby.

He didn't, and the colt, despite a bad trip in the race, finished with a rush to take third place.

Louie was still pessimistic as he moved his charge to Pimlico for the Preakness. Again, he talked of scratching the horse, and only the prodding of his girlfriend and Lamarque seemed to make him move forward to race day.

Our producer that year, Mike Pearl, knew a good story when he saw one, so he had a live camera installed at the home of the Little Sisters of the Poor, the possible beneficiaries of a Risen Star victory. Pearl's enterprise paid off, because Risen Star won the Preakness and the country saw the Little Sisters smiling softly, as if they knew all along that God—and Mr. Roussel—would take care of it.

As we stood beneath the weather vane on the winner's cupola, I invited Ronnie Lamarque to sing his song—which he did, to the tune of the classic "Way Down Yonder in New Orleans".

> Way down yonder in New Orleans,
> Risen Star is the king of kings.

He's the talk of the town, man.
You know what I mean.
That great big filly with all her colors [Winning
Colors, the Derby-winning filly],
She doesn't stand a chance.
Star's gonna win the Preakness Stakes.
He's gonna win the Belmont, too.
For the folks down yonder in New Orleans.

Three weeks later, Risen Star won the Belmont by fifteen lengths. Only his daddy, the great Secretariat, had distanced his rivals by more in the Belmont—thirty-one lengths, in one of the greatest performances in racing history. Ronnie Lamarque sang again, this time without asking permission, to wrap up a wonderfully entertaining and unexpected story. Except for his bad luck in the Derby, Risen Star might well have become the twelfth winner of the Triple Crown.

☆

Never has there been a more enthusiastic, or more sportsmanlike, owner than Bob Lewis, whose colt, Silver Charm, also came so close to winning the Triple Crown, in 1997. Lewis was the eternal optimist, constantly being restrained all through the endless spring by his young, prematurely white-haired trainer, Bob Baffert, a more superstitious type.

Baffert had good reason to be cautious after his experience the year before. In his debut at Churchill Downs in 1996, he'd felt certain that his horse, Cavonnier, had beaten Grindstone to the wire, and had started a celebration that proved to be short-lived.

He learned his lesson.

So, when Silver Charm won the Derby the following year, and he and Free House crossed the line like a team in the Preakness, Baffert wasn't jumping to any conclusions.

But Bob Lewis was. "We did it! I tell you, Bob, we won! I know we did! I'm certain of it!" cried Lewis.

Baffert wagged his head negatively.

"I don't know," he said. "I don't know. Maybe not."

Where joy had turned to sadness the year before, now caution turned to joy as the result was posted. Loser by a nose the year before, Baffert was the winner by a head this time.

Now, the colt had a chance for the fabled Triple Crown, if he could just withstand the mile-and-a-half ordeal of the Belmont Stakes.

Bob Lewis, a self-made man who loves to share his rewards with his friends, chartered a 737 to bring a hundred or so pals to New York for the race. He and Baffert—the ebullient owner and the now confident, wisecracking trainer—were a media delight, one more obliging than the other, neither making any effort to conceal his delight over the events of this dreamlike spring. The sport had given to them, and they were trying to give back.

When Silver Charm lost the Belmont by the narrowest of margins to Touch Gold, the two men showed that they could accept defeat as well as exult in victory. There were no recriminations or alibis.

☆

Horsemen are working stiffs, with long hours and little guaranteed reward. And that goes for trainers and grooms, hotwalkers and jockeys. The jockeys' hours may not be as long as the others', but they are among the bravest people in sport. Danger is their companion in every race, as they maneuver animals that weigh a half-ton through serious traffic at thirty-five miles an hour, knowing that the horse runs on cannon bones (shin bones) that are thinner than those of a man, and that might give way at any moment.

They ride hurt, in one way or the other, much of the time, protected only by a helmet and, recently, by a light flak jacket that already has prevented a number of serious injuries—or even death. Still, the last statistics I read on the subject showed, among the living, forty-seven permanently disabled jockeys.

The stereotypical jockey in the movies is a wizened, laconic character who speaks in ominous monotones. There are such riders, but I have found the men (and women) I interview to be professional, friendly, and surprisingly articulate, particularly when taking me through the rerun of a race that they have won just minutes before.

I have had usually knowledgeable sports fans argue with me that jockeys are not athletes, that all they have to do is sit on a horse and steer it. I always suggest that they come with me to the jocks' room and see these people in the buff. They are lean, but hard-muscled, as fit as any athlete you might find.

Dr. Robert Kerlan, the famous West Coast sports doctor, once administered a test of strength and coordination to athletes from a number of sports (baseball, football, tennis—the lot). The winner of the overall competition was Bill Shoemaker, all tough, sinewy ninety-five pounds of him. Shoe could bury the average weekend athlete at golf or tennis, too.

An ability to bounce back quickly from injuries or simply to endure them is vital for a jockey. With no guaranteed annual wage, his income simply stops when he is not riding. And often, owners find another rider during the injured jock's downtime, then stay with the new one.

In the autumn of 1986, Chris McCarron broke a leg in five places during a multihorse pileup and was written off as a participant in the following spring's Kentucky Derby. He not only recovered in time, but guided Alysheba to victory.

Even the most successful and wealthiest of jockeys constantly fight their worst enemy—weight. As they ride eight or nine races a day and often compete on two coasts of the country within a twenty-four-hour time span, they must somehow manage to keep their weight down and at the same time maintain their strength.

Sometimes, as a promising teenage jockey matures, his body simply becomes too big and he loses the weight battle, and his profession. Other young riders, finding themselves with a good deal of money after early success, fall into the drug trap, convincing themselves that cocaine dulls the appetite for food, or at least that it is a way of finding some sort of pleasure without eating. Soon, they are failing drug tests, getting suspended, and sliding down the scale to obscurity.

One of the saddest cases is that of Ronnie Franklin. One day back in the seventies, he appeared at the Pimlico stable gate, a pale, shy, sixteen-year-old kid saying that he wanted to be a jockey. He had no experience and his knowledge of the sport was nil. A neighbor, noticing his small size, had asked him one day if he'd ever thought of becoming a jockey.

That was all.

The stable gate guard directed him to the barn of Bud Delp, thinking that the trainer might have use for an extra hot-walker (a part-time employee who simply walks a horse around in a circle for a half hour after a race or a workout until the animal cools off). Delp brought him along, from hot-walker to groom to exercise rider to jockey. At the age of nineteen, Franklin suddenly found himself on the back of a super horse named Spectacular Bid, winning both the Derby and the Preakness, in his hometown of Baltimore. He was on top of the racing world.

But not for long.

When Spectacular Bid lost in the Belmont Stakes, Franklin blamed himself. Trainer Delp blamed the loss on a safety pin he had found in the colt's hoof that morning, saying his great regret was having told Franklin about the pin.

"I know he was thinking about the pin during the race, and that cost us," Delp told *Wide World* in 1997. His eyes misted up as he added, "I have tapes of all Spectacular Bid's races, and I look at them a lot. But I've never looked at the tape of the Belmont—and I never will."

At the suggestion of "friends," Ronnie Franklin tried cocaine.

Seventeen years later, *Baltimore Sun* columnist John Steadman found him in a recovery house in Baltimore trying to beat his cocaine addiction. After a number of attempted comebacks, each one foiled by cocaine binges, he was banned from even *attending* the Preakness.

"With drugs," he told Steadman, "you get so low you can't

go any lower, except living on the streets. I don't want to wind up in some alley."

Trainer Delp spoke with him in the late fall of 1997. At that time, he was again in a halfway house, but had no desire to get back into racing.

"Was he good?" Bud Delp said. "Jim, he could have been as good as anybody in the sport."

I found myself fortunate enough to work with two of the greatest jockeys of all time, Eddie Arcaro and Bill Hartack, the only two riders to have won five Kentucky Derbies. They were very good colleagues in commentary, and both were fascinating companions, but their personalities were totally different.

Eddie Arcaro was outgoing, pleasantly profane, and one of the greatest storytellers I have known. He loved to talk about the old days in racing. He told me about the time in New York, riding in a race with another jock he heartily disliked, when he knocked the guy off his horse, over the fence, and into the infield. He was called before the New York stewards, who were led by the formidable Marshall Cassidy. Eddie was sternly told by Cassidy, "Mr. Arcaro, it is the belief of this panel that you intentionally tried to injure another rider."

"Injure him?" said Eddie. "Hell, Mr. Cassidy, I tried to kill that son of a bitch!"

Whereupon Arcaro was suspended for a year, during which time he presumably learned to keep his temper a bit more under control.

He told me of the time he almost drowned on the race course. Thrown from his mount on a muddy track, he fell face forward into a puddle, unconscious.

"When I woke up, I was breathing water and for a moment, I couldn't move. I remember exactly what I thought. I thought, 'I've been riding these ornery creatures for twenty-five years; now I'm going to drown and some blond, curly-haired son of a bitch is going to marry my wife Ruth and get all my money!' "

Then he laughed the joyous Arcaro laugh.

Make no mistake. Although he liked to tell those self-deprecating stories, Eddie Arcaro was not called "The Master" for nothing. In my time, he was the greatest of all jockeys. Alas, he passed away in November of 1997, at age eighty-two.

☆

Despite a career only a hair less impressive than Arcaro's, Bill Hartack has suffered from bad press, even in the long years of his retirement. This is a man who won five Kentucky Derbies in only thirteen attempts. It took the great Arcaro twenty-one tries to win the same number.

Hartack was dedicated to his craft, gave his best every race, and deserves to be written and talked about as a true legend. But he was sometimes an officious kind of guy, too haughty for some tastes, and the result was bad press all through his career.

He hated, for instance, to be referred to as "Willie" Hartack. "Look," he told the members of the press one day, "my name is Bill, so don't call me Willie." From that day forward, at least one writer invariably referred to him in print as "Bill 'Don't Call Me Willie' Hartack." It was an unfair rap, but it stuck.

Years later, I asked him about it. "Jim," he said, "the way I looked at it, those guys were disturbing me at my work, and my work was what mattered to me."

Bill Hartack is incapable of dissembling. He speaks the truth as he sees it, regardless of the consequences. And there are those who honor him for that. I am among them.

One sunny winter day at Gulfstream Park, he and I were walking among the railbirds when an unshaven old fan, incongruously wearing an overcoat under the Florida sun, called out, "I know you, Hartack. I remember you—the only honest jock who ever lived."

Bill called out, "Thanks," then turned to me and said quietly, "I wasn't the *only* honest jock, but I *was* honest." I'm sure that he would settle for a tombstone inscription that reads simply, "Bill Hartack, an honest jockey."

Unfortunately, Hartack harbored some ancient grudge

against Eddie Arcaro, so they didn't communicate. When I asked Hartack about it, he wouldn't tell me the reason. And Arcaro said he didn't know what it was about.

It's a shame, because I can think of few pleasanter ways I might have spent an afternoon than listening to Eddie and Bill talk over the old days like two aging generals who'd once met in battle.

THE McKAY RATINGS—JOCKEYS

If their careers had come a bit later, Arcaro and Hartack would most certainly have been at the top of my list of the riders I consider the best that I've seen. But I only covered that one Preakness in 1948 that Eddie rode in, and saw Hartack in action almost as seldom. Still, I have watched and commented on most of the best of my time, and here is how I list them, considering not only their achievements, but their personalities and their impact on the sport:

1. Bill Shoemaker

He was so small at birth in a chilly house in Fabens, Texas, that his grandmother put him in the oven to keep him warm overnight. He never grew to be very big—just four feet, eleven inches and ninety-five pounds—but he was a perfectly formed man, and a strong one. Smart, too.

He rode in twenty-six Kentucky Derbies over the course of thirty-six years, the first in 1952, and his last in 1988.

His first Derby victory, at the age of twenty-three, was on Swaps in 1955; his last, at the age of fifty-four, came on Ferdinand thirty-one years later.

He won four Derbies, two Preaknesses, five Belmonts, and eight Santa Anita Derbies. He was the leading rider at Santa Anita for seventeen straight years.

He had more than his share of injuries. In January 1968,

the horse he was riding fell over another and Bill suffered a badly broken leg. A pin was inserted from his hip through his thigh and he was out of action for a year. On the day of his return, he won his first three races.

Despite other injuries, including a broken pelvis, he still managed to win 8,833 races, more than any other rider.

Was he perfect? Not quite. In 1957, he misjudged the finish line in the Kentucky Derby, pulled up Gallant Man too soon, and cost the horse the race.

In 1982, he flew to Pimlico on a red-eye flight to ride the favorite, Linkage, in the Preakness for trainer Henry Clark. Clark had passed up the Derby in order to make his big try in the Preakness on his home track. His grandfather had won the race long ago and Henry wanted, more than anything in his career, to duplicate his ancestor's feat.

But a local teenage jockey named Cowboy Jack Kaenel had ridden the day before at Pimlico and knew that horses on the rail had won most of the races. Kaenel sprinted out to a big lead on Aloma's Ruler, stuck to the rail, and beat Shoemaker.

If a small blemish is said to enhance a woman's beauty, then, I suppose, those two mistakes only add to the luster of Bill Shoemaker's record.

Bill rode in his first race at Golden Gate Fields in 1949 and his last at Santa Anita on February 3, 1990, forty-one years later. We were there for his last. In our interview after the race (he lost on the favorite), he had no deathless phrases to leave behind. He was the Shoe, as always—tight-lipped, impassive, polite. But I may have been the only one close enough to him to see that his eyes were filled with tears.

One Saturday, I stood and talked to Bill for a while after the races at Santa Anita. He was dapper as ever in a glen plaid suit, starting his new career as a trainer. The danger of the racetrack was behind him and the future looked bright.

Just a few days later, on April 8, 1991, driving to a restaurant to meet a friend for dinner after a golf game, he reached for his newly installed car phone. As he looked down, his vehicle slipped off the road and down an embankment. In a terrible irony, Bill Shoemaker, who had overcome every bit of bad luck that had come to him on the race course for forty-one years, was paralyzed from the neck down.

But when I think of Bill today, I always think of that magic moment in the 1986 Derby, when he silenced the critics with that daring, split-second move between horses as he rode Ferdinand to victory at the age of fifty-four.

To me, that was his golden moment.

2. Steve Cauthen

I would expect argument on this one, since the bulk of Steve's career was spent in England. But Cauthen had an impact on his sport at the age of eighteen that was comparable to Tiger Woods's impact on golf in the winter of 1997. He won the Triple Crown on Affirmed in 1978, each time outbattling Jorge Velasquez on Alydar. He was a kid not long out of his little hometown in Kentucky, good-looking, with a shy smile and a quiet manner that warmed the hearts of everyone who watched him.

The great Triple Crown champions like Citation and Secretariat were a cut above their opponents and breezed to victory in the classics. Not Affirmed. Alydar, under the experienced, canny Velasquez, challenged Cauthen and Affirmed all the way. Had the Kid and his mount not stood in his path, Alydar almost certainly would have won the Triple Crown himself. The margins of victory got closer and closer in each race that spring. Somehow the Preakness stands out in my mind—this eighteen-year-old kid having the poise and the courage to stave off the challenge of Alydar and Velasquez and win by a neck.

This was a boy wise and brave far beyond his years.

When weight became a problem, he moved his tack to England, where jockeys are allowed to be heavier. With the swift adjustment that young people can often make, he not only started winning races, but within a couple of years had unconsciously acquired a slight British accent. He became the champion jockey of England, and the only rider ever to win both the English Derby and the Kentucky Derby.

When his career ended, he returned to his hometown with his wife, a fellow Kentuckian, bought a farm, and settled down.

He was with us one year on ABC, and was just as pleasant to work with as Arcaro and Hartack. One of my most treasured mementos is a head-on photograph he gave me of Alydar and Affirmed charging down the stretch, signed by him and Jorge Velasquez.

His career was short compared with Shoemaker's, but full of explosive achievements that will be remembered as long as the sport endures.

3. Angel Cordero Jr.

In New York, where he spent most of his career, Cordero was booed more often than he was cheered by the fickle and critical New York crowds (remember, a great jockey still only wins about 20 percent of his races). He rode hard, and at times, some thought, crossed over the line between smart and reckless, dangerous riding.

Unfortunately, he will be remembered almost as much for a single controversy as he will for his great achievements. The incident came in the Preakness of 1980. The filly, Genuine Risk, was the sentimental favorite of the nation after her startling victory in the Kentucky Derby. As they turned into the stretch, Genuine Risk, ridden by Jacinto Vasquez, and Codex, ridden by Cordero, appeared to bump into each other, and Codex went on to win the race.

But what, exactly, had happened? The objection lodged by Vasquez was disallowed, while the crowd booed. This wasn't just a case of one man's version against another's. This, in the eyes of the average viewer, was male picking on female, the town bully beating up on a poor little girl.

Tabloids had a field day, with headlines like DID CORDERO MUG THE FILLY?

Bert and Diana Firestone, the owners of Genuine Risk, took the matter to the Maryland Racing Commission. For a month, the media debated the issue.

Our videotapes of the moment were shown hundreds of times across the country. Eventually, the tapes were played for the benefit of the commission as it considered the matter. TV was playing a key role in deciding the result of a major sports event, as it had in the Grenoble Winter Olympics twelve years before.

The decision was that no foul had been committed, and the result stood: Codex the winner. But Cordero is still considered by many to be a man who took unfair advantage of a female. It doesn't make sense, but the label has stuck.

Let us not forget, however, the positive side. Cordero not only won thousands of races, he was also one of the most colorful personalities in the game. Even as the New York crowd might be booing him, he would make his traditional high leap out of the saddle after each race, smiling his broad smile, large teeth gleaming in the sun.

His daring riding style was evident on the track. But those who thought that was the total Cordero were uninformed. He was a student of the sport, watching tapes at home in the evening of the races he had ridden each day, checking his technique and making notes on other horses, tucking them in his brain for races yet to come. He won three Kentucky Derbies, equaling the record of Isaac Murphy and Earl Sande and trailing only Arcaro, Hartack, and Shoemaker.

His 1985 Kentucky Derby ride on Spend a Buck was vintage Cordero. Utilizing the colt's great early speed, he rushed him to the front, got the pace that he wanted, and led the favorite, Chief's Crown, by as much as six lengths on the backstretch. By the time they turned for home, the lead was still a comfortable five lengths and the issue was no longer in doubt. He won by almost six lengths.

Cordero had "stolen" the race.

To me, Derby and other Triple Crown wins are very important in judging a rider's place in history. Jockeys who say that the Derby is just, after all, another race are like golfers who say that the major tournaments are just four stops on the tour.

Look at the record in any sport and you will see that the great events are most often won by the great athletes.

Angel Cordero Jr. belongs in that group.

4. Laffit Pincay Jr.

In his heyday, no one could beat him in a stretch drive. Margaret and I were the beneficiaries of his talent one day at Pimlico. Margaret's two-year-old colt, Sean's Ferrari, had been entered in a Maryland Million $100,000 race by our trainer, Billy Boniface. We didn't understand why—in a tune-up race ten days before the Million, the colt had finished fifth.

"Just what he needed," Billy said. Trainers live in a mystical world of their own, from which they utter phrases like "He couldn't get a hold of the track," "Something spooked him on the far turn," and "Just what he needed" after a horse finishes fifth.

The Maryland Million was an event that grew from a conversation Margaret and I had on our way back from the first Breeders' Cup—the $10 million day for the world's best horses, conceived by John Gaines of Kentucky, that had been contested at Hollywood Park. It had been more than a day of racing. It was a scene of beauty, glamour, and competition at the highest level. As Margaret and I left the racetrack, we were walking just behind Cary Grant, Gregory Peck, and Fred Astaire.

On the plane going back East, I had finished whatever I'd been reading and was really just making conversation when I said, "Wasn't that a marvelous day? Wouldn't it be great if we could have something like that on a smaller scale in Maryland?"

I should have remembered that my wife never takes anything as "just conversation"; that, she believes, is a waste of time. She thought for about ten seconds, then said, "That's a terrific idea. Why don't you do it?"

Well, the steps from that moment to the first Maryland Million were tortuous and difficult. But it happened. And now, here was Billy Boniface saying that we should actually race Margaret's two-year-old, Sean's Ferrari, in the second renewal of the event.

Sean (the correct Irish spelling of the name pronounced "Shawn") was more of a family pet than a race horse—particularly, we felt, after his fifth-place finish. The name came from a family joke. Since he had been about ten years old, our son, Sean, had been begging me to buy a Ferrari automobile, which I neither wanted nor could afford. So one day two years earlier, when Margaret and our son were leaning on the pasture fence at our farm, looking out at the baby horses, Margaret said, "Sean, see that one over there with the white blaze on his face? That's your Ferrari."

So a name was born.

The night before the race, as we were trying to go to sleep, unsuccessfully, Margaret said, "Jim, I'm afraid this is going to be embarrassing. Billy is always optimistic, but after that fifth-place finish . . ."

"Honey," I said, "look at it this way. Your colors [pale blue and white, the colors of Margaret's alma mater, the College of Notre Dame of Maryland] will be in a stakes race for the first time. Billy has brought in the great Laffit Pincay from California to ride all of his horses tomorrow. Just having Pincay on your horse is an honor. And who knows, maybe he'll finish third, and that's not bad in a big race."

The smart money seemed to agree with Margaret: Sean's Ferrari went off at 17 to 1. Pincay kept him back of the leaders but well placed in the early going. At the far turn, he was fifth—but then, fifth was his normal finish. Not this time. Pincay went to work on him and as they headed for home, he was third.

"Margaret," I shouted, "look! Look! He's third! . . . No, my

God, he's second . . . and gaining!" At this point, so help me, Margaret covered her eyes with her hands.

"I can't watch," she said. "You tell me what happens!"

I gave her a shouted, totally unprofessional call as they neared the wire. "We've got the lead! We're first! We're first! Now the favorite, King's Snow, is charging! It's only those two. The rest of the field is out of it!"

I was jumping up and down. My sunglasses fell off. "Here's the finish! Oh my God, we've won! I'm sure of it. We've won!"

Margaret uncovered her eyes. They were full of tears.

"Are you sure?" she asked.

"Well, almost." Now, I was afraid of disappointing her.

It was a photo finish between our horse and King's Snow. There was a race within the race. Kent Desormeaux, a tough young rider on the Maryland circuit, was determined to beat Pincay and prove that he was worthy of moving up to the big time, which he did not long after this race.

But it was our day.

After long minutes of waiting while the stewards examined the picture, Sean's Ferrari was declared the winner. It was the thrill of our racing lives, and Laffit Pincay had virtually carried that horse down the stretch.

When we were interviewed on ESPN, I said, "If that horse never wins another race, he owes us nothing." He took me at my word, and never won another race. His achievement on the turf was confined to that one day—the day the strong hands of Laffit Pincay Jr. drove him to victory.

Naturally, that is my favorite memory of Pincay, but his achievements on the national scene are the stuff of legend— his Derby win on Swale, his three straight Belmont victories, his six Santa Anita Derbies, six Santa Anita Handicaps, his seven wins in Breeders' Cup races. He has received the Eclipse award as the nation's leading jockey five times, more than any other rider. He is in the Racing Hall of Fame.

At the age of fifty-one, he rides on, with one more goal in sight: to break Bill Shoemaker's record of 8,833 career victories. He is less than three hundred victories short, as he and the Shoe stand alone at the head of their class—the only jockeys to have won 8,000 races.

5. A Dead Heat (five riders bunched together)

No, I'm not being chicken. I just find it impossible to separate these five jockeys on the basis of their records, their personalities, and their influence on the sport:

Chris McCarron. His feat of bringing Alysheba from his knees to win the Derby is illustrative of the talent he has shown in a long career. As a kid on the Maryland circuit he set a national record for wins in a single year that stood for a long time. He is a fine spokesman for racing and helped found the Don MacBeth Fund for injured jockeys, something in which he is still very much involved.

Jerry Bailey. He has won two Kentucky Derbies and a remarkable four straight Breeders' Cup Classics. He is an articulate spokesman for racing, whether while being interviewed after a race or while raising funds for a racing charity.

Pat Day. His career was very nearly ended by drugs, until he had a born-again experience one night after considering jumping off a motel balcony. He is the all-time leading jockey at Churchill Downs in number of victories, and finally won his first Derby in 1992 on the Cinderella horse, Lil E. Tee.

Eddie Delahoussaye. One of a number of Louisiana Cajuns on the racing circuit, he moved to California some years ago principally because he could find better care there for his physically challenged daughter. Since then, he has consistently been one of the top riders in the world's most talented jockey colony. He is one of only four riders to win back-to-back Derbies.

Gary Stevens. Yet another of the top riders on the California circuit, he made a bit of racing history when he rode to a Derby win in 1988 the filly Winning Colors, who joined Regret and Genuine Risk as the only horses of her sex to win the race.

In 1996, he won the Derby on Thunder Gulch. In 1997, he was elected to the Racing Hall of Fame and won the Kentucky Derby on Silver Charm in the same week. He won the Pimlico Special, the classic race for older horses, two weeks later, and the Preakness the week after that. Only Silver Charm's narrow loss in the Belmont marred his near-perfect spring.

THE McKAY RATINGS—HORSES

Humans proud of their ancestry should hesitate before comparing pedigrees with the thoroughbred. Long before the *Mayflower* hit the beach at Plymouth Rock, the thoroughbred's line had been started by three ancient horses of Arabian stock called the Darley Arabian, the Godolphin Arabian, and the Byerly Turk. All thoroughbreds are descended from one of those three, and 90 percent of them from a later sire, Eclipse—born in England, we are told, during a full eclipse of the sun more than three hundred years ago. The other 10 percent are descended from either Herod or Matchem, both born in the same century as Eclipse.

Imported English stallions begat the American race horse, which first competed on the dirt streets of Kentucky towns, thus starting our practice of racing on dirt rather than on the grass courses used almost exclusively in England and on the Continent.

The eventual prodigy we see today is a sensitive, high-strung, powerful animal, bred through the centuries for only one purpose: to run fast, then to reproduce itself and further the endless story of the turf.

Like an Indianapolis race car, the thoroughbred carries as little weight and as much power as possible for maximum performance. The body must be sleek, the legs slender, yet capable of carrying a half-ton of horse at thirty-five miles an hour. Just as with the race car, this combination makes for fragility. And just as the race car sometimes breaks down because of this, so, sadly, does the thoroughbred.

But there is another quality bred into the race horse, something unseen but real; horsemen call it *heart*. It is this quality that makes the thoroughbred so touching to me, this tendency to give its all every time out, without knowing why.

It is heart that wins the stretch battle when the horses are dead equal in ability, and of all the races I have covered, these stand out as the most memorable:

1. 1989 Preakness: Sunday Silence vs. Easy Goer

The connections of the two horses were as impressive as the thoroughbreds themselves. In Sunday Silence's corner was owner Arthur Hancock III, eldest son of the famous "Bull" Hancock, master of Claiborne Farm. Arthur had been "the wild son" early on and had left the family farm. He met a beautiful girl named Stacy, married her, and almost overnight, changed into a solid husband and father—eventually, the father of six. Now, he had won the Kentucky Derby with a horse of his own.

Joint partner in ownership and trainer of the colt was the ageless Charlie Whittingham, still going strong at seventy-six.

The Easy Goer people were just as impressive. The owner was Ogden Phipps, patriarch of one of the great racing families. The trainer was "Shug" McGaughey, a young Kentucky hardboot who was restoring the Phipps stable to its former eminence.

The weather on Derby Day, 1989, was miserably cold, with snow flurries—on the first Saturday in May! Easy Goer had been the odds-on favorite in the Kentucky Derby, but Sunday Silence stalked the leader, Houston, a speedball whom his trainer, Wayne Lukas, had told me might be the best he ever had. Houston couldn't stay the course. Sunday Silence moved to the outside on the muddy track and charged into the lead as they hit the stretch. Easy Goer, from sixth place, charged past other horses, but fell two and a half lengths short of Sunday Silence at the wire.

Now, they met again in the Preakness, and the stretch drive between the two is crystal clear in my mind's eye today. They were mirror images of each other, side by side. Their legs moved together. Their heads bobbed at the same time. There was absolutely nothing to choose between them. Both were using all the heart that was in them as they raced toward the finish. The roar of the crowd was not so much for one horse or the other as it was sheer admiration for the tenacity of the two rivals. This was racing the way you wished it could always be.

At the wire, it was Sunday Silence again the winner—by a nose—in the greatest horse race I've ever seen.

But Easy Goer eventually had his day. Three weeks later, on the monumental mile-and-a-half oval at Belmont Park, Easy Goer's home track, the Phipps horse beat Sunday Silence and ended his rival's bid for the Triple Crown.

2. 1987 Kentucky Derby: Alysheba vs. Bet Twice

Neither horse was the favorite (Alysheba went off at 8 to 1, Bet Twice at 10 to 1), but Bet Twice stayed close to the early leader, On the Line, then blasted him at the quarter-pole. Alysheba had a bad start, but slowly worked his way through the pack under Chris McCarron's expert handling.

By the stretch, they were fighting for the lead, Bet Twice swerving his way toward the finish line. With just over an eighth of a mile to go, Alysheba clipped heels with Bet Twice, stumbling and almost falling to his knees. That would have finished the ordinary horse's bid, but somehow, McCarron and Alysheba maintained their cool, regained their balance, and charged again, beating Bet Twice to the wire by three-quarters of a length.

When I complimented McCarron in the winner's circle for

bringing the colt back to his feet, he said, "Jim, believe me, the horse did it himself. His heart won the race."

3. 1997 Triple Crown series

The Kentucky Derby, Preakness, and Belmont Stakes of 1997 must be considered as a single story. The margins of victory, added together, were the shortest in Triple Crown history. Bob Lewis and Bob Baffert, owner and trainer of Silver Charm, made a particularly appealing personality story. The tenacity of their colt in winning the Derby and the Preakness by such narrow margins got the attention of the whole country—racing fans or not. No less impressive was Touch Gold's win in the Belmont.

After that race, Silver Charm's rider, Gary Stevens, said, "As we neared the wire, I thought, 'My God! I'm going to win the Triple Crown!' Then I saw a shadow on my right, moving fast." It was the shadow of Touch Gold, who had not been quite ready to run in the Derby, but had served notice in the Preakness that he was a force to be reckoned with.

As I was standing on the platform with Chris McCarron, Touch Gold's jockey, waiting for Al Michaels to throw it down to me for the winner's interview, Chris leaned over and whispered in my ear, "Gee, I hate to be the guy who spoiled the party."

Indeed, it was supposed to have been Silver Charm's party. On that day, the popular scenario decreed, he would become the twelfth winner of the Triple Crown. He had given his all, and lost so narrowly. But his fans didn't get down on him, as racing fans often do with beaten favorites. As Silver Charm was jogged back past the winner's circle, the crowd, the largest at Belmont in many years, gave the colt a tremendous cheer.

☆

And still, some people wonder why I love horse racing.

They are people who identify the sport with touts and

gambling, fixed races and the musical *Guys and Dolls*. That isn't the sport I love.

I love the thoroughbred, the central figure in the drama of racing. It is the most artistically conceived creature in the natural world—smooth of coat, subtly beautiful in color, explosively graceful in action. As lovely as a ballerina, as touching as a little child, and game to the point of exhaustion.

The thoroughbred is the last true amateur in sport, giving its all every time out, trying so hard and exhibiting such heart that it sometimes brings tears to the eyes of hardened horsemen. And it does it for nothing except maybe a mint or a carrot and an extra handful of feed. As trainer Ron McAnally put it when the gallant filly Go for Wand broke down in the stretch in the Breeders' Cup and had to be destroyed, "They give their lives for our entertainment."

As the filly's body was taken away in the truck ambulance, tough Angel Cordero stood with tears running down his face. And there were many tears among the elite in the Director's Room and the fans lined along the rail.

Except for terrible moments like that, I love the splendor of horse racing. It's like a novel that has a marvelous plot, wonderful chapters, and just the right setting—the varicolored silks on the jockeys and the colorful outfits of the crowd on a big racing day, from the big hats and designer clothes on the women in the Turf Club to the windbreakers and baseball caps on the railbirds. I love the lush green of the turf course contrasting brilliantly with the rich, milk chocolate brown of the dirt track.

And I love the sport's history—from Lord Derby starting a big race for three-year-olds centuries ago and naming it for himself, to those early races down the dusty main streets of Kentucky, to the great Man o' War, to the breathtaking panorama at Churchill Downs on the first Saturday of each May.

Of all the sports I have covered, it is the most beautiful and, I suspect, will be the most enduring.

Auto Racing: From Mexico to Monte Carlo

My years of covering motor racing stretched from 1961 to 1990, a fascinating period. Technical advances were remarkable, safety standards were vastly improved. Deaths on the race course became much less frequent. Drivers, once underpaid, romantic vagabonds, became international celebrities and multimillionaires.

My first motor race, and my first trip to the continent of Europe, was also the first for ABC's *Wide World of Sports*—the first of many, in both cases. Before that first trip would end, it would involve a shattered windshield, an ancient castle in the moonlight, a twenty-four-hour automobile race, a French cameraman raging in the rain, and an English-American confrontation in a ma-and-pa bistro.

There were four of us on the ABC Sports team in that first *Wide World* summer of 1961—producer Roone Arledge, director Bill Bennington, production assistant Chuck Howard, and myself. Had we read the fine print in the contract for the little Fiat we rented in Paris, we might have foreseen a problem. Buried inside was the information that the extra insurance we took covered all potential disasters and all parts of the car, *except the windshield.*

I was the designated driver as we headed south on the road to the industrial town of Le Mans, which has hosted the "24 Hours" since its inception in the 1920s. All went well for us until we reached a tree-lined straight stretch of two-lane highway just south of the cathedral city of Chartres.

At that point we got behind a laboring sand and gravel truck. Every so often, a few pebbles would fall off and bounce along our hood. That was okay, but suddenly, a large stone hit our windshield, shattering it into a translucent—but not transparent—mosaic. It was impossible to see through, so I drove with my head out the window for twenty or thirty miles until we reached the next village.

The odds on replacing the windshield, we thought, were astronomical, but we spotted a small garage and pulled in. As I pointed to the windshield, the mechanic on duty smiled and said, "Ah, oui, monsieur." He took me into another room and there, unbelievably, was a row of shining windshields—all makes, all models.

I asked him why he had all of these in such a small village. In a halting combination of French and English, he explained that European windshields were made from a different and inferior substance from American windshields. He shrugged and said, "So they break all the time, monsieur, and for that reason, they are, of course, not covered by the insurance."

Oh.

The four of us dug deep for cash, paid for the windshield, and went on our way, wiser but poorer.

Our New York travel agent, one Pierre Joseph, had been unable to find hotel accommodations for us in Le Mans—"But," he said, "I have booked you into a marvelous old castle, the Château Rouillon." Everyone in Le Mans, he said, would know exactly where it was, just outside of town.

That was not true.

No one seemed to know where it was. My map showed a tiny dot marked Rouillon, but no roads seemed to pass there. We headed in that general direction, in the dark, and soon were totally lost for several hours. Finally, a dim light appeared in a dingy farmhouse. By the side of the rutted entrance was a grimy sign reading CENTRE D'INSEMINATION ARTIFICIEL. An artificial insemination center, on this dirty farm in the wilderness?

A man came out of the farmhouse. He was unshaven, wore

a dirty blue work outfit, and, frankly, he didn't smell very good. Nor was he friendly. But I was able to find out from him in my elementary French that this was an artificial insemination center for cattle, not people.

And he did know where the Château Rouillon was. It involved numerous turns and road signs—some of which turned out not to be there. But in time, we came to a pair of huge, rusty gates, one of which was hanging crookedly from its hinges. Upon close examination, a battered sign by the gate said CHÂTEAU ROUILLON. The creaking sound made by the gate as we opened it was worthy of the scariest movie.

We drove down a bumpy dirt lane, pitch dark, with overhanging tree branches. And then, suddenly, we broke into the open. A bright full moon was shining on the château, standing tall and ghostly white in the moonlight. It was silent and the windows showed no light.

No wonder. It was now almost midnight.

At that moment, I accidentally touched the horn. A window flew open, and we made out the face of an older man, wearing an old-fashioned nightcap. "Who sounds the Klaxon?" he shouted in archaic English. He looked annoyed.

"ABC Sports," I shouted back.

"The hour is late," he replied.

The front door opened then, and a teenage girl appeared. "Well, hello," she said. "You're here at last." Her accent was British. Once inside, we found that the older man, now waiting for us, wearing a tweed jacket hastily pulled over his long nightshirt, was the Marquis de Chasteniez, owner of the château, and that the girl was a guest.

Seldom has a bed with clean white sheets looked as good to me as it did that night.

We had come to cover one of the greatest races of them all, the 24 Hours of Le Mans. It was begun in the 1920s as a test of reliability for the automobiles of that time. Each car would be driven for twenty-four consecutive hours by two-man

teams over an 8.5-mile course through the countryside near
Le Mans. The cars had to start the contest with their cloth
tops raised; they could then be lowered during the first pit
stop. Each car had to carry a suitcase, as if it were a family
car starting out on vacation.

As the vehicles evolved, becoming race cars thinly dis-
guised as modern passenger sports cars—the Aston Martin,
Mercedes-Benz, Ferrari, and even the American Cadillac and
Corvette—so did the race.

Each vehicle was painted in the assigned color of the
country from which it had been entered. Green was for Britain, blue for France, red for Italy, blue and white for the
U.S.A., orange for the Netherlands, and so on. Once, shortly
after we started televising the race in the sixties, a car was
painted in red, white, yellow, and blue by the artist Alexander
Calder.

From its beginning in the early twenties, the 24 Hours fascinated the ordinary French driver because of the cars' simi-
larity (in outward appearance, anyway) to his own family
vehicle, much as stock car racing would fascinate Americans
later on.

But Le Mans's international appeal skyrocketed in the late
twenties with the appearance of the British Bentleys. In that
gorgeous British racing green with a Union Jack painted on
the side, they created over a short four-year period (1927–
1930) a romantic legend of the race course. As a group, they
were called "the Bentley boys," led by Sir Henry "Tim" Birkin
at the wheel of his supercharged, 4.5-litre model, handsome
leather straps across the hood, pointed tail creating a stream-
lining effect behind.

After that, interest continued to grow around the world.
Americans followed the misadventures of the Cadillacs in the
1950s, entered by Briggs Cunningham, the gentleman-sports-
man from the Gold Coast of Fairfield County, Connecticut.
Cunningham wanted to prove that American cars could compete with the best of the European endurance specialists, but
the bulky blue and white cars just weren't suited to the task.

Through the years, tragedy had stalked Le Mans, just as it has every major race course in the world. The possibility of fatalities goes with the sport. But I do not subscribe to the view that death on the race course is part of the sport's appeal. I have watched crowds leaving a track after a fatal crash, and they were not on any sort of high. They were universally quiet and depressed. It is the prospect of man daring the villain Death and surviving that lures the fans. When the driver dies, the person in the stands is reminded, most vividly, of his or her own mortality.

The most deadly crash of all took place at Le Mans, before we started televising the event.

In 1954, a Frenchman named Pierre Levegh, an amateur, announced that he would "leave his mark on Le Mans" by driving the entire twenty-four hours by himself. By the closing hours of the race, he became more and more disoriented from exhaustion and was incoherent when talking to his crew on pit stops. With less than an hour to go, Levegh tore the gearbox out of the car by shifting incorrectly. The German Mercedes-Benz team inherited the race, a galling blow to Levegh and the French nation.

Two years later, as a friendly gesture to Levegh and the French, Mercedes provided him with a car to drive. As the crowd of some four hundred thousand cheered him on, Levegh barreled down the homestretch, ran up the back of an English driver's car, and flew into the crowd, killing himself and eighty-six spectators. It was racing's most terrible disaster. Unlike the driver, the spectator does not intentionally dare death. He trusts that the promoters of the event have taken the proper precautions—which they had not on the day of Levegh's crash.

But somehow, the race survived the worldwide shock over the accident.

Le Mans, when we arrived in 1961, was a blend of excitement and nostalgia, all played out from 4:00 P.M. on Saturday until 4:00 P.M. Sunday before a crowd of four hundred thousand people. Many stayed through the night, watching the race, eating at any number of temporary places, from snack bars selling Croque Monsieurs (a kind of hot ham and cheese sandwich, as popular in France as hot dogs are in America) to fully equipped gourmet restaurants. Placed around the race course were amusement parks and carnivals. The largest was located near the S-turn section of the course, with a Ferris wheel, a whip-style ride, a boxer who would take on any man on the grounds, and a freak show that would turn the stomach of the strongest viewer. The smell of frying grease blended with the aroma of zoo animals and racing fuel and popcorn. At a few places around the circuit, you could even smell the clean country air.

Sound was everywhere—the carnival barkers, roller coasters, carousel music, and always in the background the insistent, hypnotic, rhythmic sound of the race cars going round and round while the crowd murmured and the bands played on.

To tour the course at three or four o'clock in the morning, as I did, and to see thousands of people, weary or drunk, or both, still wandering through the carnival, or dining in a chic restaurant, or huddling together under a blanket in the woods, was to wonder why they were there, instead of some more comfortable place, like home.

The drivers, in those years, were the last platoon of a disappearing army, men like Masten Gregory, the American expatriate socialite from Kansas City, who was reputed to have once successfully bailed out of a race car going a hundred miles an hour, and Carroll Shelby, the epitome of the post-World War II Texan, complete with rolling walk, slow drawl, and ten-gallon hat—John Wayne goes to Europe. Shelby led a sporting invasion of Americans to the European racing scene.

There was Stirling Moss, the devil-may-care idol of Great Britain, whose every move, such as sneaking out of a London hospital while recovering from a crash, was widely reported in the London tabloids; Maurice Trintignant, unique in his own right as the mayor of a small French town when not driving race cars; and Count Godin de Beaufort, the Dutchman who eventually met his death in a Formula One race.

Much has changed since our 1961 visit. For example, the romantic running start is a thing of the past. But on that occasion, my first visit to Europe, the scenes of Le Mans made a lifetime impression.

As our expert commentator (they were not yet called "analysts"), Roone had hired the aforementioned Stirling Moss, at that time the most famous racing driver in the world. The plan was for Moss to do a stand-up piece with me as the drivers prepared to run to their cars, then to do periodic updates when his co-driver, Graham Hill, was out in the car.

Stirling and I stood in the middle of the race course at the finish line. Behind us could be seen the other drivers, poised to run; the cars sitting silently across from them; and the huge crowd, babbling in anticipation.

Behind our camera was a phalanx of motorcycle gendarmes, prepared to sweep the course of press and other outsiders so the race could start. Chuck Howard stood with a hand in the air, holding back the gendarmes while he talked with a technician in Paris who would record our interview on that still newfangled thing called videotape.

Stirling Moss was as articulate an athlete as you could find, so we knocked off the opening quickly. Unfortunately, the picture did not get through to Paris, so we had to do it again—and again. By now, the gendarmes were blipping their engines impatiently while Chuck Howard sweated. The drivers looked expectantly toward the starter. It was time.

When the fourth take failed to get through, the chief gendarme began to shout at Chuck. Using one of the six or seven French words he knew, Chuck kept repeating, "Un moment, monsieur. Un moment."

Take five got through. We went through the opening again smoothly and had almost finished when the tune of "God Save the Queen" came over the loudspeaker system. Moss, a staunch English patriot, immediately stopped talking, clapped his arms to his sides, and stood stiffly, staring at the

British flag across the way. We had only been a sentence or two from the finish, but now we would have to do it yet again.

As we started after the anthem, two things happened. They began to play the "Marseillaise" as four hundred thousand Frenchmen fell silent, and the chief gendarme pulled his gun on Chuck, indicating first that we should shut up during the French anthem, and second, that he was going to clear the course as soon as it finished. If he had to shoot Chuck in the process, well . . .

Somehow, we finished our piece, Moss ran to his pit, the motorcycles swept us all away, the flag fell, and the drivers ran to their cars. The Vingt-quatre Heures du Mans was under way, and Chuck Howard was still alive.

It was torture. We had no place to sit down, no place for our cameraman, a Frenchman named Jacques Alexandre, to leave his equipment while we wandered through the crowd, summoning our strength to sneak in again.

About midnight, we found a sort of refuge. For the first time, IBM was keeping running computerized statistics on the race. Stirling Moss took us into its headquarters. He ran through the sheets that showed the speed of each car on each lap. He pointed out that his Aston-Martin GT was going faster than supposedly speedier cars—when *he* was driving.

"Look," he said. "See how fast the car goes?"

"Yes. But look down here. You were going considerably slower."

"Of course," said Moss. "That was when Graham Hill was driving the car."

Like many great athletes, Stirling Moss was not known for his modesty.

I didn't care. I was so tired, my legs were shaking. An American IBM man noticed and said that I could sit on one of their chairs. I did. It was a small, white plastic chair resting against the wall of the brightly lit room.

It was noisy—technicians talking, computers humming, teletypes clattering. No matter. Sitting bolt upright, I fell sound asleep for a half hour.

Then it was time to sneak into the Ferrari pit again.

It had begun to rain, and as we made our way to the dreaded fence, our cameraman snapped. Holding his sodden, useless pale blue credential about three inches from Roone's face, water dripping from the end of his nose, he shouted, "Monsieur Arledge, do you know what this is worth? It is worth nussing!" He deliberately tore the credential into tiny pieces, then threw them into the wet wind.

Phil Hill was stalking the pit when we got there. He was the first American ever to win the World Championship of Drivers, a darkly handsome, intense man whose emotions were always smoldering just beneath the surface. Denise Mc-Cluggage, one of the few female racing writers of the time, had dubbed him Hamlet in a Helmet.

Now at Le Mans, his face was gray and serious as he drew on his blue Dunlop driving uniform and peaked racing helmet.

Olivier Gendebien would bring the car in on the next lap and Hill would take over. They had already won the 24 Hours three times for Ferrari and were a perfect team. It was a classic illustration of how two people from totally different backgrounds and with distinctly different personalities could join together and succeed because of their talent for a very demanding and dangerous sport.

Phil Hill loved the romance of the sport, but he also had very definite opinions about its failings and dangers, opinions that he expressed in a soft but biting tone of voice. He was, at heart, a lover of all things mechanical, an American car buff who liked nothing better than to examine a race car from nose to tail, then give a tough, critical opinion of what was wrong with it. His hobby, which today is also his profession, is the restoration of classic cars.

Gendebien, on the other hand, was the scion of an ancient and wealthy Belgian family, handsome, well mannered—the epitome of European sophistication. He and Hill couldn't have been more different, but they were the perfect combination for the 24 Hours of Le Mans.

As Hill narrowed his eyes and looked out into the rain, we turned on our lights and camera. "Phil," I asked, "what's it going to be like out there?"

Suddenly, the quiet man became a testy, impatient professional, scornful of the uninformed question. He almost spat out his words.

"What's it going to be like out there?" he repeated. "It's going to be terrible! Can't you see that there is rain falling here on the homestretch? That means there will be fog on the Mulsane Straight, the longest straightaway in racing, almost three and a half miles long! Don't you understand that my car will be going *two hundred and twenty miles an hour out there,* and there are other cars in the race—damned little *French* things—going a hundred miles an hour *slower* than I am?! I could come upon one of them in the fog without seeing it, hit it, and we'd both be killed!" He stared into my eyes. *"That's what it's going to be like out there!!!"*

Just then, the car slid into the pit, a blood red Ferrari, an open car in the rain. Gendebien, as was his habit, didn't use the door—he leaped over the side. Phil got in without a word and the car screamed off into the wet night, leaving an inch or two of rubber on the pavement. It flashed under the Dunlop pedestrian bridge and was quickly out of sight.

I approached Olivier with some trepidation and asked him the same question. "Olivier, what was it like out there?"

The answer came in softly accented English. "What was eet lahk?" he said thoughtfully. "Well, really, it was lahk nussing. We are very far ahead once again, the Ferrari ees performing *parfaitement, comme toujours,* and there are only thirteen and a half hours left in the race. It ees . . . how do you say in America? . . . It ees lahk driving to zee corner for a pack of cigarettes. And now, if you'll excuse me, I am very hungry. I must eat."

He put on his Rex Harrison–style tweed hat at a rakish angle and sauntered away toward the back of the pit.

Unbelievable, I thought, that these two men, so totally different in every way, could still mesh like the teeth of a finely made gear and become the greatest team in the history of Le Mans.

Hill and Gendebien won the race again, easily. It was lahk nussing.

Afterward, Chuck Howard and I made our weary way to a small ma-and-pa bistro we had found earlier in the week called Au Bec Fin. There were just five or six tables in the tiny dining room and only one was occupied when we walked in. Tired and dirty, our brains slightly scrambled from the long sleepless vigil, we ate and went over the things we had seen and heard.

Eventually, one of us recalled a voice that had assaulted our ears periodically throughout the twenty-four hours. It was the voice of an announcer who described the proceedings over the P.A. for English-speaking spectators. We agreed that this Englishman was pompous, overbearing, corny, and inaccurate. We laughed and imitated his manner.

After about five minutes of this, the only other person in the room rose to his feet. "Excuse me," he said, "but I feel called upon to defend myself. I am the English announcer."

I have never felt smaller than I did at that moment. Chuck and I made some sort of stumbling apology, which the stranger accepted with ultimate grace.

"Perfectly all right," he said. "I think I do tend to get carried away sometimes. Will you share a bottle with me and toast the winners?"

We did, and eventually the three of us walked back to our hotel together, assuring each other there would always be an England and that God would most certainly bless America.

I remember how exhausted I was one year after being up for some thirty-six consecutive hours covering the race. Rumpled and dirty, Chuck Howard and I flew by helicopter from Le Mans up the river Seine to Paris. As we arrived over the city, darkness was just falling. The Eiffel Tower could still be seen in that magic time called dusk. The lights of Paris flickered all around us.

We landed beside the river, just blocks from the tower, then flagged down a taxi and went to the Prince de Galles Hotel. In my room there, I took a steaming bath in the over-sized tub, sipped a Scotch, ate a sirloin steak, then slipped between the crisp linen sheets for one of the most satisfactory sleeps of my career. . . .

Today, the running start has long since disappeared, and so has the old breed of driver. Today's driver at Le Mans is much more likely to be carrying an attaché case than a monkey wrench.

And ABC's accounting department doesn't allow us to rent helicopters anymore, either.

Before I started my long odyssey with *Wide World of Sports,* I tended to think of motor racing as a sport restricted to rather boring oval courses—"round-and-rounds." Le Mans shook me out of that assumption and then some, as did all the other races we covered over the years.

The various styles of motor racing all derive from their roots.

Grand Prix racing and the endurance contests like Le Mans are the descendants of the earliest European races, in the 1890s and early 1900s, when that radical new invention the automobile was raced from city to city (the famous Paris-to-Lyons race, for example) or through the streets of a city. To this day, the Grand Prix races are contested exclusively over road circuits or city streets. They are also called Formula One races, referring to the fact that such races are held during the season for race cars with different-sized engines, each constructed according to a formula. Hence, Formula One, Formula Two, and Formula Three.

About the same time in the United States, there were road races, of which the Vanderbilt Cup on Long Island was the most prominent, but the emerging style was on the dirt horse racing tracks of state fairgrounds. From that beginning came paved oval circuits designed especially for cars. Some tracks were even made out of wood, including an immense one in Santa Monica, California, that was two miles around.

In 1909, Carl Fisher cleared a large bean field and built his dream track, a huge, two-and-a-half-mile rectangle with rounded corners, paved with brick. Almost a century later, Fisher's dream is still being fulfilled at his Indianapolis Motor Speedway.

The surface is asphalt now, except for one yard of brick at the start-finish line to validate its nickname, the Brickyard. For the first five-hundred-mile race in 1911, three thousand hitching posts were erected for spectators who came by horse, at that time still the primary means of transportation. Through the years, grandstands have been added and the infield opened to spectators, until today Indy accommodates the world's largest sporting crowd, some four hundred thousand people, each Memorial Day weekend.

Stock car racing, America's fastest-growing sport in the 1990s, was an outgrowth of Prohibition. When the "Evil Drink" was still forbidden in most parts of the South, moonshiners in the hills and crannies operated in street-model cars with souped-up engines, the better to outrun the "revenooers"—the government agents—as the illegal distillers made their rounds, distributing their wanton goods. On weekends, just for fun or on private bets, the hillmen started racing each other to prove who had the fastest of all the escape vehicles.

Bill France Sr. saw the possibility of something a lot bigger than a weekend bet. He started promoting races for ordinary American stock cars, at first on the sands of Daytona Beach, Florida. In the early years of the twentieth century, Daytona, because of the especially hard nature of its beach, had been used for land speed record attempts, until the salt flats of Utah proved better suited. France used the beach, but he had much bigger dreams.

The realization of those dreams is the Daytona International Speedway, the Yankee Stadium of the stock car world, where crowds of a hundred thousand and more gather for the sport's now world-famous race, the Daytona 500. The cars at Daytona are stock cars only in their outward appearance. Underneath, they are sophisticated racing machines, specially designed for the purpose.

Grand Prix road racing, stadium races like Indy, stock car racing—these are the three most prominent forms of motor racing. But *Wide World of Sports* has televised almost everything on wheels at one time or another—from hot rod racing to motorcycle jumping, even to motorcycle racing on ice, contested on the frozen surface of Dynamo Stadium in Moscow, in the then-U.S.S.R.

In the 2:30 A.M. darkness of a November morning in 1968, I stood on a lonely stretch of highway outside La Paz, Mexico, listening to the presidential election returns on a small portable radio. I had been hugging the radio for several hours to pass the time as Richard Nixon edged ahead of Hubert Humphrey. Peering into the darkness, I was awaiting the arrival of the first entrant to complete the tortuous course of the officially titled Baja 1,000.

This was a sadistically designed event for off-road vehicles, covering endless miles of territory that resembles nothing so much as the bleak, rock-strewn, silent surface of the moon—with cactus added. The vehicles ranged from racers specifically designed for this kind of competition, to street-version four-wheel-drives, to dune buggies, down to ordinary motorcycles.

The event was the outgrowth of one man's enterprise and spirit of adventure. In the mid-sixties, Bruce Meyers had married a Volkswagen "bug" chassis to a specially designed plastic shell and called it a "dune buggy"—suitable, he claimed, for any terrain. To prove it, he drove the length of the Baja himself in such a buggy, thereby leading to the race, which endures to the present day.

There were about a hundred drivers in the race when we televised it, professionals and amateurs, veterans and kids, male and female. The most revered figure among them was Parnelli Jones, the first driver ever to break through the once thought impregnable 150-mile-an-hour barrier at Indianapolis, and winner of the Indy 500 in 1963.

Of all the diverse forms of racing, the Baja 1,000 is the most bizarre, bordering at times on the mystical.

One driver told of seeing a white horse galloping through the night across the sandy wasteland. A mirage or a hallucination? Whatever it was, he couldn't make it go away for quite a long time. Another told of swerving to avoid another vehicle— then realizing there was none. Yet another would have sworn that the deep ruts one often encountered were actually huge snakes. The reality, that they were fissures in the parched earth of the Baja, only became apparent when his vehicle hit them and bounced a couple of feet in the air.

Even the building where the competitors register for the race on the main street of Ensenada, Mexico, has a romantic history. Now home to the Ensenada Chamber of Commerce, it was once a famous casino, to which the glamorous figures of early Hollywood would repair for rest, recreation, and gambling. As you walk through the old place, your footsteps echoing on the marble floor, you can easily imagine Douglas Fairbanks or Rudolph Valentino striding into the lobby, wearing a white linen suit with a panama hat and smoking an expensive Cuban cigar.

The casino was also famous for its chef, among whose creations was a wonderful salad that came to be named for him.

His name was Caesar.

A big crowd of friends, fans, and plain citizens of Ensenada gathered at dawn in front of the casino the year I was there, sending up a great cheer as the adventurers set off on their long journey. From the start, we followed along in a Jeep as the entrants scattered clouds of tan dust behind them in the streets of the town. Then, it was out into the country, away from civilization.

You've probably had the experience of driving a long distance through the night, alone, and suddenly feeling like your eyes are going to close whether you like it or not. On the vast emptiness of the Baja, on the lonely, desolate, southward journey from Ensenada to La Paz, the driver fights sleep for long hours with no hope of rest. For more than six hundred miles (one thousand kilometers) of mostly uncharted desert wilderness, he strains for a sight of some landmark in the dark, or shields his eyes from the blazing sun in the daytime.

There are a few scheduled stopping places along the way. One, I recall, was at a lonely ranch, and another at a tiny village, the center of which was a combination gas station and general store. My colleagues in commentary on the event were Sam Posey, race driver, artist, and author, and Jackie Stewart, the former Grand Prix world champion. We hopscotched ahead of the field of drivers by helicopter, then waited for them at a couple of the stops.

In the little village, we interviewed a few of the drivers as they refilled their gas tanks, and were about to get into the helicopter when Jackie ran back to the store. In a few minutes, he returned, smiling.

"Had to get some Snickers bars," he said in his rich Scottish brogue. "Can't live without them."

Jackie is a man of unusual, but practical habits. For example, he always travels with the English variety of Kellogg's All-Bran, claiming it is more effective than its American cousin. On long flights, he dresses in a sweat suit and has permission from British Airways to sleep on the floor—can't sleep sitting up.

As we rattled along in the helicopter, becoming fatigued from its vibration, Jackie shared the Snickers with us, and Sam shared a story about his own adventure as a driver in the race. He told us of breaking down in the middle of nowhere and fearing for his life under the broiling sun, until a rickety truck, its engine coughing asthmatically, came along. He hitched a ride in the back, and was surprised to find another race competitor already there.

Sam, whose accent is as recognizably Ivy League as Jackie's is Scottish, said, "I introduced myself to the guy, who said his name was Wayne. It wasn't until later that it came out in conversation that he was the son of John Wayne—you know, the actor."

They suffered together, the driver-artist and the Duke's son, sitting on top of the truck's cargo—a shifting mass of live turtles. It took more than a day to reach the next settlement, by which time, Sam said, the aroma of the turtles was truly beyond description.

As the night deepened, other members of our camera crew followed the race on the ground. On our return to the United States, all of the film, from the helicopter and the ground crews, would be collated and edited. Then we would add the commentary.

I felt dirty and weary by the time we landed in La Paz, a town known mostly for its fishing grounds, where Bing Crosby used to come, fleeing Hollywood in favor of the quiet waters off the Baja peninsula. A truck then took me to the lonely finish line, where I began my long vigil, waiting for the winner. The first victor of the night, at long last, was Richard Nixon, the radio told me.

Then word came that the first vehicle was about to arrive. Was it a sophisticated off-road racer, a dune buggy, or a Jeep—perhaps Parnelli Jones?

It was none of the above.

It was a motorcycle.

☆

Monte Carlo is as different from the Baja as caviar is from tortillas. No turtle-bearing trucks there; more likely, a truck making a diamond delivery for Cartier.

When we first went there in 1962, the fairy-tale wedding of the principality's ruler, Prince Rainier, and the beautiful American movie star Grace Kelly of Philadelphia, was still fresh in our minds.

The entire principality, smaller than Central Park in New

York, has a beauty and quiet unreality about it that is disturbed only occasionally by the theft of a millionaire's jewels or a broken gambler's suicide.

Its harbor is a small, sparkling jewel, inhabited in the sixties by yachts like that of Aristotle Onassis, the Greek shipping magnate, which featured a helicopter sitting on the rear deck, ready to whisk the owner wherever he might want to go. In each of the guest staterooms were priceless French Impressionist oil paintings.

The prince's palace sits above the harbor, a visual anachronism, looking much like the sand castles I used to make on the beach when I was a kid, turrets and all. I interviewed him there one day. He seemed a pleasant, serious, kind man, who wanted to talk about his plans for Monaco and the good works of his wife, Princess Grace, rather than the automobile race.

On another hilltop, in the center of the town, sits the famous casino, setting for many mystery novels and Hollywood movies. As one can picture Rudolph Valentino at the old casino in Ensenada, so you can easily imagine Cary Grant strolling among the roulette tables of Monte Carlo. In fact, he once played an attractive Monte Carlo diamond thief in a movie, *To Catch a Thief*. His costar, ironically, was Grace Kelly, before she married the prince.

For the gambler used to the lurid colors, furious action, and loud noises of Las Vegas, the casino comes as a shock. It is quiet and dignified and the action is slow-paced. Only the quiet voice of the croupier disturbs the silence. I am told there have been changes since I was last there—slot machines, for example—but I prefer to think of it as I remember it, a living relic of an earlier, more gracious time.

Monte Carlo is an escape from reality for the tourist, a tax haven for the wealthy, and a trap for the compulsive gambler. It is also, on one weekend each spring, the most glamorous and unlikely setting for an automobile race.

That first year we went there, I had the most unusual wake-up call of my career. Knocked out from the transoceanic flight to Paris, the domestic French flight down to Nice, and the exciting automobile ride across the mountain to Monte Carlo, I was totally unconscious when an unexpected and shattering sound penetrated my brain. I sat straight up in bed.

The light coming in the window of my hotel room told me it was just after dawn. And the noise—a terrifying, high-pitched scream—was the sound of Formula One racing machines, starting practice.

I hadn't realized that practice runs for the race on Thursday and Friday began at the crack of dawn so that they did not interfere with the normal traffic of the Monte Carlo morning rush hour. After practice, the guardrails were disassembled and the rush hour began.

Starting on the waterfront, visible to guests on the yachts in the harbor and to people peering out the windows of luxury hotels, the course winds through the streets of the city. Immediately after the start, it ascends a steep hill, at the top of which it turns left, passing between the glittering Hotel de Paris, where Winston Churchill spent his declining years, and the casino.

Taking a right, the cars then plunge downhill at about a hundred miles an hour to another hard right. When we first began to televise the Grand Prix, that right turn led to a sudden left at the railroad station. One driver missed the turn and ended up, embarrassingly, inside the station waiting room, car and all.

Another right takes the cars toward the sea, then into a tunnel. Out of the tunnel into the sometimes blinding sun, the driver heads for the chicane, a tricky, quick little turn (hence the word "chicanery," meaning "to deceive by clever devices").

A left at the tobacconist's shop leads to the municipal swimming pool, then around the pool to the start line once again. Of the so-called city races, the Monaco course is the one most firmly rooted into the downtown heart of a city. The race cars are often garaged within a few blocks of the course, then wheeled through the streets to the start line.

There is a tendency to think of the Monte Carlo circuit as

a sort of toy course negotiated by toy cars. In reality, it can be extremely dangerous.

The two sides of the Monaco race, the glamorous and the dangerous, were summed up for me in one twenty-four-hour period back in the early seventies. On the day before the race, on a sunny Mediterranean afternoon, I saw a bright yellow Ferrari convertible cruising past the Hotel de Paris, top down. At the wheel was Lorenzo Bandini, star driver of the Ferrari team and one of the favorites in the race. Young and handsome, with the racing world at his feet and a long, exciting future ahead of him, the Italian smiled and waved to pedestrians who called to him as he passed. He was a glamorous figure, envied by men, adored by women around the racing world.

The next afternoon during the race, Lorenzo's shiny red race car, low and sleek, its rear engine whining, blasted out of that dark tunnel along the harbor into the brilliant sunlight. Was he blinded momentarily? No one knows, because going into the chicane a couple of seconds later, Bandini lost control.

The car flipped and caught fire. As rescue crews made their way all too slowly to the scene (the incident would lead to improvements in safety precautions), one spectator ran into the flames to try to pull Bandini out of the car. It was no use.

Lorenzo, terribly burned, was rushed to the hospital, where he died the next day.

A few years later, I played golf at the little course built by the prince on terraced land high above Monte Carlo on Mont Agel. My partner for the eighteen holes was Jackie Stewart.

Jackie is a man who appreciates the romantic as well as the exciting side of life, as I do.

Standing on the tee of a par three hole in the cool air of early morning, we looked straight down to our left. Below us was the winding mountain road leading down to the city, gleaming in the morning light like the capital of some fairy-tale kingdom. Beyond the city lay the blue-green of the Mediterranean.

Turning to our right, we could see the far-distant Alps, still covered with snow on that lovely May day. We agreed that the scene was as peaceful and beautiful as anything we had ever seen.

And yet, it was on that narrow road snaking down the mountainside that Princess Grace met her death when her car careened out of control a few years later.

The beautiful and the dangerous live side by side in Monte Carlo.

Through the years, I have seen the great drivers perform at Monte Carlo, from the American Phil Hill to Stewart and Jim Clark, the two famous Scots; Stirling Moss, the idol of Great Britain in his time; Jack Brabham, Australia's world champion; and the Brazilian, Emerson Fittipaldi. I came along just after the days of the legendary Juan-Manuel Fangio of Argentina, and I haven't covered the race in recent times, which have been dominated by the more businesslike, and extremely wealthy, drivers of today.

The Monaco race I remember most vividly is that first one I saw in 1962. Phil Hill, who had won the world championship the season before, was again driving for Ferrari, but this time with a car that would prove uncompetitive before the season had progressed very far.

Still, Hill hung in doggedly at Monaco, chasing Bruce McLaren, of New Zealand, through the rain. With ten laps to go, Hill trailed by twelve seconds. Then he began to cut into McLaren's lead—reducing it to ten seconds, then eight, then five. The lead dwindled to three, then two seconds. The cheers of the crowd echoed off the hotels and apartment houses along the course.

Hill had McLaren in his sights all through the last lap, but couldn't quite catch him, losing by 1.4 seconds. As the red car coasted into the pits, spattered with rain and oil, I ran down to congratulate Hill on his virtuoso drive. A man called Commendatore Dragoni, manager of the Ferrari team, had gotten there before me.

As Hill, physically drained and soaked to the skin, pulled off his helmet, Dragoni bent over and shouted at him. Instead of congratulations, I heard him say, "You lost it! Bah! Believe me, any man who can lose by only 1.4 seconds should have won by 1.4 seconds!"

It was the beginning of the end of Hill's relationship with Ferrari and of his Formula One driving career. The Ferrari car showed its inferiority in race after race that year, never coming close to Hill's performance at Monaco.

Hill left the Ferrari team and never won another Grand Prix race, ending his years on that circuit in a badly conceived machine for a team called ATS, and later as second driver to McLaren on the Cooper team.

Phil Hill, the first American ever to win the world championship (only Mario Andretti has duplicated the feat since), never got credit for his considerable driving skills from the Europeans who dominated the sport, but his pursuit of McLaren through the rain at Monte Carlo that day remains one of the finest demonstrations of bravura race driving that I have ever seen.

The hottest sport of the nineties? The surveys show that it is stock car racing, that lineal descendant of the moonshiners racing the "revenooers." From its Southern roots, it has spread to the Northeast, the Midwest, and the West Coast. It blankets the country.

Its stars of the early days, ex-moonshiners like the legendary Junior Johnson, have given way to a new breed, led by young Jeff Gordon, who, in his mid-twenties, still looks more like a high school homecoming king than a stock car driver. Perhaps the ultimate proof that stock car racing has come of age is the fact that nowadays Jeff's picture proudly smiles at us from a Wheaties box, that uniquely American sign of elevation to hero status.

Still, as the sport's image shifts from moonshine and over-alls to chardonnay and skyboxes, my memory tends to recall most easily the track in Darlington, South Carolina, scene of the Southern 500, known locally as "the daddy of 'em all." In the days when we started going there, it was run by a threat-ening-looking man called "Mister Bob" Colvin whose eyes were hidden behind mirrored sunglasses.

In the early sixties, Mister Bob had a problem.

Spectators arriving early for the Labor Day race would come in the night before. Rattling into town in pickups and vans, motorcycles and jalopies (one well-known regular al-ways came in a hearse), they would trash the little community of Darlington. Store owners and home owners complained of fights and thefts and generally rude behavior.

So Mister Bob thought and thought, and came up with a clever idea.

Under his new rules, infield spectators were required to arrive on Sunday afternoon and drive into the infield. When all the pickup trucks and vans loaded with beer were in place, they were locked *inside* the track overnight. Police patrolled the area, arrests were made, and the most unruly were incar-cerated in a jail erected right there in the infield. There was also a small emergency hospital. The arrangement worked and still survives.

Problem solved.

The crowd favorite at Darlington in the mid-sixties was Cale Yarborough, a South Carolina native and former high school football hero. The only time I was ever mistaken for an athlete was one night when I was walking down the street in Darlington. An older couple, walking the opposite way, smiled as they passed me. The man doffed his straw skimmer and said, "Evenin', Cale. Good luck in the race tomorrow."

I thanked him.

The next day, I thought we might have lost my look-alike during the race. Barreling along between the first and second turns, Cale's car suddenly lost traction, spun, and shot up over the wall, out of sight. Where was he? Was he alive?

The race proceeded under a yellow flag. The crowd was almost silent as I did my best to comment on the possibilities.

"If his car landed right side up, he may well have survived. But of course, we don't know. There is no smoke rising from beyond the wall. That's a positive sign. . . ."

And so on, for a good ten minutes.

Finally, an official car, amber lights flashing on its roof, drove out of the tunnel into the infield and came to a stop just outside the little track hospital. There was total silence. Then the car door opened—and out stepped Cale!

To the crowd, it was a miracle: God had somehow spared their hero. Cale smiled, waved to his supporters, and disappeared into the hospital for a checkup. All he had were a few scratches. Caesar returning from the wars could not have received a more tumultuous reception than Cale Yarborough did that day in Darlington.

I visited Cale once at his South Carolina home. Thanks to his earnings on the racetrack, it was a large, attractive, tastefully designed brick house. Cale himself was a perfect host, showing me around the grounds.

At one point, he smiled and said, "Would you like to see my pet?"

"Sure."

He took me to a corner of the backyard and pointed to a cage on wheels. In the cage was a very live bear. I complimented him on the bear's appearance, then asked him where he got such a cage.

"From the county," he said. "In the old days, they used it to transport chain gang prisoners to work and back."

These days, Cale is owner of his own stock car racing team. He is a natural-born gentleman, and one of my favorites. Of course, we do look alike.

Religion was always a part of a Darlington race, in the form of an invocation before the drivers got into their cars. One minister, I recall, even called for God to bless the car manufacturers and the tire companies. But there were also occasional reminders of more prejudiced days. One Sunday morning in the early 1980s, I was stopped at a traffic light while driving to the track and was shocked to see white-robed figures approaching me and the other drivers with little baskets in their hands. They were, in fact, Ku Klux Klansmen, soliciting money for their cause.

Aside from such occasional aberrations, stock car racing then had a rich flavor of its own, and no one understood it better than Chris Economaki, the owner, publisher, editor, and columnist of *National Speed Sport News*, the weekly gospel of racing.

Experienced as he is in the folklore of stock car racing, even he, at times, has had trouble with the heavy Southern accents. One day he came to our commentary booth, chuckling. When I asked him why, he said, "I met a girl down in the pits this morning, and when I asked her who she was, she said, 'Ahm Miss Ay Ah Owr.'

"You're who?"

" 'Miss Ay Ah Owr. You know, Miss Atlanta International Raceway?' "

There was always a Miss Somebody-or-other at the stock car races, who would ride on a float representing her sponsor in the prerace parade. Often it was a woman with a remarkably well-developed figure named Linda Vaughan, who followed the circuit in that capacity for many sponsors through the years and became something of a legend.

At one race, as she came into view, the track announcer, Bob Montgomery, said in his stentorian tones, "And now, let's greet, as she stands on the magnificent Purolator float, Miss Linda Vaughan, the first lady of motor racing!"

In addition to his journalistic duties, Chris Economaki was our commentator in the pits for many years, and a regular contributor to *Monitor,* a popular NBC network radio program back in the 1960s.

One Labor Day, Chris and I made our escape from Darlington in our usual way, which was by driving around the track after the race, then exiting by a tunnel on the backstretch, which led us to a tiny grass airstrip called Moore's Airport, so stated on a rusty Coca-Cola sign at the entrance.

It was operated by Mr. Moore himself, who sat at a card table outside his office. On the table was a small radio, which served as his control tower, and several boxes of Hershey bars and Milky Ways and other popular sweets of the time, which he sold to arriving and departing travelers at a nickel over the regular price. Beside his table was a corrugated iron tub filled with ice and soft drinks. Air traffic from the little airstrip was heavy right after the race, and it was fun to sit in our small charter plane, waiting our turn to take off, and listen to the owner on the radio.

"NXS 4–6–9," he would say, "you're third for takeoff now. Watch out for the telephone wires at the end of the runway." Then, in an aside, "Whatcha got there? Two Baby Ruths, a Snickers, and a couple of Cokes? That'll be three and a quarter. Thank ya. RHL 647, just be patient and wait your turn. Y'all just shut up now."

From Darlington, Chris and I flew to Charlotte, where we would make our connections to home. As I was walking to the gate in Charlotte, I heard Chris call to me from a phone booth. When I went over, he put his hand over the telephone mouthpiece and whispered, "Jim, listen closely. I promised *Monitor* an interview with Fireball Roberts [who had won the race that day]. I couldn't get him at the track, so I'd really appreciate it if you'd be him."

"What?!"

"Come on, Jim. You're good at accents. Please. I'll only ask you one question and nobody will know the difference."

Whereupon, he said into the telephone, "Ready, New York? Okay, here we go. Fireball, whatever your strategy was, it worked perfectly. How did you plan the race?"

Doing my best Carolina drawl, I said, "Well, Chris, we decided to play it real cool for the first four hundred miles, then just let it all hang out!"

"There you have it, fans. Right from the winner's mouth. Now back to *Monitor* in New York."

The moral of the story: Don't believe everything you hear on the radio.

If Darlington is a reminder of what stock car racing used to be, then Daytona is a sharp statement of what it has become. The 500 attracts international attention now. As early as the 1970s, Big Bill France began bringing celebrity friends to enjoy the action—General Curtis LeMay and King Hussein of Jordan, for example.

Big Bill's son, Bill Jr., has since taken the sport's progress several steps farther along the road to the big time of sport. Television has had a lot to do with it. *Wide World of Sports* came first, in 1962. Today, all of the major networks cover the sport, along with a gaggle of cable networks.

The drivers we covered at the beginning are now elder statesmen—"King" Richard Petty, of Level Cross, North Carolina; Bobby Allison, the pride of Hueytown, Alabama; Junior Johnson and David Pearson, Ned Jarrett, and Coo-Coo Marlin. Many of their names are carried on in racing by their sons and nephews—Kyle Petty, Dale Jarrett, and Sterling Marlin, for example.

The Petty dynasty actually started a generation before King Richard. His daddy, Lee, once flew clear out of Daytona into the parking lot, as Cale Yarborough would later at Darlington, and like Cale, he lived to tell about it. The fans of King Richard were the ones who started the marketing of the sport, really, when they began turning up at the races in T-shirts bearing the number 43, Petty's famous number. This was before the NBA and Nike took marketing to the dizzying heights of today.

NASCAR's explosion across the nation in the nineties has been a bonanza for the economics of the sport (as with all sports today, it's mostly about the money), but to me, it still is most at home and most appealing when it is contested in the South, where lunch buckets full of sandwiches and plastic hampers full of beer are the menu for the day; where farmers and mechanics drive their pickups full of kids, cousins, and friends into the infield and stand by the anchor-chain fence, straining for a close-up look at their heroes in the pits; where another generation of Linda Vaughans still ride the floats; and where the track announcer's Southern-accented voice is a soothing syrup to the gathered thousands.

The Indianapolis Motor Speedway, like Le Mans and Monaco, has a character of its own, separate and distinct from the other American tracks, most of which are one-mile ovals.

Every level of society is represented at Indy, and in one way or another they are as segregated as royalty is from the commoner at Royal Ascot. There are the luxury suites in the motel overlooking turn two; the two hundred thousand places in the grandstand, where the varying seat prices separate the economic levels; and the great infield, filled with shirtless young people who have gathered from across the country for a Memorial Day weekend fling.

The remodeling of the Speedway golf course, several holes of which are in the infield of the track, eliminated an area near turn one known simply as the Snake Pit, where some of society's more disturbed citizens used to swill beer and indulge in disgusting behavior, reminiscent of something in a Dickensian nightmare.

Indy is Midwest America on holiday.

Even in the years since we began televising the 500, there have been great changes. In the early sixties, the cars were great, tall, ungainly, roaring, front-engine monsters called roadsters. The driver sat straight up in his seat, visible to the crowd as he wrestled the wheel. We were there when Parnelli Jones, driving one of those stately old beasts, became the first to break the 150-mile barrier, once considered as unbreakable as the four-minute mile had been before Roger Bannister. Just a few years later, the same Parnelli Jones was whooshing quietly, but swiftly, around the track in a jet car that approached two hundred miles an hour. Today, the two hundred barrier has long since disappeared; two-fifty will be the next to go.

The jet car appeared briefly, then was outlawed, but a much more lasting imprint was put on the race by the Australian Grand Prix (Formula One) champion Jack Brabham. Brabham came to the Speedway in the early sixties with a modified version of his Formula One car. It was small, sleek, and underpowered as it lined up with the hulking roadsters, looking like a midget among giants. But it flew through the corners with an agility that shocked the experts as Brabham finished in an impressive eighth place.

It took a few years for the roadsters to join the dodo bird, but their death knell had actually sounded on the day Brabham arrived.

I remember talking with Phil Hill, asking him why the small, light, underpowered car could outrun the bigger, more powerful ones. Phil, a born teacher, thought for a moment, then said, "Look. A dog could outrun a horse if they were racing around your living room. Right?"

Of course.

Another driver from the Grand Prix circuit was responsible for a singular improvement, less noticed than Jack Brabham's, but to the drivers, at least, quite necessary.

Graham Hill was a quiet, erect Englishman with a guardsman's mustache, a Formula One world championship to his credit, and a sly sense of humor.

Shortly after his arrival for his first Indy 500, he was dining with track owner Tony Hulman when Hulman asked him if everything was all right—his hotel room, his treatment at the track, and so forth.

"Oh, yes," he said. "But since you ask, there is one thing. I was rather shocked to find that there are no doors on the stalls in the garage area men's rooms. Rather uncivilized, don't you think?"

The next morning, carpenters were hard at work, installing doors on the stalls.

Anything else? Well, yes.

"Tell me," Graham said. "In the entry list, there is the letter R next to my name. What does that mean?" Hulman explained that it stood for "rookie."

"And what does 'rookie' mean?"

"Why, it means that this is your first Indy, that you are a beginner here."

Graham's eyebrows shot up. "Beginner?" he said, wonder in his eyes. "Well, I am, after all, a world champion, so I'm hardly that. Beginner, indeed."

Then, Graham Hill went out and won the Indy on his first attempt, just as he had won out in the situation with the men's room doors. But not so with the rookie issue. If you check the record book, it will say that the winner that year was, "Hill, Graham, England—R."

Graham later met his death, not on the race course, but in a private plane crash, trying to get home from a European race on a Sunday night. His name lives on, though, in the person of his son, Damon, a champion Grand Prix driver in his own right.

☆

I am a sucker for nostalgia, so I love all the old, traditional things about Indy, like the parade around the track before the race, complete with war heroes, old race cars, minor movie stars, and the Purdue University marching band, led down the stretch by "the Golden Girl" as the crowd cheers wildly. And I'll admit it, I always got a tear in my eye when Jim Nabors sang "Back Home Again in Indiana" while the varicolored balloons floated into the sky and the fireworks boomed.

One year before Nabors took over the chore, the anthem was sung by a former champion, Peter DePaolo, and the pace car was driven by a local automobile dealer. DePaolo's singing was enthusiastic but off-key. The car dealer lost control of the pace car, sending it crashing into a hay wagon loaded with photographers and almost fatally injuring a visiting South American doctor. These incidents, occurring on the same day, prompted someone to say, "Next year they're going to get it right. They're going to have the car dealer sing the anthem and let Peter DePaolo drive the pace car!"

If the great variety of venues was a surprise to me during the thirty years I covered motor racing, so have been the varied personalities of the drivers. And, as always, it's the human beings I find most intriguing.

And so on to my list of favorite race drivers, based not just on their feats, but on their personalities and their positive impact on the sport.

THE McKAY RATINGS

1. Jackie Stewart

First of all, please don't call him Jack, or he'll correct you. That would be like calling Willie Mays Bill, or Jack Nicklaus Johnny, or Jim McKay James. He is Jackie to the world of motor racing, to the dozen and more sponsors he represents and visits around the globe, to the British and European royalty he counts among his friends, and to the television audiences of several continents. "Jackie" is his trademark, and as an astute businessman, he recognizes its commercial value.

He was not "to the manor born." His dad ran a garage and automobile dealership outside Glasgow, Scotland. He himself did not finish high school (only much later in life did he discover that he was a victim of dyslexia, when one of his sons was diagnosed with that handicap). As a teenager, a big date with his girlfriend Helen (later to become his wife) was to take her out to Prestwick airport to watch the airplanes land and take off.

"It was cheaper than a movie," Jackie told me.

Two things were to influence his life strongly. His older brother, Jim, was a racing driver, good enough to compete at Le Mans. That piqued Jackie's interest in the sport. The other influence was skeet shooting. He was very good at it, good enough to become Scottish champion and narrowly miss qualifying for the British Olympic team.

In that sport, he met a number of wealthy men, and that, in time, led to his lofty social and business associations.

His racing achievements are the stuff of legend. He broke Jim Clark's world record for number of victories on the Grand Prix circuit (Jackie won twenty-seven to Clark's twenty-five), drawing crowds wherever he went.

He never won at Indianapolis, but they came to love him there. Once, when his car broke down during the 500 and he was forced to walk back to the pits, the crowd gave him a great cheer as he walked along, smiling and waving.

Stewart always seemed to be in the middle of some interesting news story. One evening in Indiana, he was being driven to a speaking engagement by a state trooper when the trooper recognized a stolen car. They gave chase and ended up capturing the miscreants.

"Would you believe it, Jim?" Jackie said. "As we were running after the kids, I saw a bagpipe band marching down the street, kilts and all."

Stewart was the first of the Grand Prix drivers to realize the commercial value of racing fame. He never failed to wear his little black cap, part of his image. He signed autographs until he was near exhaustion. And he accumulated sponsors at a dizzying pace.

Once, on the day before a Southern 500, on which he and I were going to comment, I sat with him in one of those dark, damply chilly Southern motel rooms, where the bath mats are made of paper and the television set is bolted to the wall, watching a PGA Tour golf tournament. At that time, golf was about the only major sport to hold out against the wearing of commercial logos.

As we sat there, Jackie groaned.

"Oh, Jim," he said. "It's such a waste. Look at that chap. If I were in his position, I would start with a tasteful logo for my airline sponsor on the shirt pocket. The cap, of course, is the logical place for the Ford automobile company I represent.

The only thing I have seen on the caps is the name of the Amana fridge company, and I'm told they get precious little money for wearing that."

He went on with his suggestions until the golfer was arrayed, in his mind's eye, with signs and stickers like a Formula One race car. "Oh, well," he said finally. "I'm sure Mark McCormack [founder and head of International Management Group and Jackie's agent] will take care of it shortly."

Which, of course, he did.

Stewart was as brave as any driver ever to pull on a helmet. But he was perhaps more intelligently cautious than any other. In 1973, his final year on the Grand Prix circuit, he had a physician accompany him to all the races, suspicious as he was of the medical precautions taken by the various race organizers. And when his teammate, the talented young Frenchman Francois Cevert, was killed in qualifying the day before the final race of the season at Watkins Glen, New York, Jackie withdrew from the competition.

He never drove his last race.

2. A. J. Foyt

Foyt epitomized the Indianapolis 500 driver, from the days of the tall, front-engined roadsters to the winged, rear-engined technical marvels of today. He won the great race four times, in both types of cars. And he did much more, driving any sort of race car that was presented to him, be it the powerful sports car of Le Mans, the burly stock car of Daytona, or a tiny sprint car at some little Texas track when he had a free night. Dirt track or asphalt, oval or road course, it was all the same to A. J., as long as there was a race to be won.

He raced them all, and he won them all, but Indy was his home track, the place he loved, and he was the image of Indy racing for a long, long time.

If Jackie Stewart enchanted reporters with his carefully honed, shiny public persona, A. J. dominated them with his tough, open-faced, challenging Texas manner. He was part car designer, part mechanic, part PR man, and most of all, captain of his ship. He was fiercely loyal to his faithful pit crew, especially to his father, Tony Foyt, whom he referred to as "my daddy."

If you walked by his garage door at Indy and it was closed, you never knocked. All you would get was a muffled snarl: "I'm busy!!" But if the door was open, you were welcome—if he knew you. And then his face would light up with a boyish smile.

When Foyt walked from Gasoline Alley into the pit area, a great cheer would go up. It was Babe Ruth striding to the plate at Yankee Stadium, Arnold Palmer hitching up his trousers on the first tee. He would smile and wave to the fans, then turn deadly serious, inspecting his bright orange race car from nose to tail, grabbing a wrench from a mechanic to attend to some small detail.

He was probably the most versatile race driver of his time, and still receives cheers wherever he goes, but my most lasting mental picture of him—and of the Indianapolis 500—is A. J. in the winner's circle, a strong, slightly overweight figure in a sweaty white racing uniform, wearing a smile as the Texas prairie, and holding aloft the traditional glass of milk given to the winner, while the crowd goes wild.

A. J. was their man. He was ecstatic in victory, furious in defeat. He was Texas. He was Indy. He was an American hero.

3. The Unser Family

Racing has been in the family blood for three generations now. Uncle Louie started the Unser tradition in the Pikes Peak hill climb, a tradition continued through two later generations. Uncle Louie himself drove in the event until he was well into his sixties, to a point where the organizers were becoming concerned for his safety. He wasn't about to stop, so they put in an age limit that applied to all entrants. But in most people's opinion, it was, in reality, the Uncle Louie Rule.

The Unsers must be treated as an entry because, among them, they have won nine Indianapolis 500s, and because their story is a family story, full of happiness, but dotted with tragedy.

There were three brothers who raced at Indianapolis. Jerry, the eldest, was killed there, but the two others carried on the name with great distinction. Al, the youngest, won the Indy 500 four times, tying A. J. Foyt for most Indy wins. Bobby, the middle brother, won three. And Al's son, Al Jr., has won twice.

And their younger sister died in a dune buggy crash.

After his retirement from racing, Bobby Unser became lost while on a snowmobile hunting expedition. He and a friend were found after spending two days in the freezing wilderness, during which time Unser came close to dying of hypothermia.

The Unser racing tradition continues today.

4. Mario Andretti

Some years ago, while on an overnight flight from New York to Milan, Italy, I was drifting off to sleep. The dinner service was over, the lights had been dimmed, the sound of the engines had a soporific effect. I pulled a blanket over my knees.

And suddenly, a bizarre and scary thought crossed my mind. Years before, the American Phil Hill was on the verge of becoming the first of his country to win the World Championship of Drivers. If he won the Grand Prix of Italy on the track at Monza, the prize would be his. And the only man with a chance to deprive him of the title was his Ferrari teammate, the German count Wolfgang "Taffy" von Trips. Trips crashed in the race, but it was only when the event was over that Hill learned his teammate was dead.

Phil stood on the winner's platform, a champion with a victory wreath around his neck and tears streaming down his face. He was beyond words, but his face spoke volumes.

Now, I was thinking, I'm headed for Monza, the same track, for the Grand Prix of Italy, the same race. A young American, Mario Andretti, has the opportunity to become only the second of his country to win the world championship. Again, the only other driver to have a chance at the title is his teammate, Ronnie Peterson of Sweden. The comparison was chilling. It felt like some kind of presentiment to me and I couldn't sleep at all.

When Peterson was involved in a multicar crash shortly after the start of the race, I waited fearfully for word on his condition. He was alive, the officials told me, but his legs were badly crushed. The Swedish driver was taken to the hospital by helicopter as Andretti went on to win the race and the championship.

The final tragic news didn't come until the next morning. Peterson had died when particles of bone filtered into his bloodstream. Only two Americans have won the World Championship to this day, and both won it at Monza, under nearly identical, and tragic, circumstances.

Mario Andretti actually was born and raised, until his early teens, in Italy. At the end of World War II he lived with his family, for a time, in a displaced persons camp in Trieste. It was there that he and his brother, Aldo, first sat in a race car, a small, less powerful version of the beautiful machine he now drove. Mario was hooked, and when his family moved to Nazareth, Pennsylvania, he already knew that his ambition was to be a race driver, and more specifically, the World Grand Prix champion.

That would take time. First came the country midget and sprint car tracks of Pennsylvania. Then the big track itself— Indianapolis. His success there was quick and dramatic, and he won the 500 in 1969.

With his prizefighter features, his ready smile, and his very slight Italian accent, he was an immediate idol of the sport. It was assumed that he would win more 500s, perhaps even more than his great rival, A. J. Foyt. It didn't happen.

Although he competed at Indy for a quarter-century, he never won again. Hard luck dogged him. If it wasn't a crash in practice or qualifying, it was a blown engine or an unavoidable accident in the race. He drove everywhere in the U.S., on what was then the USAC circuit and in NASCAR, but always in the back of his mind was the boyhood dream—the Grand Prix Championship. When he finally achieved it, the cloud of Ronnie Peterson's death hung over it.

But his fans never lost faith in him. He was a sympathetic figure, never pitied, even in defeat, but admired for his talent, his persistence, his decency, and his positive influence on the young, which continues as his career winds down.

Today, as in so many motor racing families, his son Michael carries on the family name as one of the sport's top drivers.

5. Phil Hill

How's this for a movie script? A young Californian grows up with Shirley Temple as his neighbor and boyhood crush, races midget cars near his Santa Monica home, then finds his way to Europe in post-World War II days. Encouraged by a tall, adventurous Texan named Carroll Shelby, who had become a sort of Pied Piper luring Americans to the Grand Prix circuit, the young man hooks on with the famous Ferrari team.

He becomes a romantic figure, a career bachelor who spends his evenings listening to classical music on the stereo set he takes with him everywhere or dining on great food and fine wines in the French restaurants he loves. He absorbs European culture—it becomes a part of him.

He has great success, winning the 24 Hours of Le Mans with his driving partner, the Belgian sophisticate Olivier Gendebien. He and his Formula One teammate, a dashing young

German count, battle for the world championship. The Californian wins when his teammate is killed in the final race of the season.

Hill is reduced to tears on the victory stand.

But the esteem of Enzo Ferrari, the George Steinbrenner of race car owners, doesn't last past the next season. Fired by Ferrari, the quietly intense Californian becomes a loner, making his way across Europe as a member of an ill-conceived and ill-fated team called ATS.

Then, he joins ABC as a commentator, speaking his mind plainly but obviously uncomfortable without a race car to drive.

And suddenly, he meets a beautiful, statuesque blond European schoolteacher named Alma. Well into his forties, he finally falls in love. They marry and return to Santa Monica, to the very house where he used to stare longingly out the back window, hoping to catch a glimpse of little Shirley Temple, tiny idol of a nation, whose house backed up to his backyard.

Here, he and his wife have two children, a boy and a girl. He makes a new career in what had been his hobby, the restoration of old automobiles, which he does right in the garage on his property. At the same time, he continues two other unusual hobbies, player piano rolls and antique music boxes—not the little ones, but great, impressive cabinet jobs.

He and his wife grow older together as their daughter turns into a beautiful young woman and their son becomes a handsome, talented race driver.

Some script. But it is, of course, the real-life story of Phil Hill.

Everything that Phil is and represents was summed up for me one night when Margaret and I came to California for a show to which I had been assigned.

I called Phil from the Beverly Hills Hotel and asked if he and Alma could come up from Santa Monica and have dinner with us. He said dinner would be a great idea, but that we would eat at a place he liked near his home, and that he would come get us.

I insisted that we could drive down in my rental car, but he would have none of that. He would pick us up at 7:00 P.M. sharp.

The entrance to the Beverly Hills Hotel just before seven o'clock each evening is always quite a scene. Limousines pull up one after another. Mercedes convertible follows BMW convertible, which follows Rolls-Royce Silver Shadow. The shrill sound of women's laughter blends with the rumble of CEOs' pronouncements, as the expensively dressed hotel guests eye each other to see if anybody there *is* anybody.

That night, we topped 'em all.

On the dot of seven, as we waited outside the lobby, we heard an old-fashioned automobile horn, the kind that goes *Ah-OO-gah!* Pulling up to the entrance was a gorgeous old Bentley painted in British racing green. It was a cloth-topped open sedan—a touring car—of the sort "the Bentley Boys" used to drive at Le Mans in the late 1920s.

At the wheel sat a smiling Phil Hill, wearing a duster, a cap, and goggles. He leaped down from the car, helped Margaret and me into the backseat, and roared off through the streets of Beverly Hills.

The sound of the great gears shifting and the engine roaring had heads turning as we reached Santa Monica Boulevard. To us, it seemed that Phil was going at racing speed as the Bentley careened around corners and the wind ruined Margaret's hair. But it was wonderful.

On our arrival at the Hill house, Alma greeted us and we went on a tour of the garage where Phil restores his vintage cars. When Margaret admired a royal blue sedan he had been working on, Phil said, "No, look carefully along the side. There's a ripple there. It looks like a bag of walnuts. It needs work!"

Inside the house, he showed us the music boxes. I had never seen such things. They were beautiful pieces of cabinet-work, some five or six feet tall, with matchless sound.

The most unexpected pleasure came to us in the living room. Phil brought us drinks as we sat in front of the fire. In back of us was a grand piano, but a different sort of grand. It was a player piano. Gesturing toward it, Phil said, "Would you like to hear Rachmaninoff play the piano?"

"Sure," I said, having no idea what he was talking about. I'm not exactly a classical music freak, but I did know that Rachmaninoff was dead.

He pulled from a drawer a piano roll, not much different from the ones I had played on my grandmother's old upright.

"Look," Phil said. "This is a piano roll, but a special kind. Instead of the holes just banging out the notes, this roll actually has recorded the *touch* of the person playing. This particular one is a piece composed by Rachmaninoff and *played* by Rachmaninoff."

So we sat there, sipping our Chivas Regal and listening to the ghost of the great composer actually playing his own music.

☆

These, then, are my top five motor racing personalities. It is difficult to leave out such men as Johnny Rutherford, Parnelli Jones, Rodger Ward, and Rick Mears for their pure driving skill at Indy. Similarly, Jim Clark, the quiet Scot; Emerson Fittipaldi, the versatile Brazilian; and the aforementioned Graham Hill belong in any Grand Prix Hall of Fame.

"King" Richard Petty is a NASCAR legend by anyone's standards. As Stewart epitomized Grand Prix and Foyt was the image of Indy, so Petty, with his good looks and infectious smile, his ever-present cowboy hat and sunglasses, his great driving skill, and his positive influence on the young, represented all that is good about stock car racing.

And I must mention Sam Posey, of Sharon, Connecticut. Sam never won a Grand Prix race or the Indy 500. He did finish a quite creditable fifth in his first try at Indianapolis, but unaccountably was not named Rookie of the Year. Some claimed this was because he was not a member of the Indy clan.

I put Sam in my memorable group because of his racing, writing, and speaking skills. To say nothing of his painting. Educated at the highly respected Rhode Island School of Design, Sam used to say he wasn't sure whether he was a race driver who paints or a painter who drives race cars.

As a racing commentator, as he sat beside me in the booth speaking in his Ivy League accent, he could make the design of a favorite race car sound like a sculpture by Michelangelo. To him, the driving of A. J. Foyt was as admirable as the violin playing of Jascha Heifetz. As he described a driver stalking another in the closing laps of a race, he made it sound like James Bond closing in on the KGB's top agent. He finds both of his worlds—art and sport—worthy of respect.

Today, he and his wife, Ellen, an artist, live and work in Connecticut, where he paints, writes, and designs houses.

I came to motor racing with a preconceived mental picture of laconic mechanics in grease-stained coveralls going round and round in noisy, smoke-throwing monsters. It has been one of the pleasant surprises of my career to have found a fascinating sport, populated by some extremely interesting, diverse, and articulate people, competing on a wide variety of race courses around the world.

They do not, I can assure you, drive because of a death wish. Rather, every one of them, each in his own way, has an inner curiosity to see how close he can come to death and still cheat the Grim Reaper. And each is totally convinced that he *will* win over the dark forces.

It's too bad that it doesn't always work out that way.

200 Times Around the World: 1961–1998

The tale of our *Wide World of Sports* show sprawls over four decades, five million miles, a thousand or so airplane rides, and an equal number of hotel rooms, ranging in comfort from a truck stop in Oregon to Holiday Inns and Quality Courts around the U.S.A., Claridge's in London, the Ritz in Paris, and the old National in Moscow.

That first summer of 1961 set the tone. The ten years that followed were a decade of discovery—discovering new sports for television and new exotic locales for me, arrayed all over the world.

Not that I really got to know these stopovers. My trips lasted days, not weeks, and we were working all the time.

The way we began to get the hang of covering international sports was from our fascinating, but excruciating, experience in Moscow in July of 1961—perhaps the hottest time of the Cold War.

It took a great deal of audacity for the producer of a summer replacement sports show (that's what it was then, just a summer fill-in) to think he could penetrate the Iron Curtain, but Roone Arledge has never lacked for audacity, nor has he ever allowed budgetary problems to stand in the way of progress. So he decided that we would go to Moscow and televise the U.S.-Soviet track-and-field meet.

This took a lot of doing. We were in the depths of the Cold War at that time. The Bay of Pigs disaster had occurred less than three months before. The Soviet government was suspicious of all American visitors and extremely reluctant to issue visas. In addition, Roone intended to take our own equipment and technicians with us—twenty tons of equipment and half a hundred engineers.

Frustration followed frustration in dealing with the Soviets, and with less than a week to go it looked like our trip might not occur. Someone from ABC sat in the Soviet embassy for days, waiting for the permits that were promised, but didn't come. A big decision had to be made. If the technicians and equipment weren't sent on their way, they would never make it in time for the event.

Roone took the gamble and sent them to the Netherlands, where they waited for permission to fly on to Moscow. Just in time, the necessary documents were obtained and the ABC men flew on.

They had no idea what awaited them on arrival. How would they get all their equipment from the airport to the stadium? Where would they set up when they got to the site of the event, Lenin Stadium?

Arriving in Moscow that July was a true culture shock. The airport terminal was large, but had something of the feeling of an abandoned World War II air base. Nobody seemed to be minding the store, except for an extremely ominous-looking customs inspector. He had a narrow forehead, a drooping mustache that accentuated his melancholy manner, and piercing eyes that told you not to cross him.

In front of me in the line was a Soviet citizen returning from a foreign trip. The customs inspector not only opened his bag, but took out every single item of clothing that the man had with him. He turned each item over, glancing up at the man after he had studied each piece. It took him a good twenty minutes to finish with the single bag. His final act was the most alarming. There were two bars of soap, which he unwrapped. Then he took a knife from his pocket and slit each one horizontally in half. There was nothing inside, so he pushed all the man's belongings to the end of the counter, gave him a curt nod that he could leave, and left him to repack his bag.

It was my turn. If he took that long with a Soviet citizen, how long would he take with the enemy? His approach was different. No friendlier, but different. He put my bags aside and beckoned me to a bare adjoining room. We waited there for some forty-five minutes until we were joined by a friendly young man, speaking near-perfect, American-accented English, who identified himself as our guide.

When we asked him about our luggage, he said it would be in our rooms at the National Hotel when we arrived.

The ride into town had the same feeling of an abandoned village that the airport had had. We saw no private cars, only the occasional army truck rumbling across a desert of potholes and one official car with flags on the fenders that resembled a 1949 De Soto. At one point, we passed a huge, rusting tank trap.

"It is there," our young guide explained, "to remind us that the Nazis got that far—to the outskirts of Moscow—but no farther."

Sure enough, our bags were waiting for us at the hotel, and sure enough, our clothes were just rumpled enough to indicate that the luggage had been thoroughly searched.

All during our stay, Moscow had the feeling of a big city in which most of the people were unseen except at the morning and evening rush hours, when they would flood into or out of the beautiful subway stations. Downtown, the great boulevard was wide enough to accommodate an army. That may have been its purpose, because there certainly was no civilian traffic.

The National Hotel was a relic of czarist days. It had the appearance and feeling of a great house that had been inherited by someone who didn't have the funds to keep it up.

Roone and I were assigned to be roommates in an immense chamber with two big, heavy-looking beds. There was no decoration on the walls. For light, there was a chandelier left over from the old days and two tiny bed lamps. The weak lighting reminded me of Mel Brooks's line about Zagreb. When asked what the city was like, Brooks said that it was the kind of place where the whole city was lit by one forty-watt bulb.

Tom Moore, the president of ABC, had come with us on the trip. One morning he, Tom Jr., and I visited the tomb in Red Square, which at that time held the bodies of Lenin and Stalin. We agreed with Tom Sr. that it was a hell of an embalming job. I considered his opinion to be an expert one, since at one time he had been an executive at Forest Lawn Cemetery in Los Angeles.

We made the required trip to the huge GUM department store, where we saw women waiting in an endless line to buy some rather tacky-looking winter hats—and this was in July! Most of the counters seemed to be out of whatever it was that they were selling.

Eating dinner was not a simple matter. In the hotel dining room, a big, spare echo chamber, glum waiters in what looked like leftover fancy uniforms from czarist days stood in the corners talking to each other. Surprisingly, there was a menu of many pages, listing all sorts of meat and fish dishes—surprisingly, that is, until we noted that almost all of them were crossed off. Borscht seemed to be the best bet, washed down with your choice of warm beer or warm champagne.

It was a far cry from today's Moscow, with its gourmet restaurants for the elite, and McDonald's for the ordinary citizen—if he can afford it.

Room keys were huge things worthy of a medieval castle's front gate. They were kept by stern, elderly women stationed on each floor, who made sure that you left the key when you were out and identified yourself before picking up the key when you returned.

One landmark did strike me as a great idea. It was a huge outdoor swimming pool, perhaps an acre in size, in which thousands of people frolicked in the July sunshine. That was impressive in itself, but I really paid attention when our guide told me that it was open in the wintertime, too. How was that possible? Well, the swimmer changed his clothes in a mammoth locker room, then entered the heated pool through an underwater tunnel. When he swam out into the open air, he was in warm water, his head surrounded by the warm steam rising from the pool. I wasn't sure I believed him, but on a later trip to Moscow, I saw it in operation.

The only real signs of life and enthusiasm we found on that trip to Moscow were at the scene of the event—Lenin Stadium. The track-and-field meet between the U.S. and the Soviet Union was obviously to be a showpiece. The stadium was scrubbed and freshly painted. The track was a modern synthetic one. Workers were scrambling to get everything in perfect condition for the athletes—and for our cameras.

Still, our every move was monitored very carefully. Roone requested a camera position at field level to get tight close-ups of the athletes in action and reacting after victory or defeat. After a long wait, the cameras were okayed, but when we arrived the next day, Soviet cameras were right beside ours, proving once again that imitation is the sincerest form of flattery.

The one thing that could not be duplicated was our video-tape equipment, and that would prove to be the technical marvel of the weekend for the crowd in the stadium. Rather than put our tape machines in a truck, as we do normally at home, or in a room under the stadium grandstand, the Soviets put them on one of the ramps leading to the upper seats. As a result, several thousand fans were able to peek over the railings and see what was happening with the machines. The first time our technicians played back something that had just happened, a gasp went up from the people. How was this possible? The race had just finished on the track, and now they were seeing it again!—no film in the world could be developed that quickly! Word spread and crowds began coming from other sections to see this magic.

The reason for the spectators' surprise was that videotape was at that time unknown in the Soviet Union. In fact, two of our technicians had been instructed to sleep with the tape heads under their pillows to prevent espionage.

Two athletes in the competition—one American and one Soviet—stand out in memory. The American was the late Wilma Rudolph—Wonderful Wilma, as she was called. She dominated the women's sprints as few have, before or since. But she also had an unself-conscious charisma that communicated itself to all who watched her.

She was a handsome, long-legged woman, serene in manner—until she burst from the blocks. For the first few meters, she would be even with the field, then she would slip smoothly into another dimension, and at that moment a roar would start from the crowd. As she left the others behind, it was a roar of appreciation somewhat like the one that accompanied Secretariat as he won the Belmont by thirty-one lengths, or Babe Ruth as he circled the bases after yet another home run.

Less than a year before the Moscow meet, in the Rome Olympics, this girl who had been stricken with polio as a child had captured the world as she won three gold medals, in the 100 meters, the 200 meters, and the sprint relay.

Now, on that July day in Moscow, it mattered not to the ninety thousand in the crowd that she was defeating the home team. It was just a display of excellence that would always be remembered by those who saw it. I remember white, Mississippi-born Tom Moore, standing beside me in the booth, shouting as the black woman came to the wire, "Come on, Wilma. Pour it on, baby!"

The other memorable athlete was the Soviet high jumper Valery Brumel. Young, tall, slender, and handsome, he looked more like an American wide receiver than the idol-to-be of the Soviet Union. He had failed in his quest for an Olympic gold medal the year before. He and his teammate, Robert Shavlakadze, each had cleared 7' 1", but Shavlakadze won on the basis of fewer misses during the competition. Now Brumel would make his mark before the crowd in Lenin Stadium and on the TV screens of millions of American living rooms.

As the event proceeded, the skies darkened. The other

jumpers failed, one at a time, but Brumel sailed over height after height and by late afternoon was the only one left. Now it was pouring rain, but he signaled to raise the bar again. He would go for a world record. The crowd loved it as he stood staring at the bar, rain dripping from his chin, a picture of total concentration. We were huddled under a big piece of plastic that someone had produced.

Brumel bobbed his head once, stalked the bar, increased speed, then flung himself up and forward—and safely over! The height—7' 4¼", a new world record. The stadium erupted. Soviet soldiers threw their caps in the air, red balloons floated into the sky, a male Russian coach ran up and kissed Brumel on the lips, as is the Russian custom (although I had noticed earlier that when the burly, scowling Soviet female shot-putter, Tamara Press, had won her event, the same coach just shook her hand).

The most pleasant person we met over there was our guide, Nikolai. He had a great interest in things American, and patiently, sometimes persuasively, explained the Soviet point of view to us. When I asked him why they felt they had to dominate Eastern Europe the way they did, he told us that his country had suffered twenty million dead in World War II.

"My mother was reduced to chewing on shoe leather during the siege of Leningrad," he said. "We will never let these things happen again."

When it came time to leave Moscow, I met Nikolai in the lobby of the hotel. I asked him if there was anything he would like me to send him from America.

His answer surprised me.

"Perhaps you cannot do it," he said, "but I would like very much to have a button-down-collar shirt." On the spot, I opened my suitcase and gave him an oxford-weave, light blue button-down shirt, complete with the little loop in the back of the collar. I hope that capitalist garment didn't get him into trouble with the dictatorship of the proletariat.

Moscow, then, was a trip to remember, but I was more

than ready to leave. There was a final strange surprise on the way to the airport. As I got into the car, the leather sole of my right shoe came totally loose. The entire bottom, except for the heel, would flap as I raised my foot, then make a slapping noise as it hit the ground again. It was a ludicrous sight, one that Roone and Chuck Howard found deliriously funny. We'll never know whether the shoe had been examined one day in my absence from the room by the KGB or not.

This might be considered a paranoid thought by some, but you never knew in those days. Maybe they thought I might have a telephone in my shoe, like the TV comedy character Maxwell Smart.

It was certainly embarrassing for me. But as we were checking our bags, a Russian baggage handler beckoned to me to approach him. He held out his hand, smiling, indicating that he wanted my shoe.

I gave it to him, whereupon he took from his back pocket something that looked like an ice pick. He used it to punch holes all around the edge of the sole, then ran to a side room and returned with a big roll of coarse wire. He threaded the wire through the holes, and there it was, a crude but certainly usable shoe with an attached sole. Our entire group cheered him, he smiled and bowed, and we went to the plane.

That trip to Moscow really set up the whole odyssey of ABC's *Wide World of Sports*.

Looking back on it all, over the four decades, here are the other memories that have stayed with me, that I know I will never forget.

THE SIXTIES

For kids growing up in America and for the world at large, the sixties were perhaps the decade of disillusion, but for us, in our circumscribed little world of sport, they were the decade of discovery.

In addition to major events like the U.S.-Soviet track meet, the 24 Hours of Le Mans, and the World Figure Skating Championships, we found sports we had never seen before, and a few of which we had never heard. And the most important thing we discovered was the intensity of interest the participants had in the most obscure events.

In the beginning, there was a temptation to treat some of the sports and the athletes with tongue in cheek, but I learned a lesson about that, to my embarrassment, one day at a down-at-the-heels little racetrack in Islip, Long Island. The event was the "World" Demolition Derby Championship, staged by a melancholy man named Larry Mendelson.

Larry was the inventor of the Demo Derby concept and the sport's "commissioner" and absolute ruler. He had decreed that anyone who won a Demo Derby anywhere in the world during the regular summer season (the "world" being a circuit that stretched all the way from New England to Pennsylvania) would be eligible for the season-ending World Championship at Islip. Islip, which has long since fallen on hard times like the cars that used to fill its infield, was at the time the Demo Derby equivalent of the Indianapolis Motor Speedway.

The event was won that day by a young man from Manassas, Virginia, whose name I fear has been lost somewhere in the sands of time along with the records of Demolition Derby championships.

Remarkably, the Manassas man had won the event for the second year in a row.

As I made my way down to the course, filled with the smoking, dented shells of the losing cars, I thought of his achievement as something like hitting the lottery. Here was an event that seemed to require little, if any, skill, that was simply a matter of old, beat-up cars smashing into each other until only one was left.

Approaching him for an interview with an unseemly smirk on my face, I asked him, "Well, Mr. Lucky, how do you account for winning the World Championship two years in a row?"

I thought he would be as amused as I was at the absurdity of it all.

Instead, he looked at me very seriously, thought for a few seconds, then said, "Well, I worked real hard on gettin' my car ready—and I go to church a lot." There was no humor in his voice.

I felt my face flush in embarrassment. I had committed an unforgivable bit of gaucherie, looking down on this man in a condescending manner during what he considered the greatest moment of his life.

I learned a lesson that day. Since then, I have tried to approach all sports, no matter how small or how odd, through the eyes of its competitors.

Rodeo looked to me in the beginning like simply a bunch of crazy cowboys taking wild risks. Then I went behind the chutes and saw that almost every contestant was wearing some sort of brace or bandage under his working clothes. I found that they had to perform week after week, indoors or out, in small towns and big cities, with injuries major and minor, if they were to make a decent living.

I watched the rodeo clowns and enjoyed their broad humor, then developed respect for them when I came to realize that their most important function is not to make people laugh, but to distract the wild bull when he is about to attack a cowboy lying helplessly on the ground. The clown's job is the most dangerous in a dangerous business.

He must be funny and brave at the same time.

There was the time at the World Barrel Jumping Championships when the seventeen-barrel barrier was broken. You might laugh at a "World" championship being conducted on the little ice-skating rink at Grossinger's Hotel in New York's Catskill Mountains, and you might snicker at someone comparing leaping over barrels on ice skates with the historic barrier of the four-minute mile. But you wouldn't if you had been there, as I was, the day that Kenny Lebell, of Lake Placid, actually broke that seventeen-barrel barrier.

Like running the sub-four-minute mile, clearing seventeen barrels had been considered an impossible feat by most people in the sport. But on that bitter winter's day, as I sat at my table describing the event, with our eight-year-old son, Sean, standing behind me, I realized that this was a moment to be respected.

As Kenny soared over the barrels and landed successfully, looked back to make sure the barrels hadn't been disturbed, then leaped joyfully in the air, the crowd around the Grossinger's skating rink, mostly New Yorkers on holiday, burst into cheers. Kenny's supporters swarmed around him and lifted him to their shoulders as his wife's tears flowed. To that dedicated little band of skaters, this was Bob Beamon's leap in the 1968 Olympics, Mary Lou Retton's vault at Los Angeles.

Even our son Sean, a low-key personality at the age of eight, as now in his position as president of CBS Sports, jumped up and down, cheering.

The promoter of that event is worth mentioning here, because he had been a world-class athlete of note. As a young man from the asphalt jungle of New York, Irving Jaffee had beaten the favorites from the frozen tundra of Scandinavia in the 1932 Winter Games at Lake Placid, winning gold medals in both the 5,000- and 10,000-meter speed skating races.

Standing beside the rink at Grossinger's before the barrel jumping that day, Jaffee told me how he became famous in an event often ignored by the media. The day before the 10,000, Irving went up to the famous radio sports announcer Ted Husing of CBS, who also narrated the newsreel, and complained that there was no way he could get publicity should he win the race. It was a long race to begin with, taking almost twenty minutes to complete. And the newsreels, the closest thing there was to television in those days, were certainly not going to shoot a twenty-minute race.

"No," Husing said. "They probably won't show the race. But—" Husing said, his eyes a-twinkle, "if you should throw

yourself across the finish line and slide headfirst to victory,
then, I guarantee you, they will show it!"

Jaffee explained that he, or whoever won, probably would
win by a hundred yards or more in a race that long. There
would be no need to throw himself across the finish line. It
would look ridiculous.

"Just do what I tell you," Husing said.

Sure enough, Jaffee slid to an easy victory, the newsreels
used it, and Irving became a national celebrity—the American
who slid to the gold.

We shared our discovery of faraway places with the *Wide
World* audience. Everywhere we went in that first decade, we
did an introductory piece about the city or country where the
event was being staged.

In Prague, at the 1962 World Figure Skating championships, I told the story of my entry into the country. While
changing money at the airport, I noticed a worn, sepia picture
of the city on the wall behind the old man changing the money
for me.

Making conversation, I said, "It looks like you have a beautiful city here."

He didn't raise his eyes, just kept sorting the money,
squinting through his steel-rimmed glasses. Then he said,
"Well, it used to be. But then, you will see for yourself." It was
a dangerous thing for him to say in a country then held in the
iron fist of the Soviet Union.

Without getting government permission, Roone had us
drive our cumbersome mobile unit through the streets with a
camera mounted on a cowcatcher attached to the front of the
truck. We shot everything we saw, including a statue of Stalin,
which had a wooden scaffolding around it. In my commentary, I explained that the government had told the people they
were going to take down the statue because the foundation
was weakening. In fact, a citizen of Prague told me they were

taking it down because they were afraid that if they didn't the people would tear it down first.

One morning while walking downtown on my way to the skating arena, I saw a man driving a motorized street sweeper being applauded by people on the sidewalk. He was Emil Zátopek, a national hero, winner of the 5,000 meters, 10,000 meters, and the marathon at the Helsinki Olympics in 1952. It was a fantastic performance, but now Emil, a political dissident, had been reduced by the government to sweeping the streets.

The applause was the people's answer. And it was not an isolated occurrence. Our interpreter told us quietly that the applause had become an almost daily phenomenon in the repressed city. Zátopek's face, he said, was more recognizable to the public than that of any of the politicians then ruling the country.

The citizens made a political statement with their cheers in the competition, also, when a brother-and-sister skating pair, Otto and Maria Jelinek, won the gold medal. And a tremendous roar rocked the arena when they came out for a postcompetition exhibition wearing the peasant costumes of another time and skating joyfully to polka music.

The very appearance of the Jelineks in Prague was a reminder of happier days to the Czech audience. Otto and Maria had been born in Czechoslovakia, but, as small children, had fled across the border with their parents one dark night in 1949 and made their way to Canada. The parents still were barred from their native land, but the youngsters received special permission from the Communist government to travel to the championships, with a guarantee of safe conduct.

We filmed our mini-travelogues everywhere we went. When we went to Copenhagen for waterskiing, we did pieces on Hamlet's Castle, Hans Christian Andersen, The Little Mermaid statue, and the famous Tivoli Gardens amusement park. For ski racing and bobsledding, we took our viewers to St. Moritz, winter refuge of the rich and famous, where the local grocery store's most popular item is caviar; and for rodeo we

took them to the Strip in Las Vegas, where the flashing electric signs included one that said, MINISTER, MARRIAGE LICENSE,
24-HOUR SERVICE, FEE INCLUDES MUSIC AND FLOWERS. The music,
of course, was recorded, and the flowers were artificial.

In May 1964, we visited Paris in the spring for one of the
most unusual of all our *Wide World* events. A team of mountaineers, three Frenchman and an Englishman, decided, for
reasons best known to themselves, to scale the Eiffel Tower,
from the outside, using only the rivet heads for footholds.

The event was televised live on Eurovision before an immense on-scene crowd of Parisians and tourists. It was a
lovely day, and as our camera panned around the city from
the second level of the tower, I described Paris as looking like
"a pretty girl with flowers in her hair." I tend to get carried
away in Paris.

Before making their final assault on the top, the mountaineers stopped at the first, and then the second, level. Instead of resting and planning their strategy, the Frenchmen
went into the tower restaurant for some jovial conversation,
accompanied by cheese and a suitable wine. The Englishman
tagged along.

Just after they left the second level, there was an added,
and unwelcome, starter. As I sat in the restaurant sipping my
own glass of wine, I saw a fellow suddenly clamber onto the
intricate grillwork of the tower, and begin climbing! I shouted
for the police and pointed. A chase ensued, at the end of
which, fortunately, the intruder was captured, unharmed.
Under questioning, the inebriated man explained that he had
once worked on the tower as a painter, and that he had bet
some of his friends that he could climb the Eiffel as easily as
the mountaineers.

Meanwhile, the professionals scaled the final few feet,
pulled themselves over the fence at the top, and received their
reward, champagne—not over their heads, as at the World
Series, but inside their mouths, in the more intelligent French
way.

Three years later, there was another *Wide World* event that I will never forget.

Sir Francis Chichester, a man in his sixties who had, in his words, "willed away" cancer a decade earlier, sailed around the world—alone. *Wide World* covered his arrival back home in Plymouth, England, and his press conference.

Someone asked him if the conclusion of his journey was a great victory. He stuttered for a moment, then said, "See here! You're talking to a man who's been alone for months, like living in a cave or something like that. I've been through terrible storms rounding Cape Horn, and all sorts of things. When you've tried so very hard to do something, victory means nothing. It's the trying that counts."

Chichester was an example of excellence in the human character, the true mark of a hero, for which I have always searched.

Not all of our events were minor, or unusual, ones, and none of them were of the "Made for TV" variety. The small sports I have mentioned all existed before we came along. Each, in its way, had its own dignity and tradition. They were legitimate sports—not the contrived events where men carried refrigerators on their backs or tried to lift up a car.

We covered international track and field, the British Open, Canada Cup (now World Cup) and Bing Crosby Invitational golf, Grand Prix motor racing, NASCAR racing, the Indianapolis 500, horse racing from England, Ireland, and France, the Pan American Games from Brazil, the Wimbledon men's singles final, international ski racing from Sun Valley, and many other sports. With commentary by Howard Cosell, *Wide World* covered the career of Muhammad Ali, nee Cassius Marcellus Clay, from his first stunning victory over Sonny Liston to the very end.

Years after his retirement, on our thirtieth anniversary program, he was a special guest. As the host, I said to him,

"Muhammad, you always told us you were the greatest. Now, looking back on your career, we know you were right."

Ali, suffering from an advanced case of Parkinson's disease, had walked slowly onto the stage, stood with his head down, and mumbled, "Thanks, Jim, but we're all gettin' on in years now, aren't we?" Then he walked off, to a standing ovation. That picture, contrasted with memories of the handsome, quick-witted, lightning-fast Ali we had known, provided a touching and memorable moment.

On April 22, 1967, *Wide World* became a participant, an actual competitor, in an odd event, the London-to-Brighton run for veteran cars. It is an annual race to the sea, commemorating the "Emancipation of the Automobile," the day in 1904 on which it was no longer the law in England that every automobile had to be preceded on the highway by a man carrying a red flag! The "newest" cars allowed in the run are 1904 models.

A wealthy classic car enthusiast from Oklahoma named Jim Leake provided our car, a 1904 Reo (the initials of its manufacturer, Ransom E. Olds, who also invented the Oldsmobile before selling out to General Motors). Phil Hill, the former World Grand Prix driving champion, and himself an old-car buff, was the driver. I was the "navigator."

London to Brighton, a distance of about fifty miles, is not really a race. It is a "run," in which every car arriving before 4:00 P.M. (after having started at 8:00 A.M.) is awarded a little pennant to fly from its fender—or "wing," as the English would have it.

Dressed in the driving clothes of the time—capes, deerstalker caps, and goggles—Hill and I made our snaillike way to Brighton in the open car, under overcast skies and through occasional showers, breaking down four times. Once, we stopped at a country pub for a shepherd's pie and a pint of bitter, and altogether were having a wonderful time, until we realized that it was nearing four o'clock, and we were in danger of not reaching the finish line in time to win our pennant.

Suddenly, Phil was transformed from a hobbyist enjoying

himself into a champion race driver in danger of losing the day. Bending over the wheel, he pushed the car furiously to its limit (about ten miles an hour). At one point, he started to pass our camera car, which was riding in front of us, documenting our progress with a camera mounted on the tailgate.

"Phil," I shouted into the wind, "you can't pass the camera car. That's why we're here!"

"Maybe that's why *you're* here," he screamed back, "but *I'm* here to get to Brighton!"

Fortunately, we weren't able to pass the camera car.

Finally, we reached the Brighton waterfront. It was quite a sight. On the heights above the road, a crowd estimated at a hundred thousand was gathered, cheering home the old cars. Then, our car stopped again. It was three minutes to four.

Hill's best efforts could not get it started, so he leaped back into the driver's seat. "Push, Jim!" he ordered me. "Push, dammit!" So, I pushed and pushed, while the crowd cheered me on and the P.A. announcer said, "Here come the Yanks! Can they make it? Let's encourage them!"

Encourage they did, shouting and applauding, until I pushed the little car across the line. At that moment, somewhere in the distance, a church bell chimed four o'clock. We'd earned our pennant.

We had named the car Emmy, after the TV award, and darned if the London-to-Brighton segment wasn't instrumental in bringing *Wide World* an Emmy later that year.

Our decade of discovery had taken me farther than I had ever dreamed.

THE SEVENTIES

The decade that brought the world Watergate, the end of the Vietnam War, the breakup of the Beatles, and people saying "Have a nice day" also saw *Wide World of Sports* still chasing around the globe in pursuit of games large and small.

Recognition, in the form of Emmys, Peabodys, and other

awards for the show, began to line the walls of Roone Arledge's big corner office. I won some myself. The onetime summer replacement program had by now become a staple of American television. Our signature phrase, "The thrill of victory and the agony of defeat," had become part of the American language. It appeared regularly in newspaper stories. Comedians referred to it in their routines. People used it more and more in ordinary conversation.

I even saw a billboard in Oklahoma advertising a podiatrist who claimed that he could cure "de agony of de feet!"

At the very beginning of the decade, in the winter of 1970, a little-known athlete appeared on *Wide World*, and with one startling, and unintended, action, earned himself a place on our weekly opening sequence, where he would remain for a long time to come.

We were covering the World Gymnastics Championships in Lyubjyana, Yugoslavia, when our producer, Denny Lewin, came down to lunch in the hotel, wagging his head.

"I just saw something live on Eurovision that I guarantee you will be on our show next week. At the ski flying in Germany, a Yugoslavian guy went off the jump on the side and almost killed himself and an official standing there! It was unbelievable!"

So it was, but true. And Denny was right in his prediction: Not only did the ill-starred jumper show up on *Wide World* the next week, but he has been appearing on the opening of our program every week, with the end not yet in sight. To this day, people approach me to ask, "Whatever happened to that ski jumper?" or "Who was that guy who fell off the ski jump? I heard he was killed. Was he?"

Well, he is a man named Vinko Bogataj (rhymes with "bowtie"). He wasn't killed or seriously injured. Just a slight concussion, and he lived to jump on many other days, albeit not too successfully. He was a true amateur, whose day job was driving a forklift truck in an anchor chain factory. On the side, he is something of an artist.

For *Wide World*'s twentieth anniversary dinner in 1981, at

the Waldorf-Astoria Hotel in New York, Vinko was flown over to join us. He had no clue as to why he was famous in America—he certainly wasn't back home—but when it was explained to him, he just smiled and shrugged.

Dressed for the occasion in black-tie regalia, Vinko sat, rather stunned, as we showed the fifteen hundred dinner guests a tape of his crash. Then I introduced him and asked him to stand. His reception was tumultuous, a standing ovation. The only other standing ovation that night was for the U.S. hockey team, which had beaten the Soviets and won the gold medal in the previous year's Winter Olympics.

After dinner, Vinko diffidently presented me with a water-color of the ancient Yugoslavian town of Dubrovnik, painted by him. In the lower-right-hand corner, he had signed, "To my friend, Jim . . . Vinko."

The next day, he returned the tuxedo and went back to Yugoslavia and his forklift.

The watercolor hangs on the wall in our home.

In 1971, I was introduced to cricket by the English talk show specialist David Frost at the sport's holy of holies, Lord's Cricket Ground in London. In Pensacola, Florida, I covered the U.S. Air Force Fighter Interceptor Rocketry Meet, with a man colorfully named Colonel Jimmy Jumper as my expert commentator. Colonel Jumper was the handsome embodiment of an air force recruiting poster and was, in fact, the inspiration for the hero of the adventure comic strip *Terry and the Pirates*.

The Little League World Series, in Williamsport, Pennsylvania, became a staple during the seventies, and I was usually the play-by-play man. A highlight for me was the year that Ted Williams was signed as my analyst. I had admired the famous hitter from afar for many years, but had never met him until

I entered the restaurant of the Holiday Inn in Williamsport to meet him and our producer, Denny Lewin, for dinner.

I was two or three minutes late, and as I looked around the dimly lit room I heard a loud voice shout, *"Well, here he comes—finally! The famous sportscaster, fashionably late—to meet the worn-out old ballplayer! Get the hell over here, McKay!"* The voice did not sound friendly.

"Oh, my God," I thought, "are all the horror stories I've heard about Williams true? Does my hero have feet of clay and a voice of thunder? Does he hate me even before we've met?"

As I walked up to the table, I made a quick appraisal of the heavy man who sat with Denny Lewin. No longer was he the "Splendid Splinter" of memory, but the face was still handsome, and the eyes were as keen and wary as when he was facing some hard-throwing pitcher in the old days. His mouth was serious, but I sensed there was a twinkle behind the eyes. I took a chance.

"What the hell are you talking about, Ted?" I said, with a smile. "It's only two minutes after seven."

He stared at me angrily, then erupted in a loud laugh. "Okay, come on," he said. "Sit down and let's have a drink." Apparently, the raucous greeting had been some sort of test, and I had passed it.

For the rest of the weekend, I found Ted to be a pleasant and fascinating guy. He was wonderful with the Little League kids, but with adults, his friendliness was always tinged with caution. In his playing days, he had been ravaged by some of the Boston press for too many years not to be defensive.

Ted Williams remains an American hero to me, on the baseball field and in the air as a U.S. fighter pilot. I wonder what baseball records he would have set if he had not gone to war for his country—twice.

☆

When a man named George Willig suddenly, and illegally, scaled the World Trade Center Building in Manhattan one day

in 1977, attracting a huge crowd of spectators and half of the
New York City Police Department, he became an overnight
celebrity. Willig, it developed, was not a nutcase, just an experienced mountaineer having a little fun. In the ensuing
months, we traveled George around the country to climb various rock faces for our *Wide World* audience.

☆

In October of the same year, we covered the farewell game of
soccer's greatest star, Pele, at Giants Stadium in New Jersey.
A crowd of more than seventy thousand was on hand for the
occasion, as the charismatic Brazilian stood in the middle of
the field at a microphone and said, "Please say with me three
times the word 'love.' " The hardened denizens of the metro-
politan area complied like a huge chorus of children, shouting, seventy thousand strong, "Love! Love! Love!" It was a
strangely touching moment in the stadium where Giants football fans on a later afternoon would throw icicles and snow-
balls at the players.

☆

I visited China in January of 1977 for a gymnastics competition between the People's Republic and the U.S. It was an experience.

Early each morning in Beijing's Tiananmen Square, we
saw thousands of people doing centuries-old slow-motion ex-
ercises. They were not young people being prepared for military service, but mostly older folk, staying in shape. Later in
the morning, tens of thousands pedaled their bicycles through
the downtown streets on their way to work. The only cars I
saw were official vehicles.

The sight of all that exercise sent me back to my hotel
room to do a few push-ups.

We visited the Forbidden City and the Summer Palace and
had tea at the American embassy. And we saw evidence of
either preparedness—or paranoia.

Our guide took us to a tailor shop on a small side street.

There, behind the counter, an attendant lifted a rug, revealing a door in the floor. When the door was lifted, we descended a staircase into a strange and fascinating world. It featured long, lighted corridors, dining rooms with chandeliers, kitchens, large rooms for sleeping, ventilation—everything to sustain life over a long period of time. The main tunnel, our guide said, ran some twenty miles to the suburbs of Beijing.

I asked him what it was for.

"In case of invasion," he said.

"By us?" I asked.

He shook his head. "No," he said. "The Soviet Union. They came and told us we were brothers, but we came to find that they only wanted to make us their satellite."

The same attitude surfaced when we went to the Great Wall of China.

"Who was this built to guard against all those centuries ago?" I asked our guide.

"The same as today," he said. "The people from the north."

He pointed in the general direction of the Soviet Union.

It was at the Great Wall that I indulged myself in a whimsical feat. During the long hours on the plane from New York to Tokyo on the way to China, I somehow took it into my head that it would be fun to hit a golf ball over the Wall, so I bought a Mizuno pitching wedge and a sleeve of three Titlists at the Tokyo airport.

Our day at the Great Wall proved to be a cold one, but I was determined to fulfill my folly. Shedding my coat, and with our cameras rolling, I stood beside the Wall. Because of the steepness of the terrain, I was only able to stand about twenty feet back from it. I hit the first ball thin, and it bounced off the Wall and back down the hill. The second ball was high enough, but landed on the Wall itself, scattering confused Chinese tourists in several directions.

I had only one ball left. The pressure on me had to be at least as extreme as if I were putting on the final hole of the U.S. Open.

I was—umm—up to it. I can still see ball number three

arcing gracefully over the Wall into what I referred to on the show as "history's most unplayable lie."

So, the show went on.

But in mid-decade, there was a change. Spurred on by the success of Howard Cosell's segments with Muhammad Ali, and in a ratings battle with the other networks, *Wide World*'s schedule became top-heavy with boxing segments—actual fights, live or on tape, some competitive, others ludicrous mis-matches; interviews with boxers; and on one occasion, even a segment on the cancellation of a fight. By my own count, *Wide World* in the seventies featured 159 segments on boxing. To me, that was far too many, and endangered our show's reputa-tion as the place to go for a broad variety of sports.

The story of Muhammad Ali was certainly one of the most compelling of our time, in any sport. But it was a far cry from the incredible skills, unpredictable antics, and brave political stands of Ali to some of the deplorable stuff that was offered on *Wide World* through the seventies.

And there was something else. On March 25, 1972, the tra-ditional "cloud no bigger than a man's hand" appeared, in the person of one "Super Joe" Einhorn. On that date, *Wide World* showed Mr. Einhorn doing a motorcycle jump in San Jose, California.

It would not be the last such jump we would show. On November 11, 1973, we introduced to our audience a man named Robert Knievel, who for professional purposes had dubbed himself "Evel" Knievel. He was not misspelling "evil"; Evel was just his name. And it had a ring to it.

He wore a star-spangled suit and carried a silver-headed walking stick, which also served as a container for a few shots of bourbon. And he was the most sparkling athletic conversa-tionalist to come along since Muhammad Ali.

Motorcycle jumping had been going on for a long time, at state fairs and carnivals, but never in the national theater of television, and never by a self-promoter as talented as Evel, who was ready to put his body on the line with no assurance of success.

In fact, it was Evel's failures that made him famous. Like the wild crash in Las Vegas. And the attempt to clear a gaggle of London buses in Wembley Stadium. Frank Gifford, doing the commentary, had to rush to Evel's rescue on that one, when he crashed and slid across the stadium floor.

The most spectacular failure of all was the ill-fated Snake River Canyon affair in Idaho. Knievel's boast had been that one day he would jump over the Grand Canyon. When challenged on that promise, he scaled it down to the Snake River Canyon, which was still quite a jump, requiring a special jet motorcycle.

For a week before, his fans trooped in from all over the country; it became a "happening." Some of the fans indulged in public behavior that made "the Snake Pit" crowd at the Indianapolis 500 look like a meeting of theology students. David Frost, my colleague in cricket commentary, was the announcer for the historic occasion, his British accent lending a small note of much-needed elegance.

Once again, Evel failed with a flair, parachuting to safety in the canyon only a few seconds after takeoff, and missing some nasty rocks by just a few feet.

Well, Evel was more show business than sport. And the gaggle of boxing matches, I thought, overwhelmed the basic concept of *Wide World*. But it must be said that, of the ten highest-rated programs in *Wide World*'s history, five were fights, three were Evel Knievel jumps, and two featured the Harlem Globetrotters.

Still, to me, that period was the beginning of a long, slow descent for our show as the leader of its class.

THE EIGHTIES

By the early eighties, both Margaret and I were weary of my schedule: leaving home almost every Thursday, returning on Monday. To be sure, the kids were both out of college and living away from home (they had been eight and six when *Wide World* began), so Margaret could travel with me more, but in most places, there wasn't that much for her to do. We visited a good many more Darlingtons and Bulgarias on *Wide World* than we did London and Paris.

There were a few highlights for her, like the time we went to Dublin to televise the Irish Derby. We stayed at an honest-to-God Irish castle with our friend Mike Roarty, of Budweiser, and his guests. On the day of the race at the famous Curragh in Kildare, I was in the commentary booth while Margaret stayed in the stands with the Budweiser group.

As the horses were led to the post for the big race, there was a sudden, shocking announcement over the public-address system.

"Ladies and gentlemen," the announcer intoned in a deep, portentous Irish brogue, "there is a bomb threat on the Derby. The race will be delayed, and it will be necessary to evacuate the entire stand. Please leave quietly and proceed to the infield of the course."

Margaret was a bit frightened until she found herself being escorted gallantly from the grandstand by two fellow guests. On one side she had Steve Garvey, the handsome retired baseball player, and on the other John Forsythe, at the time the idol of every woman on both sides of the ocean as the star of *Dynasty*.

After an hour, during which the horses had to wait at the post, no bomb was found and the race was run. As soon as I could, I went looking for Margaret and found her standing with Garvey and Forsythe.

"Are you all right, honey?" I asked, with proper husbandly solicitousness.

"Of course," she said. "John, Steve, and I have been having a lovely time."

Many of our traditional *Wide World* events were wearing a bit thin through repetition by now, and at times, the new events presented on the show were less than impressive, e.g., the World Frisbee Championships, the Calaveras County Frog Jumping Contest, and the National Croquet Championships. My notes show that on January 10, 1987, *Wide World* even presented something called the Bruce Willis Music Video (or did I just dream that?).

This is not to say that there were no interesting new events. There was the Fifth Avenue Mile, for example, in which some of the world's best middle-distance runners scampered down New York's most fashionable thoroughfare. And the Iron Man Triathlon in Hawaii, which begat other triathlons, mini and mega, all over the civilized world.

The most dramatic of these found the leader in the women's division in 1982, Julie Moss, staggering and falling just yards from the finish line of the marathon, the third and final phase of the grueling competition, then crawling, stunned and only half conscious, as Kathleen McCartney passed her and won the event. But Julie did finish, and became a national symbol of grit and determination.

When *Wide World* presented Pro Beach Volleyball, it was considered a peripheral sport, but a decade later, it was in the Atlanta Olympic Games. And surfing, a staple of our show since its inception, will be an Olympic event in Australia in 2000.

☆

Through the years, the sports most consistently and dramatically advanced by *Wide World* have been figure skating and gymnastics. The athletes in these competitions, and particularly the women, have provided some of the most beautiful and dramatic moments in every decade.

In skating, we have watched Peggy Fleming and Dorothy Hamill; Janet Lynn and Katarina Witt; the great Russian pairs skaters like the Protopopovs and Rodnina and Zaitsev; the superb English ice dancers, Torvill and Dean.

But through the years, the women's side of the sport has been dominated, more and more, by extremely young girls doing remarkable stunts on the ice. Children thirteen and fourteen years old have become international celebrities.

And it is their very youth that has, frankly, made it difficult for me to enjoy the sports of figure skating and gymnastics. They now appear at ages when most girls are cheerleading for their high school team and having their first dates.

Hardly into their teens, the tiny athletes twist their undeveloped bodies on the uneven bars in gymnastics or perform triple jump after triple jump in figure skating. Their childhood simply doesn't exist. A few have somehow combined their sport and normal teenage life, but they are the exceptions.

The youngest of the young have made the sport more acrobatic than artistic. Dick Button, our erudite analyst and one of the great figure skaters of all time, has often mourned the passing of the artist.

"Look," he said to me once. "You can teach a ten-year-old to play the 'Minute Waltz' in a minute, but that doesn't make them an artist." Which is not to say that he doesn't admire the amazing triple jump combinations that he sees today; he, after all, was the first human to ever do a triple jump in competition, back in the 1950s, and he remains the sports' most articulate spokesman and biggest fan.

Things were different when Dick competed. He found time to graduate from Harvard University in addition to winning world and Olympic championships, and for many years has been president of his own thriving television production company. Tenley Albright, who dominated women's skating as Dick did men's at the same time, became a mother and successful surgeon.

It is the very contrast between the days of Button and Albright and today's youngsters that spoils skating—and gymnastics—for me. The extreme youth of the girls and the backstage envy and backbiting that occurs—climaxed by the notorious attempt of one skater to have the leg of another broken—have made it very difficult for me to enjoy figure skating and gymnastics the way millions of other people do.

I'm sorry this is so, because through the years I have met

many interesting people in the two sports. One of the best was, and is, Scott Hamilton, a small, balding young man who conquered childhood illness and his short stature to become a world and Olympic champion. Recently recovered from testicular cancer, he skates on as a professional today. Just as appealing as his achievements is his personality—direct and confident, but tempered with humility.

When he skated off the ice after his final free skating performance in the Sarajevo Winter Games of 1984, he shook his head and said to his coach, "I'm sorry." The performance had not been up to his personal standards.

Moments later, the marks were displayed—and Scott's performance had been good enough to win the Olympic gold medal.

Despite moments like that, by the mid-eighties, I was asking ABC not to assign me to figure skating or gymnastics anymore. They agreed.

So *Wide World of Sports* went on, but to me, it wasn't the same. In 1986, I was sixty-five years old, and most of my old school friends had retired. I wondered if I should do the same.

Then Dennis Swanson took over as president of ABC Sports.

After twenty-five years of overseeing the day-to-day operation of our department and changing the nature of TV sports coverage forevermore, Roone Arledge would concentrate now on his job as head of ABC News.

I had never met Swanson until he took over, but we got along well from the start. Still, I had no idea of what to expect when he called one day and said he would like to come down to our farm in Maryland to talk about my future—or would it be my *lack* of a future?

When he arrived, Margaret made us lunch; then, as we sat on the screened-in side porch, he opened his attaché case and took out several sheets of lined yellow paper.

"Lunch was great, Margaret," he said. "Now. I have a feeling that you two are getting tired of *Wide World*'s weekly grind, but, frankly, we need you. So I am going to read to you our schedule for the next year. You two tell me which events you'd like to do and which you wouldn't. As for the money, can we keep it the same as it is now?"

Absolutely.

Dennis read the schedule to us, we made our choices—mostly horse racing and golf, plus a few special events—and he checked them off as we went. From thirty-five or forty events, suddenly we were down to less than twenty. It was unbelievable.

"Well, that's that," Dennis said. "Now, can we take a walk around the farm and look at the horses?"

As Roone had given me the opportunities that shaped my career—*Wide World*, hosting the Olympic Games, almost a hundred major golf championships, and travel to all of the continents except Africa—so now was Swanson extending my career.

When my contract was running out again the year before he left for NBC in 1996, he came to the farm again. At the end of that visit, I was under contract to ABC until the year 2000, at which time I will be seventy-nine.

THE NINETIES

As the calendar turned to the nineties, my involvement in the week-to-week, round-the-world activities of the program declined sharply, as did *Wide World*'s concentration on its original concept.

To be sure, the search for new and different events continued, and some were discovered, like the Iditarod sled dog race in Alaska, satellite coverage of the Antarctic Expedition Finish, and the Disabled Skiers Championships. But the well seemed to be running dry, and many of our traditional events were being imitated on the numerous cable channels that were springing up like weeds. It was no longer a novelty to televise from distant lands—that was happening every night on the evening news.

My focus now was on horse racing, golf, and a few special events, like the World Cup of soccer in 1994, for which I was host.

ABC's *Wide World of Sports* had started that day at the Penn Relays in 1961 with limited expectations—a decent rating for twenty weeks was all that the network hoped for. In the end, it had changed the face of TV sports coverage everywhere, and put my career on a course that curved steadily upward for almost four decades. It brought me a place in the Television Academy Hall of Fame, a medal from the West German government for my commentary during the Munich Olympics tragedy, thirteen Emmy Awards, a George Foster Peabody Award for lifetime achievement, and a George Polk Memorial Award.

It was more than enough.

But as the nineties wore on, the show relied more and more on figure skating, as it had with boxing in the seventies. And still, the ratings went down. The *Wide World of Sports* I had known was fading like an old photograph, left too long in the sun.

The magic was gone.

☆

On January 3, 1998—thirty-six years, eight months, and five days after its first appearance as a summer replacement show—ABC's *Wide World of Sports* ceased to exist in its original form, an hour and a half each Saturday afternoon. The name continues in the form of a studio host operation that links together ABC's various sports programming—golf, basketball, horse racing, etc.

All that remains from the original is the words that I've said since the early days:

Spanning the globe to bring you the constant variety of sport;
The thrill of victory and the agony of defeat,
The human drama of athletic competition.
This is ABC's *Wide World of Sports.*

There is one other thing that remains.

Every weekend, as he has since 1970, Vinko Bogataj still leaps from the past out of your TV screen, sliding off the side of the ski jump in-run, nearly decapitating the official and flying off into sports history.

Time now for the Jim McKay Ratings, remembering that I have considered only athletes whose fame arose primarily from *Wide World of Sports*, and in sports which I covered. Boxing, for example, was Howard Cosell's beat, Evel Knievel was Frank Gifford's, etc.

THE FIVE ATHLETES I'LL MOST REMEMBER FROM ABC'S *WIDE WORLD OF SPORTS*: 1961–1998

1. Valery Brumel, U.S.S.R.

The young, handsome Soviet high jumper became the first foreign athlete to acquire American fans when he broke the world record for his event three times on our program—in Moscow in 1961, before ninety thousand spectators; in Palo Alto, California, in 1962, before eighty thousand in Stanford Stadium; and in Moscow again, before another ninety thousand, in 1963.

On the first occasion, his achievement, and the goodwill generated by the other friendly athletes in the competition, helped save our show from cancellation in the middle of its first summer. At Palo Alto, as he was cheered on by the huge American crowd, he was a sign that all was not lost between our two nations, at least not on the field of sport. And in Moscow again, his world-record jump caused Nikita Khruschchev and American ambassador Averell Harriman to hug each other joyously before our cameras.

He was named our Athlete of the Year, and in an unusual move in those days, was allowed to travel to New York to accept the award at a big dinner. Soviet ambassador Anatoli Dobrynin flew up from Washington through a violent rainstorm to be on hand.

Valery Brumel may have been a sign of a maturing, more sophisticated sports audience in the U.S.—he was the first foreign athlete to achieve popularity in America, and he was from an "enemy" nation, at that.

2. Scott Hamilton, U.S.A.

As a small boy, he spent months in a hospital, battling for his life against Schwachman's Syndrome. He won the battle, but the disease stunted his growth. He couldn't compete in most sports, but he found his destiny in figure skating, and in Sarajevo in 1984, he won the Olympic gold medal.

Still, he was almost in tears when he finished the gold medal performance, saying to his coach, "I'm sorry. I let you down. I didn't skate my best."

Continuing his career as a pro, he was an inspiration to undersized kids everywhere. Then, at age thirty-nine, he was stricken with testicular cancer.

Four months after surgery and the ensuing radiation and chemotherapy, he returned to the ice. His first day back? "Devastating," he said. "I couldn't even do the little bunny hop that three-year-old beginners do. I'd fall on nothing."

A month and a half later, he said, "Now, I'm competitive with a six-year-old."

Three months after that, he was back skating with his professional show, a winner yet again.

3. Julie Moss, U.S.A.

She is the young woman who endured the rigors of the Ironman Triathlon (a 2½-mile swim, 112-mile bike race, and a full 26-mile, 385-yard marathon), only to collapse while in first place within yards of the finish line. She lost, but crawled to the finish and completed the race.

Julie epitomized the skill, courage, and determination exhibited by so many women on *Wide World of Sports* through the years—wonderful Wilma Rudolph conquering polio and the world of women's track; Peggy Fleming, Dorothy Hamill, Janet Lynn, Katarina Witt, and many others in figure skating; Bonnie Blair in speed skating; Olga Korbut, Nadia Comaneci, Cathy Rigby, and Mary Lou Retton in gymnastics.

They all played as important a role in the emergence of the American female as other women did in business, television, and politics.

4. Every Kid Who Has Ever Played in the Little League World Series

These kids' behavior on the baseball field in Williamsport, Pennsylvania, has been a lesson in sportsmanship to us all. No cursing, no belittling a beaten foe, no showboating. Just playing baseball as hard as they can, and at the end, leaping over each other in joy or trying, often unsuccessfully, to restrain the tears of 12-year-olds, that age when it sometimes seems there is no tomorrow.

They have provided a lesson that should shame any big leaguer who has ever brought discredit to the game.

5. Len Chalmers, England

The Leicester City soccer star who played the entire second half of the 1961 F.A. Cup Final, England's football championship game, with a broken leg. At that time, no substitutes were allowed in big-time soccer, so Chalmers played on rather than leave his team a man short. Once again, an example of excellence in the human character.

☆

F. Scott Fitzgerald said, "Show me a hero and I will show you a tragedy." I can't agree. It is true that some of those mentioned above have faded rather quickly from the scene— Brumel's career ended in a motorcycle accident; Julie Moss and Len Chalmers were, to the public, one-day wonders; only a small fraction of Little Leaguers have fulfilled their dream of lasting fame in the big leagues; Scott Hamilton certainly had to overcome tragic circumstances to succeed—but all earned their moment in the sun, and all can treasure the knowledge that, at least once, they had chanced failure, and found success.

☆

I also remember those who have thrilled us, but are now gone, and to whom we have paid tribute on *Wide World*. Athletes like the racing drivers, World Champion of Drivers Jim Clark of Scotland and Peter Revson, the handsome, charismatic heir to the Revlon cosmetics fortune; Vince Lombardi, who taught us that "fatigue makes cowards of us all"; Jackie Robinson, who changed the face of sporting America from snow white to a much more attractive black and white checkerboard; Abebe Bikila, the great Ethiopian marathoner; Steve Prefontaine, the talented young American runner, sadly killed in an auto accident at the peak of his powers.

And Chuck Howard, who died of a brain tumor in 1996. He was the production assistant on the very first *Wide World* program, then rose through the ranks to become the leader and spirit of the ABC Sports production staff. He could be grouchy and grumpy in the control room, but it was always in the effort to make the show better and was never, to use producer Bob Goodrich's word, "personal." In private, he was easily moved to laughter or tears.

On the road, we enjoyed hundreds of dinners and endured as many airplane rides together. I never tired of his company.

He and his wife, Caroline, were very good and faithful friends to Margaret and me. And Caroline still is.

To our son, Sean, Chuck was an idol in his boyhood, and a friend and mentor later on.

Epilogue

The journey has thus far taken me some five million miles. It hasn't ended yet, but I'm spending more and more time at the farm in Maryland. If there were no other peripheral benefits of my job, the farm alone would be worth it.

As Margaret and I walked out to the garden this morning, the screen door slammed behind us. They tried to sell us on a metal screen door ("This will last forever; the wood will rot and need replacement before you know it"), but we stuck with the wood, because a metal door just doesn't slam like a wooden one.

A slamming screen door goes with other summer sounds remembered from our childhood, like a dog barking in the distance or the tinkle of the Good Humor man's bell.

The garden is Margaret's creation. In the early years of our marriage, she was the one digging dirt. She kept at it until one summer evening when I returned home from an assignment and found her digging away, her hands covered with mud, perspiration ruining her hair.

"I can't have you doing that, Margaret," I said. "It fills me with guilt."

"Well then," she said, handing me the trowel, "you do it."

I smiled at her nervously and, passing over the suggestion that I do the digging, promised her I would always earn enough money to pay someone else to do it. That has been our deal ever since, although sometimes it was pretty close on the money part.

The garden she has designed and presented to our (strictly part-time) gardener is breathtaking in the spring. Some four thousand tulips of many colors lead the parade in April, followed by the subtler colors and marvelous aromas of mock orange and peonies in late May and June. The geraniums are in flower all summer long. Various perennials also bloom, one after the other, all summer. In the fall, chrysanthemums are everywhere, along with a perennial called sedum, which ever so slowly changes from light green in August to deep purple in October. That one is my favorite.

The house at Bellefield Farm is 170-year-old brick painted white, a four-square, honest-looking edifice, three stories high. The floors and doors are the same ones that were installed in 1830. Some of the window glass has that wavy appearance that marks it as being very old. Margaret has filled the house with the furniture we have acquired along the route of our fifty-year marriage. She says that her decorating is of no particular style, that it simply reflects who we are and what we like.

Some of the pieces are true antiques, purchased when times were good, but many came from tag sales, too. No one would guess this from walking through the house—it has the stamp of Margaret's taste, which is exquisite.

As you look past the white fences of the pastures, you see a graceful turn in the road. Coming down that road from the airport after yet another assignment, coming around that curve and seeing the farm open up before me, all forty acres, is one of the supreme pleasures of my life.

As we were walking in the garden this morning, looking around us, we had the simultaneous realization, as we often do, that we actually own this place, free and clear. It is not rented or leased. It is ours, and that's sometimes difficult to believe.

At our age, the questions naturally occur: "Has it been worth it? And how did we really get to this point, anyway?"

Well, I have always felt that there is a price tag on everything in life, and the price is seldom money. It's more subtle and less predictable elements. The trick is to give the right answer to the question "Am I willing to pay the price?"

For Margaret, the price has been high. For more than thirty years, she was alone almost every weekend—actually Thursday through Sunday, or Monday morning. A social life virtually didn't exist. Not that her social life was a priority with her—raising two children and trying to find time to write her syndicated column more than filled the hours. But it had to be lonely. And the fact that Roone Arledge seldom finalized our schedule until the last minute made it difficult to plan anything ahead.

As for me, I missed Margaret, Mary, and Sean very much, all the time. I covered a lot of sports in which I had little interest (try synchronized swimming championships at a neighborhood pool in Houston on a steamy Easter Sunday morning, or the World Amateur Wrestling Championships, outdoors, in Sofia, Bulgaria—in the rain).

Semi-hypochondriac that I am, I was always fearful of getting sick in the Soviet Union or some other Communist-dominated Eastern European country. Once I did get sick in London from bad seafood, sick enough that I couldn't sleep all night, with the Wimbledon final to do the next morning. And there was that time at the World Table Tennis Championships in Sarajevo when a guard with a gun sat outside my hotel bedroom. I didn't sleep all that night, either.

But I had the companionship of a very pleasant bunch of guys who traveled with me. I have had some marvelous meals in Paris and Lyons, and enjoyed those wonderful walks on the seaside golf links of Scotland, listening to the musical burr of the Scottish spectators' speech as they commented on the relative abilities of the competitors we were watching in the British Open. I saw Moscow in all its imperial drabness under the Communists and Copenhagen in its shining simplicity (imagine a country where the national hero is a teller of fairy tales, Hans Christian Andersen, rather than some military braggart).

Margaret had only the kids, her column, and somehow working out our finances, a tough job much of the time.

From the flower garden, we walked on to our very small vegetable patch. Last year, we tried corn, tomatoes, asparagus, peppers, string beans, and cucumbers. This season, we are going to settle for the tomatoes only. It seems we were always waiting for vegetables to harvest, but it never happened. We waited three years, until this spring, for the first crop of asparagus. All we ended up with was some tall, spindly growths that looked like weeds.

Waiting. We should be used to it by now.

We've had to wait for just about everything in our lives. In the early years of our marriage, Margaret had to wait for me to finish growing up. We had to wait for children, finally and gratefully realizing that it was our destiny to adopt two irresistible babies, whom we named Mary and Sean.

The eleven years at CBS were full of waiting and frustration.

By the time we finished the first summer of *Wide World* on ABC, I was forty years old, and *Wide World* was considered anything but a choice assignment. It took years for it to be recognized.

Personal recognition came to me for the first time after the 1972 Munich Olympics, when I was fifty-one. Not long ago, I heard a sports commentator complain that he was already thirty-three years old and hadn't done the World Series yet.

I've tried to let it be known that the success I have had is the product of two people's efforts, not just mine.

Margaret had to wait for thirty-two years in Connecticut and New York before finally convincing me that I could get to my assignments just as easily from a horse farm in Maryland as I could from New York. My fault. I never realized until we moved back how much Margaret had missed our beloved home state.

So, was it worth it? We decided, as we stood looking around us, that it was.

Our fifteen years back home have been one pleasant, and
often surprising, experience after another. We have renewed
old friendships and found new ones. We've gotten involved in
horse racing, both as thoroughbred owners and breeders and
as founders of a new event called the Maryland Million, that
single day of racing each year on which a million dollars in
prize money is awarded to the winners, all of whom must be
the progeny of Maryland-based stallions.

A few years ago, we were surprised by a phone call from Peter
Angelos, inviting us to be part of a group that was trying to
buy the Baltimore Orioles baseball team. We are certainly
among the smaller investors in that great organization, but it
has been a wonderful ride as the Birds have risen from medi-
ocrity to their present prominence.

Our daughter, Mary, a board-certified counselor, has
moved to Maryland from California, bringing with her our
grandson, James, who is the light of Margaret's life and my
frequent companion and golfing partner. He's just sixteen.
Mary, James, and our daughter's husband, Dr. Alex Guba, live
within a fifteen-minute ride of our farm.

Our son, Sean, comes down every few weeks from New
York, where he is president of CBS Sports, to enjoy his mother's company and counsel and to join James and me on the
golf course. Sean and his wife, Tracy, have an apartment in
New York and a house in Connecticut.

There is little more we could ask for.

There have, of course, been unexpected bumps in the
road. Life treats us all that way. Both Margaret and I have had
heart surgery, and more recently, she had to have a kidney
removed. But such things happen, and when they do, what
better place to be living than in Maryland, where Johns Hopkins Hospital is one of our home teams, rated number one in
the nation for seven straight years. Number one in football is
nice, but number one in hospitals is better. Our doctors have

not only gotten us through the tough times physically and emotionally, they have also become our friends.

As to how we have gotten to this point, in work and marriage, the answer is simple: Margaret and I are a team. A good team is a product of good chemistry, and that takes a lot of blending. Put the wrong elements together, and it may all blow up. We didn't achieve it in a year, or even a decade, but with Margaret's patience and my eventual maturing, we did it.

And what were, in the end, the magic elements?

Just these: common backgrounds, common interests, common goals.

At the risk of sounding preachy, I'll explain how they worked for us. We are both of Roman Catholic backgrounds, went to Catholic parochial grammar schools and private Catholic colleges. The colleges, Loyola and the College of Notre Dame of Maryland, are located next to each other on Charles Street in Baltimore, but we never met until some years after graduation. Both of our fathers were of full Irish descent. Both of our mothers were Irish-German. Our German grandmothers, who never met, even had the same recipe for German potato salad. Celery seed was the secret ingredient.

So when we talked about our childhoods, we found we had a lot of things in common. Our big common interest when we met was the reading of and working for a newspaper—the *Baltimore Evening Sun*. In time, that interest shifted into the new medium of television, but we are still avid readers, and critics, of newspapers.

We love good plays, good movies, good books, and, yes, good television shows. Margaret was not a lover of sports when we met, and her interest was little more than casual until the last few years.

Until we became involved with the Orioles, she hardly knew whether it was four balls and three strikes or the other way around. Now, she has progressed to the point of reading George Will's scholarly tome on the sport and second-guess-ing manager (and now ex-manager) Davey Johnson. She is in love with the double play. "A double play is so beautiful," she says. But only, for Margaret, when the Orioles are the ones making the twin killing.

Common goals? Margaret wanted to be the first woman White House correspondent for the *Evening Sun,* and she was well on her way when the man from New York offered me the television job. I didn't realize it at the time, but that was the moment when career and marriage could have taken a different turn.

Finally, we both are competitive, but not with each other. We love to win, we hate to lose. We are willing to take the chance of losing (few teams go undefeated) and like to think that we know how to take a loss when it happens.

Although we both preferred news to sports in the beginning, we have never looked down on what I do for a living.

The essayist Roger Rosenblatt summed it up nicely in the June 9, 1997, issue of *Time* magazine.

". . . Keep up your love of sports," he wrote. "Sports are about clean victories and perpetual renewals; every old game has a definite end, and every new game is a world reborn. Jogging is nice, but be sure to play something you can win.

"Winning is nicer."

Amen.